I Was a Teer
the Americar

The Battle of Lexington Green, first engagement of the Revolution, April 19, 1775. Drawing from an engraving by Amos Doolittle, a Connecticut militiaman (National Archives).

I Was a Teenager in the American Revolution

21 Young Patriots and Two Tories Tell Their Stories

ELIZABETH RYAN METZ

McFarland & Company, Inc., Publishers
Jefferson, North Carolina, and London

LIBRARY OF CONGRESS CATALOGUING-IN-PUBLICATION DATA

Metz, Elizabeth (Elizabeth R.)
    I was a teenager in the American Revolution : 21 young
patriots and two Tories tell their stories / Elizabeth Ryan Metz.
        p.   cm.
    Includes bibliographical references and index.

    ISBN-13 978-0-7864-2509-9
    softcover : 50# alkaline paper ∞

    1. United States—History—Revolution, 1775–1783—Personal
narratives.   2. United States—History—Revolution, 1775–1783—
Biography.   3. Teenagers—United States—History—18th
century.   I. Title.
E275.A2M37   2006
973.3092'2—dc22   2006009909
[B]

British Library cataloguing data are available

Cover art ©2006 Pictures Now

Manufactured in the United States of America

McFarland & Company, Inc., Publishers
    Box 611, Jefferson, North Carolina 28640
    www.mcfarlandpub.com

Acknowledgments

For this book, I have selected 1765 to 1792 as the era of the American Revolution. The following accounts reflect the experiences—many involving hardships and sacrifices—of teenagers during this period.

Maps are based on those that appear in James Truslow Adam's *Atlas of American History* (New York: Charles Scribner's Sons, 1943).

I wish to express appreciation to the staffs of all the libraries I visited for research, and to the following in particular: Syracuse University Department of Special Collections; town of Manlius Library; and the Indian River County Library in Vero Beach, Florida. The historical societies in Charleston, South Carolina, and Putnam County, New York, and the Library of Congress in Washington, D.C., all provided information and services.

Contents

Contents

Introduction

Teenagers were critical to achieving victory in the Revolutionary War. At that time 90 percent of the people in America lived on farms or in country villages. Of the population of 2,780,000 in 1780, half were 16 or younger. At the beginning, many volunteered. However, as the war progressed, boys aged from 16 to 19 were drafted, along with able-bodied men up to 60. Members of families and neighbors were organized in militias to protect their local areas. Sons and fathers often served together. As British soldiers moved through the countryside, militias were called to action. Teenage soldiers played an essential part throughout the war in militias, in the Continental army, and at sea.

Young women were equally important in support of the war. Teenage women and their mothers kept the farms going to provide the food for all. They cared for the animals and raised the grain and harvested it. They processed the wool from the sheep and made linen from the flax grown on the farm. They spun the wool and flax into thread and yarn. They knitted stockings and mittens. Even in the large cities, they bent to their spinning wheels and looms to produce the needed homespun outfits. As the war passed through their areas, they visited the hospitals and cared for the injured and ill. Some even found ways to collect information on enemy movements. Often they put themselves at risk of getting smallpox and cholera, so prevalent at that time.

The troubles arose after the British expelled the French in 1763 at the end of the French and Indian War. The king of England then claimed all the territory on the eastern coast of North America from Canada south to Florida and west to the Mississippi River. For the next 20 years this was the site of contention between the colonists and the king over their respective rights.

In 1764 the British king and Parliament imposed taxes on the American colonies to pay for the cost of the war with the French. Many colonists believed that bills to raise revenue must be voted upon by the assemblies of those who would pay the tax, not by a parliament 3,000 miles away. The cry became, "No taxation without representation." Next, Parliament passed regulations governing exports and manufacturing, which limited the colonists' freedom to carry on business as they chose.

The dispute dragged on. In 1768, when the British sent troops to Boston to enforce the new laws, crowds of Bostonians protested. On March 5, 1770, British soldiers standing guard were pelted with snowballs and stones. In turn, they fired their guns into the crowd, killing five and wounding several others. The outrage of the Bostonians over this "massacre" led to the removal of the troops to an island in the harbor.

Some taxes were repealed, except those on tea. However, only special agents of the government could sell the tea. Colonial merchants objected. On December 16, 1773, several "Sons of Liberty" disguised as Indians boarded the ships carrying the tea and dumped it into the harbor in what became known as the Boston Tea Party.

Angered, the British imposed a set of laws known as the Intolerable Acts. The troops that had been moved to Castle William Island were sent back to the city to be sheltered and fed by the citizens. Major-General Thomas Gage arrived to assume command as the new royal governor. Effective June 1, 1774, he ordered the port of Boston closed until the city paid for the destroyed tea.

News of these actions spread throughout the colonies. The result did not isolate Boston as the British intended. The Massachusetts colony set up a special provincial congress in Concord and sent delegates to the First Continental Congress meeting in Philadelphia in September. They proposed terms of a peaceful settlement to the king.

All changed on April 19, 1775, when 700 British troops marched out of Boston to Lexington and Concord looking for ammunition they suspected was stored there. Paul Revere was one of those who alerted the colonists. The militias gathered on Lexington Green. As the British approached a shot was fired and returned. The war had begun. Seventy-three British soldiers were killed and 26 were missing in the resulting skirmishes as the armed colonists followed the troops back to Boston and set up a siege around the city. The Americans lost 49.

On May 10, 1775, the Second Continental Congress convened in Philadelphia. In June, the members voted to form the Continental army and send rifle companies from the middle colonies and Virginia to join the forces outside Boston. The next day they appointed George Washington to command "all the continental forces, raised or to be raised for the defense of American liberty." The signing of the Declaration of Independence on July 4, 1776, set the course. The rebels were challenging the most powerful armed force in the world.

The battles and skirmishes took place in back yards, behind barns and fences, around rural taverns, in tobacco fields, and over stands of corn and wheat. Many young men served at sea on privateers, privately owned vessels commissioned by Congress to capture enemy ships. Each family had to decide whether to support the rebels, to remain loyal to the king, or not to favor either. Everyone was affected as the war continued until the surrender of the British general Lord Cornwallis in Yorktown on October 17, 1781. British colonials, at last, became free Americans with the signing of the peace treaty in Paris on September 3, 1783.

The following accounts reveal what it was like to be a teenager then. Some were written at the time, others later in memoirs. A few were handed down in family histories. John Greenwood was at Bunker Hill. Israel Trask and Ebenezer Fox served at sea. Enduring long voyages away from home, they were captured and imprisoned on filthy prison ships. Abigail Foote kept a diary of her daily tasks as she processed the wool and flax grown on her farm into cloth and clothing. She milked the cows, made soap and cheese, weeded the garden, knitted and wove on the loom. Mary Slocumb hurried to care for the wounded in a battle in North Carolina between Loyalist clans and patriots. Michael Smith guarded the New Jersey coast when the British fleet anchored in New York harbor.

It was also a difficult time for teens who lived in Loyalist families. John Enys was a British soldier sent to Canada to fight rebels. Walter Bates was arrested and tortured as a suspected spy. During the war an unknown number of Loyalists left for Britain, Canada and the West Indies. After the war thousands more accompanied the retreating British.

Sybil Ludington rode her horse through the night to warn of the approaching British soldiers when they raided Danbury. Ebenezer Fletcher, captured at Hubbardton, vividly describes his experiences as a wounded prisoner after the retreat from Fort Ticonderoga. Escaping into the woods one night, he brings to life the terror of losing his way in the dark as wolves howled nearby. David Holbrook met the British at Bennington as Burgoyne lost nearly a thousand soldiers killed, wounded, or taken prisoner on his way to surrender at Saratoga.

The most influential teenager in the Revolution was not an American. He was a wealthy French orphan, the Marquis de Lafayette. When he heard of the English colonies' Declaration of Independence, he bought a ship and crossed the Atlantic to become part of that effort. As he turned 20, he was injured at the battle of Brandywine. Serving without pay, he was an important link to the alliance with the French.

Henry Yeager was only 13 when he became a drummer in the militia as it met the British in several actions around Philadelphia. He was threatened with hanging as a spy when he visited his parents in the city. Sally Wister kept a diary while living near Philadelphia during the British occupation of the city. She described her fear as British and American troops skirmished nearby and American officers occupied her home.

African-American James Forten was free when he volunteered to serve on a ship. On a second voyage it was captured. Imprisoned on the *Jersey,* he describes the horrible conditions and his final exchange. Another African American, James Armistead, spied for Lafayette at Yorktown and was granted his freedom for his service.

Eliza Wilkinson was filled with terror when British soldiers occupying Charleston entered her home and stripped it of everything they wanted. Dicey Langston acted as a spy/courier to pass information about the enemy to the patriots at the risk of her life. Grace and Rachel Martin dressed in their husbands' clothes to hold up a British courier near Fort Ninety-Six in South Carolina. They passed his messages along to patriot General Nathaniel Green.

Pursued at times by Loyalist bands, Paul Hamilton chronicled warfare in the Carolinas. The future president, Andrew Jackson, was only 14 when he was captured with his brother. Imprisoned at Camden, South Carolina, the boys caught small pox. Only Andy survived. Joseph Plumb Martin summarized the thoughts of many when the war was over.

The teenagers' experiences in these accounts open a window on that period. They let the reader learn about the courage, sacrifices, and hardships and how the teenagers risked danger and death to achieve the freedoms we have today. The defeat of the British made it possible for the colonists to unite in forming a government based on the consent of the people, by the people, and for the people. America became a beacon of freedom for the world.

1

John Greenwood Was There at the Beginning of the War

John Greenwood recalls many of the events leading up to the Revolutionary War during his early years in Boston. Later he went to live with an uncle in Maine. He relates his experiences in trying to go back home to see his parents. His story is set against the Battle of Bunker Hill (Breed's Hill) and the withdrawal of the British from Boston.

I was born in Boston, America, May 17, in the year 1760, and educated in the North School until thirteen years of age; but as children were not at that time taught what is called grammar, or even correct spelling, it must not be expected to find them in this relation. All that we learned was acquired by the mere dint of having it thumped in, for the two masters who had to overlook and manage some 300 or 400 boys, could pay little attention to us except so far as flogging went, which right was rather freely indulged in.

While I was at school the troubles commenced, and I recollect very well of hearing the superstitious accounts which were circulated around: people were certain a war was about to take place, for a great blazing comet had appeared and armies of soldiery had been seen fighting in the clouds overhead; and it was said that the day of judgment was at hand, when the moon would turn into blood and the world be set on fire. These dismal stories became so often repeated that the boys thought nothing of them, considering that such events must come in the course of nature. For my part, all I wished was that a church which stood by the side of my father's garden would fall on me at the time these terrible things happened, and crush me to death at once, so as to be out of pain quick....

I remember what is called the "Boston Massacre...." The British troops fired upon the inhabitants and killed seven of them one of whom was my father's apprentice, a lad eighteen years of age, named Samuel Maverick. I was his bedfellow, and after his death I used to go to bed in the dark on purpose to see his spirit, for I was so fond of him and he of me, that I was sure it would not hurt me. The people of New England at that time pretty generally believed in hobgoblins and spirits, that is the children at least did.

About this period I commenced learning to play upon the fife, and, trifling as it may seem to mention the circumstance, it was, I believe, the sole cause of my travels and disasters. I was so fond of hearing the fife and drum played by the British that somehow or other I got possession of an old split fife, and having made it sound by puttying up the crack, I learned to play several tunes upon it sufficiently well to be a fifer in the militia company of Captain Gay. This was before the war some years, for I think I must have been about nine or ten years old. The flag of the company was English; so were they all then.

I saw the tea when it was destroyed at Boston, which began the disturbance, and likewise beheld several persons tarred and feathered and carried through the town; they were tide-waiters, custom-house officers—I think they called them informers.

At the age of thirteen I was sent eastward to a place called Falmouth (Portland), 150 miles from Boston to live with my father's only brother whom I was named after. He was a cabinet-maker by trade but had concerns in the shipping business likewise, and was looked upon to be an able, or rich, man. His wife was dead, he had no children and I was his favorite. The whole country at this time was in commotion and nothing was talked of but war, liberty, or death; persons of all descriptions were embodying themselves into military companies, and every old drunken fellow they found who had been a soldier, or understood what is called the manual exercise, was employed of evenings to drill them. My uncle was lieutenant of an independent company (the Cadets), and of course, I was engaged to play the fife while they were learning to march, a pistareen [Spanish coin] an evening for my services keeping me in pocket-money....

I stayed with my uncle two years, until the time arrived when we had an account that the British troops had marched out of Boston, attacked the country people at a place called Lexington, and killed a number of them. I had frequently been inclined to return to Boston that I might see my father, mother, sister, and brothers, but as I was not permitted to do so, I took it into my head, saying nothing to anyone about it, to go alone on foot in the beginning of May 1775. The distance was 150 miles, and the country was so thinly inhabited that I had to traverse, at times, woods seven miles in length, and I had never traveled before more than three or four miles by land into the country. I concluded to set out on a Sunday, for then they would not be so apt to miss me, and not having mentioned my determination of going, they would not think it possible so young a boy would, without any manner of cause, attempt such a journey. My reason for going was I wished to see my parents, who, I was afraid, would all be killed by the British, for, as I observed before, nothing was talked of but murder and war.

Sunday morning, when in New England all is still and no persons are in the streets, having eaten my breakfast, I took a handkerchief and tied up in it two or three shirts and a pair or two of stockings and with what clothes I had on my back and four and a half pistareens in my pocket, jumped over the fence in the back yard and set off. I walked rapidly through the town without meeting any one I knew, as it was breakfast-time, and when once beyond the outskirts, being a very strong-constitutioned boy, off I went with a light heart and a good pair of heels; sometimes I ran and sometimes trotted like a horse, and I really believe I accomplished forty miles the first day. I do not recollect that I was the least tired during my whole journey. As I traveled through the different towns the people were preparing to march toward Boston to fight and as I had my fife with me—yes, and I was armed likewise with my sword—I was greatly caressed by them. Stopping at the taverns where there was a muster, out came my fife and I played them a tune or two; they used to ask me where I came from and where I was going to, and when I told them I was going to fight for my country, they were astonished such a little boy, and alone, should have such courage. Thus by the help of my fife I lived, as it were, on what is usually called free-quarters nearly the entire route.

As nigh as I can remember it took me four days and a half to reach Charlestown, opposite Boston; but on Charlestown Neck there stood a Yankee soldier or sentry who stopped me, telling me that I must not go past him. I attempted, however, to get by him and run, when another fellow caught me and carried me to the guard-house, which was a barn standing not far off. Here I was kept all night when they let me go, informing me that in order to go down to Charlestown ferry a pass must be obtained from General Ward, at Cambridge; but by no means would I be permitted to go into Boston to see my parents, as all communication was cut off between the British and the country people. The war had begun, they told me; the British had marched out into the country to Lexington, to the tune of "Yankee Doodle," and they had made them dance it back again.

I immediately set off for Cambridge after my pass, got it, and traveled back for Charlestown ferry; but I was not allowed, after two years' absence from home, to go over and see my parents. Everything on the opposite shore was familiar to me, and I was well acquainted with the person who kept the ferry, Mr. Enoch Hopkins, whose son used to go to school with me. There I stood alone, without a friend or a house to shelter me for the night, surrounded by women and children, some crying and others in different situations of distress, for the Boston people were flocking out of town over the ferry in crowds, with what little furniture they were permitted to take with them. The British governor, or more properly calling him "Granny Gage," gave permission to the inhabitants before the battle of Bunker Hill, to leave the town, but placed a fellow by the name of Cunningham (the notorious master of the New York provost during the war) at the ferry stairs, to search their trunks and little bundles and take from the women and children their pins, needles, and scissors, in short anything he pleased, which, with his noted cruelty, he would throw into the river while the poor helpless creatures were weeping. O British magnanimity! Brave Fellows!

This, however, is nothing to their boasted valor. They dared not show their faces to us over their breakfasts after Bunker Hill frolic. They then found out to their sorrow what kind of stuff Yankees were made of; they lost in killed and wounded upward of 1100 of their best troops, and we lost about 200. The British had ten men to our one, as history will inform you, and I was an eye-witness.

But to return; Charlestown was at the time generally deserted by the inhabitants and the houses were, with few exceptions, empty; so not knowing what to do nor where to go and without a penny in my pockets, if

1. John Greenwood Was There at the Beginning of the War

I remember rightly, I entered a very large tavern that was filled with all descriptions of people. Here I saw three or four persons whom I knew, and my fife sticking in front of my coat, they asked me, after many questions, to play them a tune. I complied forthwith, but although the fife is somewhat of a noisy instrument to play upon, it could hardly be heard for the din and confusion around. Such a scene cannot be described, nor hardly conceived, save by those who have beheld something similar to it.

After I had rattled off several tunes, there was one Hardy Pierce who, with Enoch Howard and three or four others, invited me to go up to Cambridge to their quarters, as they called it.

When there, they tried to persuade me to enlist as a fifer, telling me that it was only for eight months and that I would receive eight dollars a month and be found in provisions; moreover they calculated to quickly drive the British from Boston, when I would have an opportunity of seeing my parents. I waited four or five days to see if I could get into Boston, living meanwhile in their quarters. The army which kept the British penned up in the city at the time was no better than a mob, the different companies not being formed as yet, that I could observe, into regiments or divisions. This was in the latter part of May 1775. Concluding finally that it would be best for me, I enlisted for eight months in the company of Captain Bliss, which was quartered in the house of the Episcopal minister, who with his family had deserted it at an early period of the disturbances and gone into Boston.

There we stayed; to call it living is out of the question for we had to sleep in our clothes upon the bare floor. I do not recollect that I even had a blanket, but I remember well the stone that I had to lay my head upon. Not more than two or three weeks passed by when I began to think if I had not some friend or relation near Cambridge, and happened to recollect a great-aunt then living in a town twenty miles from the camp. I procured a furlough or permit from my captain to go and see her, and set off briskly after breakfast without a penny in my pockets. With a spirit too proud to beg a mouthful to eat, I traveled onward, and late in the afternoon arrived within a few miles of the town, which is called Andover. I was now so hungry that I thought a piece of live sheep in the neighboring field would be relishable, but although so near the town, at this point, strange as it may appear—unaccountable, improbable, or whatever else you may please to call that which I am

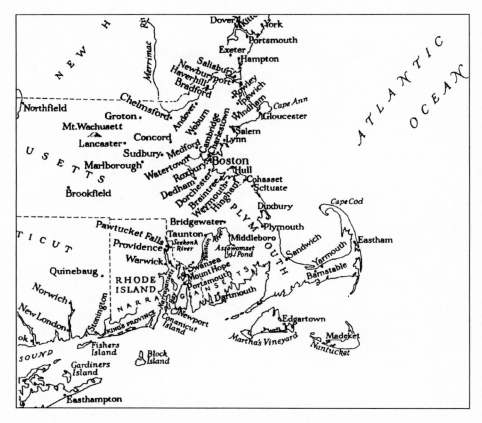

New England in the Revolutionary War (From *Atlas of American History,* by Kenneth T. Jackson, Charles Scribner's Sons, © 1984, Charles Scribner's Sons. Reprinted by permission of the Gale Group.)

about to relate—I yet assert it as a fact, and am willing to take my oath, that, as I was proceeding onward, there was a certain something that prevented me from going forward; it seemed to push me back, or, as it were, insist on my returning. I attempted still to advance but could not, yet on wheeling around to retrace my footsteps, I could do so without uneasiness and with pleasure; moreover I traveled very fast.

I proceeded a considerable distance on my way back, as I walked some time after dark but became so fatigued and hungry that I was obliged to stop at a farm-house to beg something to eat and ask permission to lie on the kitchen floor that night. They gave me some mush and milk and a blanket to lie down on, and I was soon sound asleep. Early the next morning, before the people were stirring, I had again started for Cambridge, or the camp.

At dawn of day I heard the firing of great guns, which caused me to quicken my pace, for I supposed the armies were engaged and, being enlisted, I thought it was my duty to be there. By ten o'clock I had reached Cambridge common, where I met a man I knew, by the name of Michael Grout, who informed me that my mother, who had come over the day before from Boston, was in his house, where he had left her only a few minutes before. His house, he told me, was just behind the meeting-house. When I reached the house I had been directed to, I found my mother; surrounded by weeping women and children. She had no sooner seen me that she exclaimed, "Johnny, do get me away from here!" and appeared no more frightened if nothing had been the matter. "Go," said she, "up to Cousin Fuller's and get his (riding) chair immediately." It was nearby so off I set, but found that Mr. Fuller who was one of the leading characters in the Provincial Congress had gone to Watertown; so I procured a horse and side-saddle, but found on returning to the house where I had left my mother that she had gone.

I forgot to mention that as soon as my father heard I was among the rebels he went to Governor Gage and got a permission for my mother to visit the American camp, provided with money to hire a man in my stead. She was also to procure a permit for me to go to Boston. Accordingly she came over the day before that attack on Bunker Hill, but was not allowed to return, although she had powerful friends and relations among the rebels, as the British called us. After the arrival, however, of General Washington, when she had been absent from Boston then about six weeks, she applied to him in person. He consented immediately—and that against the will of a great many officers and others—to her returning to my father. She was the first and only person who had permission "to go into Boston after the Battle of Bunker Hill." I did not see my mother again until she left the camp, and meanwhile she had believed me dead, as some person informed her, a few days after the battle, that I had been killed in the engagement.

As I was observing, previous to this digression, not finding my mother at Mr. Grout's on my return, and not knowing where she was,

I let the horse go, saddle and all, to find the way home the best way it could and down I went toward the battle to find the company I belonged to, then about two miles off. As I passed through Cambridge common I saw a number of wounded who had been brought from the field of conflict. Everywhere the greatest terror and confusion seemed to prevail, and as I ran along the road leading to Bunker Hill, it was filled with chairs and wagons, bearing the wounded and dead while groups of men were employed in assisting others, not badly injured, to walk. Never having beheld such a sight before, I felt very much frightened and would have given the world if I had not enlisted as a soldier; I could positively feel my hair stand on end. Just as I came near the place, a negro man, wounded in the back of his neck, passed me and his collar being open and he not having anything on except his shirt and trousers, I saw the wound quite plainly and the blood running down his back. I asked him if it hurt him much as he did not seem to mind it; he said no, that he was only going to get a plaster put on it, and meant to return. You cannot conceive what encouragement this immediately gave me; I began to feel brave and like a soldier from that moment; and fear never troubled me afterward during the whole war.

As good luck would have it, I found the company I belonged to stationed on the road in sight of the battle with two field-pieces, it having been joined to the regiment commanded by Colonel John Patterson from Stockbridge (afterward the 12th Massachusetts Bay Regiment). Captain Bliss who had given me permission the day before to go a distance of more than twenty miles was astonished to see me, and asked me how I had returned so soon. I thought I might as well appear brave as not and make myself to be thought so by others so I told him that, having heard cannon firing early in the morning, I considered it my duty to be with my fellow-soldiers; that I had run all the way back for that purpose, and intended to go into the battle to find them—which I certainly would have done, as big a coward as I was on setting out to join my companions. The cause of my fears then was, I presume, being alone, for I cannot say that I ever felt so afterward. I was much caressed by my captain and the company, who regarded me as a brave little fellow.

The British received such a warm reception from the Americans that they dared not advance one inch farther from the spot they had possession of. If they had we were ready at our station to give them another battle, as we were placed there for that purpose and to cover a retreat. The next morning we began, in sight of them, at the distance of half-cannon shot, to build a fort on Prospect Hill and they likewise began to build another opposite to it.

One of the British soldiers was asked, after the engagement at Bunker Hill, by a comrade who had been in Boston during the battle, how it was, and what sort of fellows the Yankees were. "Faith!" replied the former who was an Irishman, "don't bother me, for I can tell you all about it in a few words—it was a diamond cut diamond—and that's the whole story, my dear honey."

As my father lived near the ferry my brothers were at this point and, the river being only half a mile wide, saw the whole battle.... The wounded were brought over in the boats belonging to the men-of-war, and they were obliged to bail the blood out of them like water, while these very boats carried back the fresh troops who stood ready to reinforce those engaged. My brother told me that the wives or women of the British soldiers were at the ferry encouraging them, saying: "D ... the Yankee rebels, my brave British boys, give it to them!" He observed likewise that the soldiers looked as pale as death when they got into the boats, for they could plainly see their brother redcoats mowed down like grass by the Yankees, the whole scene being directly before their eyes. The Americans were all chiefly marksmen, and loading their guns each with a ball and five buck-shot, reserved their fire until the English troops had advanced within pistol range. I was told the enemy fell like grass when mowed, and while they were filling up their ranks to advance again the Yankees gave them the second fire with the same effect, two and three dropping at the discharge of every gun. The British then began to fall back and retreat, and it was with some difficulty their officers could rally them to the charge. The Yankees stood their ground and waited until they had advanced within a hundred feet, when they fired again, continuing it for some time about half an hour, when the British retreated a second time. After they had received additional troops they again pushed forward, but on being welcomed as before, pretty warmly, they were again obliged to retreat.... From the Boston side the British officers were seen to drive their soldiers onto the charge with swords and bayonets—this is a fact well known to many living witnesses at this day.

With a reinforcement, for they were all the time sending troops over from Boston, they came on again, and the sound of the guns firing appeared like the roll of a hundred drums. At last the bayonet went to work and as the majority of the Americans using fowling-pieces, had no weapons of this kind, and as many even had no more powder, they clubbed their guns and knocked the enemy down with the butt-ends. But at last for the want of bayonets and powder, they were obliged themselves to retreat and leave the English in possession of a dear-bought little piece of ground...

It is falsely reported that the Americans were intrenched in a strong fort; it was no such thing. The case is this: about 800 men were ordered to make a fort the night before the battle on a rising piece of ground directly opposite Boston. This was called Breed's Hill, and there was a very gentle slope down to the river, so that at the distance of a quarter-mile from the bank one could easily roll up a loaded barrow. These 800 men were without spades or pickaxes, or at least a sufficient number of them, for it is well known that the mob or army could not at that early time be supplied with these articles, and I cannot believe that there were more than, if as many as, 300 tools to work with. It was twelve o'clock at night before they commenced, and being persons unaccustomed to such labor it is reasonable to suppose that one-half of them were idle and looking on, while a great number were playing—I judge by what I have seen myself on similar occasions. Well, even admitting they were all at work hard during the entire night, is it not natural to think they would be tired by morning? But you find it was not the case. They fought like hell-hounds more than six hours, these very men, who, they say, were building this great fort the night before. Now the fact is this: there was nothing that could with any propriety be even called a breastwork, much less a fort. A little earth had been heaved up in a pile; in some places it was as high as a man's waist, but the chief part of it would only reach his knee. It was entirely open on the back, and was not half so good a defense as a common stone wall. All the cannon in it consisted of two field-pieces and 3-pound balls, one of which, in the beginning of the battle, had the carriage shot away by a 24-pound shot from the Boston side at Copp's Hill, while the other was of little use on account of the scarcity of powder.

Toward the middle of the engagement the British by firing what are called carcasses, struck several houses in Charlestown, one of them lodging in the steeple of the meeting-house, and the town, which is situated at the foot of Bunker, or Breed's Hill, was soon in a light blaze. The fools! It was of no great advantage to them, as it made a great smoke which the wind blew directly on both combatants.

After the battle, little else was done by either party except the building of breastworks and forts. The enemy were by this time convinced we would sell every inch of ground at as dear a rate as we could...

In that single afternoon, the British suffered 1,150 casualties— 40 percent of their entire North American army. They also lost one in four of all their officers killed in the Revolution. Washington sent Colonel Henry Knox to Ticonderoga to obtain needed cannon and ammunition. Sixty tons of cannon were loaded onto slays. With eighty yoke of oxen, Knox successfully hauled the precious armory more than three hundred miles down the Hudson Valley to Claverack, then eastward across Massachusetts snows and frozen rivers to the outskirts of Boston.

John Greenwood tells of the night they installed the cannon on Dorchester Heights behind straw-filled breastworks called fascines ingeniously devised by engineer Colonel Rufus Putnam. The guns overlooked the British forces and ships in Boston and the harbor.

At the latter work we went (March 4) with about 3000 or 4000 men, and having all the fascines ready made, the British were in the morning surprised at beholding a fort which would have so great a command over them. The British Admiral (Shuldham) told the General (Howe) that the place must be attacked immediately or he could not remain with his ships in the harbor. Accordingly 5000 or 6000 men were sent off in boats to take the fort but such a storm arose that they were obliged to give up the design. Had they succeeded in landing they would certainly have been overpowered, for it was a steep hill and the Americans had a number of hogsheads and barrels filled with sand to roll down upon them, and intended to sally out of the fort upon them when in confusion, and they would have liked no better fun....

The British perceived that it would be impossible to drive us from Dorchester Heights without another Bunker Hill frolic, or one much worse. They concluded to quit the town, not burning it, if we let them go quietly. We permitted them to depart, with their braggadocios, in peace.... The first thing they did was to march from Bunker Hill in the night leaving the cannon in the fort. Two effigies stuffed with straw stood sentry with guns upon their shoulders, etc. They passed over to Boston and, in a short time, embarked on their ships and were off for Halifax.

John Greenwood's first term of enlistment had expired at Christmas 1775, during the siege, and he had enlisted again for one year. He served on the Canadian expedition with Benedict Arnold and in the battle of Trenton. Later he went to sea on a privateer engaged in capturing British shipping. After the war he became a dentist in New York City and cared for General Washington's needs until his death.

Bibliography

Greenwood, John. *A Young Patriot in the American Revolution 1775–1783.* 1809. Reprint, Chicago: Westvaco, 1981.

2

Israel Trask Sees Washington
for the First Time

After Lexington and Concord, the militia from miles around
Boston came to lay siege to the British. As a ten-year-old, Israel
Trask joined the militia at Gloucester, Massachusetts, with his
father. Soon they moved to Cambridge. He describes the first time
he saw General Washington, after the Virginian assumed command
of the rebel troops. As a 12-year-old he began serving at sea and
remained a sailor until the end of the war. His experiences provide
an eyewitness view of the Revolutionary War by a young boy and
teenager on land and at sea.

In the year of our Lord 1775, having completed the tenth year of
my age on the fifth day of February of that year, I volunteered in the
Service of the United States as a soldier in a company commanded by
Capt. John Low....

Captain Low and the officers under him as well as the soldiers were
bivouacked and under light tents during the summer months and part
of the autumn. When cold weather set in we were put under barracks
and quartered on Winter Hill during this period.

I had various duties assigned me such as the care of the baggage
and the property of the mess. When the officers were called on duty,
which was daily the case, either to mount guard or fatigue duties in fortifying the camp, the entrenchment of which had a line of continuity
from Winter Hill to Watertown when finished, my duty alternately was
to take the edibles prepared at the mess to the officers on duty, which
in some instance [were] miles distant.... This term of service expired the
thirty-first December, 1775...

The day immediately following the expiration of my first term of
service, I recommenced my duty in the service of the United States for

another term the first day of January, 1776 ... having previously engaged to do so some day in the month of December 1775, great exertions having been made by all the patriotic officers who had determined to continue in the service of the country to induce the soldiers to reenlist for another term during the whole of said month, this period being looked for with intense anxiety and frightful apprehensions, lest the enemy should take advantage that the time of disbanding one army and forming another gave them and make a sortie from Boston and Bunker Hill and attack the then half-finished works defended by a force so greatly diminished, and seemed to be the only theme of discussion among the officers....

Sometime before the winter months of 1776 ended, the regiment was ordered to remove to Cambridge, the officers of which were quartered in the second story of the college buildings. It was at this encampment I saw for the first time the commander-in-chief, General Washington. A description of the peculiar circumstances under which it took place may not be thought foreign to the object of the present narrative but tend to illustrate not only the intrepidity and physical as

George Washington takes command of the Continental army at Cambridge, Massachusetts, July 3, 1775. Engraving by C. Rogers from a painting by M.A. Wageman (National Archives).

well as mental power of the commandant-in-chief, measurably show the low state of discipline then in the army, and the great difficulty of raising it to a proper standard.

A day or two preceding the incident I am about to relate, a rifle corps had come into camp from Virginia, made up of recruits from the backwoods and mountains of that state, in a uniform dress totally different from that of the regiments raised on the seaboard and interior of New England. Their white linen frocks, ruffled and fringed, excited the curiosity of the whole army, particularly to the Marblehead regiment, who were always full of fun and mischief. [They] looked with scorn on such a rustic uniform when compared to their own round jackets and fishers trousers, [and they] directly confronted from fifty to an hundred of the riflemen who were viewing the college buildings. Their first manifestations were ridicule and derision, which the riflemen bore with more patience than their wont, but resort being made to snow, which then covered the ground, these soft missives were interchanged but a few minutes before both parties closed, and a fierce struggle commenced with biting and gouging on the one part, and knockdown on the other part with as much apparent fury as the most deadly enmity could create. Reinforced by their friends, in less than five minutes more than a thousand combatants were on the field, struggling for the mastery.

At this juncture, General Washington made his appearance, whether by accident or design I never knew. I only saw him.... With the spring of a deer, he leaped from his saddle, threw the reins of his bridle into the hands of his servant and rushed into the thickest of the melee, with an iron grip seized two tall, brawny, athletic, savage-looking riflemen by the throat, keeping them at arm's length, alternately shaking and talking to them. In this position ... the belligerents caught sight of the general. Its effect on them was instantaneous flight at the top of their speed in all directions from the scene of the conflict. Less than fifteen minutes time had elapsed from the beginning of the row, before the general and his two criminals were the only occupants of the field of action. Here bloodshed, imprisonment, trials by court-martial were happily prevented and hostile feelings between the different corps of the army were extinguished by the physical and mental energies timely exerted by one individual.

19

The regiment continued to be quartered in and about the college buildings without any occurrence worthy of remark, except the occasional interchange of shot and shells with the enemy from the advanced works, until part of the army was marched to take possession of Dorchester Heights, and some days after, in the month of March, the main body of the army was put in motion sometime in the night, marched into Boston about the dawning of day, when the last of the enemy were leaving it....

Sometime in the course of the summer, part of the army took up its march for New York.... I was directed by my father to return home and hold myself ready to start when I received orders to do so ... My father quit the army, prostrated by sickness brought on by hardships and privations incident to a retreating army scantily supplied ... my father never returned to the army, being confined to his room nearly two years by the same sickness he brought home with him.

During his next few months at home, Israel decided to go to sea for his next duty. Privately owned ships were issued licenses (letters of marque) by the continental or state governments. When the ship captured an enemy vessel, the profits from sale of the cargo and the ship were divided among the owners, the officers and the crew. These privateers ranged from 100 to 500 tons and carried up to 20 guns. The average crew was 100 men. During the early part of 1777, as a 12-year-old veteran of two short tours in the war, Israel entered the sea service on the privateer schooner *Speedwell*.

Cruised in and about the banks of Newfoundland and captured four prizes; all arrived safe at Gloucester. The latter part of the same year, was fitted and commissioned as a letter of marque, the same vessel and same commander; went to Martinique and returned in safety. Early in the year 1778 I entered on board the ship *Black Prince* of Salem, Capt. Elias Smith, Lieutenants Bordman and Nathaniel West. A few days out, captured after a smart action a brig of sixteen guns commanded by a lieutenant of the British Navy. Cruised off the coast of Ireland, and in the Irish channel captured many prizes. Sent seven home; all arrived safe.

In the autumn of the same year, the same ship sailed on second cruise under the command of Nathaniel West. Not many days out, fell in with an English privateer the *Ladies Adventure,* mounting twenty guns. Not suspecting our character, she was unprepared, and shot poured into her with such rapidity, prevented all preparation for action. She surrendered without firing a gun. We cruised in the Bay of Biscay, took one more prize, went into Bilboa [Bilbao] to refit, sailed again, crossed the bay, cruised off the Land's End, the south and west coast of Ireland, captured some thirteen prizes, some of which were recaptured, and returned with the ship in safety to Salem early in the spring of 1779.

The British at Halifax on June 10, 1779, sent a force of ships and 650 men to build a fort at the mouth of Penobscot Bay. As it was two days' sail from Boston, it was a threat to New England. The Americans responded by sending a frigate, four brigs, a sloop, 2,500 troops on 22 transports, and numerous privateers. Together they mounted some 316 guns, against 190 of the British. The *Black Prince* was one of these. However, lack of agreement by the commanders delayed action until the British were able to bring reinforcements from New York. The Americans were forced up the Penobscot River where there was no escape. To prevent capture by the British, the American commander ordered the burning of all the ships not captured by the British. Israel relates his experiences.

The *Black Prince* shortly after her arrival at Salem from the latter cruise, was taken into the service of the Bay State [Massachusetts].... On board this ship I entered a volunteer, I believe in April 1779, and sailed from Salem the forepart of summer of said year and arrived at an eastern port I believe then called Townsend, where we lay many days waiting the arrival of other armed vessels and transports destined for the expedition to Penobscot. I continued on board this ship until she was blown up at the head of navigation on Penobscot River, from whence, with many others, I escaped to the dense forests and traveled through the wilderness about three hundred miles with a pack on my shoulders containing a light blanket, a small piece of rusty pork, a few biscuits, a bottle wine, and one shirt, wending my way across streams and through underbrush until the second day's march my shoes gave way. The rest of the way I performed on my bare feet until I reached home ... the month of September, '79.

Late in October, 1779, I again volunteered in the ship *Rambler,* twenty guns of Beverly.... Cruised on the Atlantic, Bay of Biscay, and entered Bilboa in December, where the ship was visited by the Honorable John Adams and his son John Quincy on their way through Spain to Paris. Sailed from thence the latter part of January, 1780. In one of the heavy gales of that severe winter, we were partially dismasted, lost main yard and mizzenmast. Arrived at Beverly the following March, 1780. Early in April, I again sailed in the brig *Wilkes* of Gloucester, fourteen guns. Took two prizes and sent home. Afterwards captured by the *Ferry*, sloop of war. Carried into St. John's, Newfoundland, where I was forced from the prison ship at the point of the bayonet on board the *Vestal* frigate and compelled to do duty until the arrival of Admiral Edwards, whose humanity, at the instances of a pathetic petition, ordered that I should with fourteen others be returned to the prison ship. Soon after, an exchange of prisoners took place. I returned home under the cartel.

In the winter of 1781, I sailed in the brig *Garland* of Newburyport, letter marque, Captain Knap, for Martinique. On the return voyage, was captured and carried into Bermuda. After some months' detention, I returned home under the cartel flag of exchange. In the summer of 1781 I served in making two voyages in safety to Martinique and back, first in the brig *Ranger* ... second in small brig from Gloucester.

In the spring of 1782 I entered on board the ship *Betsy*, eighteen guns, of Gloucester ... Second day out, captured by the *Perseverance* and *Ceres* frigates, the former rated forty-four, the first of that class ever launched from the navy yards of Great Britain. Here we experienced the full force of the insolent pride and lofty arrogance so prevalent in the navy and army of Great Britain at that period.

On board the *Perseverance* the prisoners were driven down under the haulup deck, their only beds large ironbound water casks, with a stifled, impure air to respire. Only four in the daytime and one at night were allowed to leave this dungeon to catch the pure air or answer the calls of nature. In about a fortnight we were relieved from these impurities to be thrust into a filthy prison ship at Halifax, a large old condemned East Indiaman. On her three decks were housed, or entombed, some hundreds of our countrymen, many of whom had been her occupants for three long years. The gloomy aspect of the ship, the cadaverous appearance of the prisoners, made death preferable to a lengthy abode in this horrific Avernus.

2. Israel Trask Sees Washington for the First Time

With spirits still alert and energies unrelaxed, the eighth day of confinement, two of our intrepid companions and expert swimmers swam in ice-cold water two miles to a fortified island and brought off, in the obscurity of a foggy evening, two boats within breath hearing of a sentinel. The smaller of the boats, unperceived, reached the ship, into which I was the last to enter. At the moment the alarm was given to the guard, and a volley of about forty muskets was poured in us before we had pulled a stroke. Only one ball entered the boat. Before a recharge could be made, we were hid in the obscurity of the night and succeeded, by hauling our boat on uninhabited islands in the daytime and embracing the night for progression, in making good our escape. After a fortnight of great suffering, we got on board of an American cruiser and reached our home a little over a month from the time we left it.

Israel made three more trips to the West Indies. News of peace reached him in Guadeloupe. He had made ten voyages on privateers and naval vessels, was captured three times, impressed into the British service once, and exchanged twice.

Bibliography

Trask, Israel. *1832 Revolutionary War Pension Application.* Washington, D.C. Veterans Administration Archives in the National Archives, Record Group 15, Microcopy 805.

3

Ebenezer Fox Runs Away to Sea

Listening to all the talk about freedom, 12-year-old Ebenezer Fox thought about liberty for himself. He began his Revolutionary War adventures when he ran away to sea on the night before the battle of Lexington and Concord, April 18–19, 1775. Serving on board several ships during his career, Ebenezer endured battles at sea, capture and imprisonment on the infamous *Jersey*, as well as near-drowning. Born in the east parish of Roxbury, Massachusetts, January 30, 1763, Ebenezer recalled that, when he was seven,

My father, who was a tailor, being poor and having a large family, thought that my physical powers were adequate, at this time of life, to my own maintenance; and placed me under the care of a farmer named Pelham. The house in which that gentleman resided was situated in what was then called Roxbury Street.

With him I continued five years performing such services in the house and upon the farm as were adapted to my age and strength. I imagined, however, that I suffered many privations and endured much hardship; which was undoubtedly true, were my situation compared with that of many other boys of my age at that time....

I had for some time been dissatisfied with my situation, and was desirous of some change. I had made frequent complaints of a grievous nature to my father; but he paid no attention to them, supposing that I had no just cause for them, and that they arose merely from a spirit of discontent which would soon subside....

Almost all the conversation that came to my ears related to the injustice of England and the tyranny of government....

I, and other boys situated similarly to myself, thought we had wrongs to be redressed; rights to be maintained ... I thought I was doing myself great injustice by remaining in bondage, when I ought to go free; and the time was come when I should liberate myself....

I sought a friend and found one in a companion with whom I had long associated, John Kelley, who was a little older than myself. To him I imparted my views and wishes in regard to future operations.

We held many consultations in secret, and mutual confidence being established, we came to the sage conclusion that we were living in a state of servitude that ought to be scorned by the sons of freemen.

In our opinion we were abundantly capable of providing for our own wants, of assuming all the responsibilities of life, and needed no protectors.

Our plan was soon formed, which was nothing less than to furnish ourselves with whatever we thought needed for our undertaking, to leave home privately, and take the most direct route to Providence, R. I. where we expected to find employment as sailors on board some vessel.

Our greatest trouble was to raise the means for the expedition. Having collected what few articles we possessed and securing them in two small bundles, we secreted them in a barn at some distance from our habitation.

The place for our meeting was the steps of the church.... I found my friend Kelley on the spot at eight o'clock in the evening on the eighteenth of April [1775], the night before the memorable battle of Lexington.

Kelley's first question to me was, "How much money have you got?" I replied "A half a dollar." "That is just what I have got," said Kelley, "though I might have taken as much as I wanted from the old Tory; but I thought I would not take any more than what belonged to me...."

Kelley had lived with a gentleman named Winslow, who was highly esteemed for his benevolence and other virtues: but being a friend to the royal government, he was stigmatized with the epithet of "Tory," and considered an enemy to his country and was finally obliged to leave the place when the British evacuated Boston. After spending some time making arrangements, we started about nine o'clock at night, and travelled till we arrived at Jamaica-Plain and stopped on the door-steps of the Rev. Dr. Gordon's church to rest ourselves and hold a consultation.

We concluded to continue on our route and directed our course to Dedham, where we arrived shortly after ten the same night.

As I have observed, this was on the night previous to the battle of Lexington. At that time, much excitement prevailed in the public mind. Great anxiety was manifested in the country in the vicinity of Boston to know what was going on there. People were out in all directions to hear the "news from town." As we were too young to be very well informed in regard to coming events, and were ignorant of the great plans in agitation, our fears induced us to think that the uncommon commotion that appeared to prevail must have some connexion with our escape, and that the moving multitudes we saw were in pursuit of us....

After making some cautious inquiries at Dedham, we directed our course to Walpole with the intention of reaching it that night.

About eleven o'clock, finding ourselves excessively fatigued, we determined upon taking up our night's lodging on the ground by the side of a stone wall.

With feelings of despondence I stretched myself upon the earth, with my bundle for a pillow, and observed to my companion, "This is hard lodging, Kelley, but we may have harder," little anticipating the hardship and suffering I was to endure in some succeeding years. After a cold and uncomfortable night's rest, we started before day and reached Walpole about ten o'clock in the morning.

Before we entered the village, we stopped at a tavern and called for a bowl of bread and milk, the price of which was three pence; but the kind-hearted landlord refused to take any compensation....

We stopped at Mann's tavern in Walpole and here a multitude of people collected, having some great object in agitation. Being seen coming in the direction from Boston, we were again assailed with more questions than we knew how to answer consistently with our safety. The tavern-keeper excited our apprehensions by abruptly asking us whither we were going?

"To seek our fortunes," we replied.

"You have taken hard times for it," and he advised us to return home.

During this conversation, the stagecoach from Boston arrived at the tavern, where the passengers were to dine. They brought the news of the Lexington battle, with an exaggerated account of a loss on the side of the British of two hundred men, and on that of the American of only thirty. This was received with loud shouts of exultation, while the militia marched off full of ardor and zeal....

British losses on April 19 were 73 killed, 190 wounded, and 22 taken prisoner. American casualties numbered 49 killed, 39 wounded, and five missing.

Tired of walking, our next object was to drive a bargain with the coachman for a ride to Providence.... After a great deal of haggling, a bargain was made to carry us both for two and eight-pence. We left Walpole about one o'clock and arrived in Providence about sunset.

Solitary and desolate, we felt as it were "strangers in a strange land...." Hungry and weary, with but thirty coppers in our pockets, we thought it would be, we thought, unjustifiable extravagance to indulge our appetites with the luxuries which a tavern might afford; we accordingly, seated upon the steps of a church, attempted to appease the cravings of hunger upon some provisions in our bundles, with which we had the precaution to provide ourselves before leaving Roxbury. Having finished our scanty meal, we found night approaching, and that it was necessary to obtain lodgings somewhere at a small expense.

Our design in coming to Providence naturally led us to the part of the town where the shipping lay. We found a vessel at a wharf, which appeared to have no person on board. We went on to her deck and finding the cabin doors open, entered, took possession of two vacant berths in which we slept soundly till morning, when we left the vessel without meeting with any person belonging to her.

We strolled about the town with spirits considerably depressed and breakfasted upon what remained of the cold food on which we had supped the previous night.

I and my companion then thought it best to separate for the purpose of seeking employment, in different directions; and we parted without thinking to fix upon any time or place for a subsequent meeting. I have since ascertained that Kelley found employment on board a vessel and went to sea.

Ebenezer visited an aunt who was living in Providence. First she tried to persuade him to return home. As he obstinately refused, she helped get him ready for a voyage.

After seeking for a situation on board of some vessel for several days, I at length found one in the service of Capt. Joseph Manchester, who was in the employ of Nathanial Angier. I shipped in the capacity of cabin boy, for a compensation of twenty-one shillings per month to go to Cape François in the island of St. Domingo...

The vessel was hauled off into the stream, and shortly after, we sailed for our destined port. This being the first time I ever was at sea, I experienced a considerable amount of "sea-sickness;" but in a few days I became accustomed to the motion of the vessel, and recovered my usual health and spirits. Being what is termed a "green hand," I had everything to learn that belonged to my duties; and of course made some blunders for which I received more curses than thanks.

Among other misfortunes, I unluckily placed a large pot of butter in the larboard locker, without the precaution to fasten it in its place. It rolled out in the course of the night and the fragments of the pot, together with the contents, were scattered about near the foot of the cabin steps. At the time of the accident the captain was upon deck, and having occasion to go below, he stepped into the midst of the greasy particles and measured his length upon the floor. The butter received a stamp of considerable magnitude in the form of a head, which although it served to protect the captain's from any lamentable damage, did not shield mine from a volley of oaths and threats arising from the irritation of the moment at the awkward predicament in which he found himself placed.

After a pleasant voyage of about fourteen days, we arrived in sight of our destined port. That part of St. Domingo in which Cape François is situated was then in possession of the French; and in regard to certain articles, trade was prohibited between the inhabitants and the American colonies. Some management was therefore necessary to obtain the cargo we wanted. A boat was sent ashore to inform certain merchants, who were expecting us, of our arrival. In the morning a pilot came to our assistance, and we were soon anchored in the harbor of Cape François.

We carried our staves and hoops in a state of preparation to be converted into hogsheads; and I worked at coopering till we were ready to receive our cargo. Having filled the hogsheads with molasses, which was apparently all our cargo, we set sail and afterwards took on board a quantity of coffee, a prohibited article, which was conveyed to us by vessels employed for that purpose.

Our loading being thus completed, we directed our course for Providence, and after a passage of about fifteen days we arrived at Stonington, Connecticut.

During our absence from home, the Revolutionary War had commenced, and we found that the British had begun their depredations upon our commerce and maritime towns.

We left Stonington in the night, entertaining the hope, that, with a favorable wind, we might get into Providence without being discovered by the British cruisers, which we knew were cruising somewhere between Newport and Providence.

If the breeze had continued favorable, we should have effected our object; but unfortunately, the wind subsided a little before daylight, and in the morning we found ourselves close by the enemy, consisting of two ships of war, and a small vessel called a tender between them and the land. The American commander, Commodore Whipple, with a naval force greatly inferior to the British, was seen by us, higher up the bay, out of reach of the enemy, making signals for us to press all sail and approach. But unluckily we were ignorant of the meaning of the signals, and did not know whether they came from a friend or an enemy. As the cruisers were to the windward of us, we tacked one way and the other, hoping that we should be able to beat up the bay; but finding that the tender was about to intercept our progress in one direction, while the cruisers approached us in the other, and no chance of escape appearing, we bore away and ran our vessel ashore.

Preparations were hastily made for leaving the vessel. Our captain gave permission to all, who were disposed to run the risk, to make their escape. The mate and crew jumped overboard and swam for shore where they all arrived safe, although fired upon by the British tender.

Captain Manchester, supposing that I should be unable to reach the shore by swimming, kindly advised me to remain on board with him and be taken prisoner. I hesitated a short time about taking his advice, but finally concluded to run the risk of being drowned; and with nothing on but a shirt and a pair of trousers, I plunged into the sea and swam for the shore. I arrived without injury, but nearly exhausted from fatigue and fear, not a little augmented by the sound of the bullets that whistled around my head while in the water. In dread of pursuit, I ran into a cornfield, and finding my wet clothes an encumbrance, I stripped them off and ran with all speed through the field.

At a little distance in advance of me, I could discover a number of men, whom I soon found to be our ship's crew, who had landed before me. My appearance among them in a state of entire nakedness excited not a little mirth. "Holloa! my boy," exclaimed one of them, "you cut a pretty figure; not from the garden of Eden, I can swear for it, for you have not even an apron of fig-leaves to cover you with; you were not born to be drowned, I see, though you may live to be hanged." But after a few jests at my expense, the mate took off one of the two shirts which he had taken the precaution to provide himself before he left the vessel, and he gave it to me. This garment answered all the purposes of a covering as it effectually covered my person from my shoulders to my feet. After travelling about half a mile, we came to a house, where the good woman, taking pity on my grotesque and unique position, gave me a decent suit of clothes.

I immediately proceeded to Providence, where I arrived the same day, and lost no time before visiting my good aunt, although I had great doubts and fears of the reception I should meet with. She was glad to see me again, but did not lose the opportunity of giving me a long lecture upon the folly of my conduct in leaving home; and appealed to my candor to acknowledge the justice of her reproof, by comparing my present condition with what it formerly was. The anxiety and distress of my parents, too, were described to me in all the eloquence of female affection, as an additional inducement to return to them.... Finding me obstinately resolved upon undertaking another voyage, to obtain, as I thought, some remuneration for the misfortunes experienced in the first, my aunt showed a disposition to assist me as readily as before and I was soon comfortably fitted out for a second expedition.

Four days after my arrival in Providence, I fortunately met with a ship-master named Thomas, and engaged in his employ for a voyage to Cape François, the port to which I sailed on my former voyage. We had a short passage, and arrived at our destined port without anything having transpired worthy of notice during the voyage.

We took on a cargo similar to the one we received on my former voyage, and set sail for Providence, where we arrived after a pleasant voyage of eighteen or twenty days. I worked on board the vessel several days, assisting to unload her, and then received my wages, which had been stipulated at four dollars per month.

With my money in my pocket, the largest sum I ever before possessed, and much elated with my success, I visited my good aunt once more, who received me with much joy. She assisted me with her advice in purchasing some articles of clothing, that I might make a respectable appearance among my friends....

After securing my clothing in a small pack, I slung it on my back and started on foot for home, from which I had been absent about six months. This was the latter part of November, 1775.

My finances being rather low, after deducting the expense of my clothing, I found it necessary to exercise economy on my journey, and not indulge myself in entertainment at public houses. I found a ready welcome at the dwellings of the farmers on the road, and was treated with an abundance of bread and milk without compensation. I was hospitably received at a respectable farm-house the first night on my journey; and on the second, arrived at the American camp in Roxbury on Saturday evening. Ascertaining that my parents had, during my absence, removed to Dorchester, a distance of about three miles, I felt too much fatigued to seek their residence that night, and found comfortable accommodations in one of the barracks.

Early on Sunday morning I started for Dorchester, and soon, to my great joy and satisfaction, found my parents in the enjoyment of good health, except my father who was afflicted with a bad cold. My mother gazed at me with the amazement of one who had seen a spectre.... She had concluded that I had gone to sea, and that, in her estimation was equivalent to being lost.... Intimating that I was hungry, having had no breakfast, she postponed the gratification of her curiosity to attend to my animal wants.

My father with much gravity and solemnity of manner, addressed me as follows: " My son, I am much surprised and grieved that you should have left home in the manner you did without giving us any means to ascertain your fate, or what your intentions were. If you had any cause for complaint, and thought yourself ill-treated, why did you not inform me, and I would have seen justice done?" With the sense of wrongs, either real or imaginary, still rankling in my breast, I replied that I had done so. "Since you have been preserved from any serious disaster," continued my father, "and no evil consequences have resulted from the imprudent steps you have taken, I hope you will abandon all such schemes in the future. You can remain at home until you are old enough to learn a trade, and then choose one for yourself...."

During the winter I improved the time in attending a school and making myself useful in various ways to my parents.... [In the spring] I found employment in the shop of Mr. John Bosson, a barber and manufacturer of wigs ... In Mr. Bosson's service I continued until I was sixteen years old and made laudable progress in the mysteries of his art.

The war at this time was fiercely maintained between the United States and Great Britain; and as soldiers were wanted, a draught was made upon the militia of Massachusetts for a quota of men to march to New York, to reinforce the American army then in the vicinity of that city. My master was unfortunately among the number draughted for that service ... he wanted someone to take his place.

The spirit of adventure had been suppressed, but not destroyed within me. The monotonous duties of the shop grew irksome, and I longed for some employment productive of variety. The opportunity seemed favorable to my desires; and I resolved upon offering my services.

Mr. Bosson accepted my proposition to act as his substitute with a great degree of satisfaction and gratitude, which he evinced by a liberal supply of clothing and equipment for the service. He did not suffer my zeal to cool, but immediately gave directions to have me enrolled and enlisted for three months, in a company commanded by Capt. William Bird of Boston, in a regiment under Colonel Proctor.

Early in the month of September, 1779, being not quite sixteen, the age required at that time for the militia service, our company was paraded on Boston common, and with a heavy knapsack on my back, and a gun on my shoulder, superior in weight to those carried at the present time, we took up the line of march.

We halted at Roxbury to take under our protection six baggage wagons of ammunition, and commenced our march for Peeks-kill in the state of New York.... After a fatiguing march of five or six days, we arrived at Peeks-kill, and delivered to the commander there our wagons and then marched to Albany. We remained here about six weeks, when,

General Washington having changed his plan of operations, and abandoned his design of attacking New York, and our services being no longer needed, we were discharged, to get home in the best way we could.

My clothes were much worn and damaged in the service, and upon our return were found in a very shabby condition, especially my shoes. Of these I had two pairs, but the good judgment of a thief was shown by stealing the better pair one night while I was asleep, leaving me no other alternative but to go barefoot, or secure the remaining shoes to my feet by winding rope-yarn around them in the form of bandages.

My feet were covered with blisters while I marched over the frozen ground and snow; and thus, almost crippled, and worn down with fatigue, I arrived at my father's...

After resting a few days at home, and recovering my strength and spirits, I returned to Mr. Bosson, abundantly satisfied with the specimen I had experienced of a soldier's life, assuring him that nothing would again induce me to officiate as a substitute for him or anybody else.

I continued to perform my duties in the shop, and was contented with my employment till I was about seventeen years of age, when a spirit of roving once more got possession of me; and I expressed a desire to go to sea.

The condition of the country was at this time distressing; and, as my master had not more business than he and one apprentice could perform, he expressed a willingness to consent, upon condition that he should receive one half of my wages and the same proportion of whatever prize money might fall to my share.

Our coast was lined with British cruisers, which had almost annihilated our commerce. The state of Massachusetts was building a twenty-gun ship called the "*Protector,*" commanded by John Foster Williams. She was to be fitted out for service as soon as possible, to protect our commerce, and to annoy the enemy. A rendezvous was established for recruits at the head of Hancock's wharf, where the national flag, then bearing thirteen stripes and stars, was hoisted. All means were resorted to, which ingenuity could devise, to induce men to enlist. A recruiting officer, bearing a flag and attended by a band of martial music, paraded the streets, to excite a thirst for glory and a spirit of military ambition.

I Was a Teenager in the American Revolution

The recruiting officer ... was a jovial, good-natured fellow, of ready wit and much broad humor. Crowds followed in his wake when he marched the streets; and he occasionally stopped at the corners to harangue the multitude in order to excite their patriotism and zeal for the cause of liberty.

When he espied large boys among the idle crowd around him, he would attract their attention by singing in a comical manner the following doggerel:

> All you that have bad masters,
> And cannot get your due;
> Come, come, my brave boys,
> And join with our ship's crew.

A shout and a huzza would follow, and some would join in the ranks. My excitable feelings were roused; I repaired to the rendezvous, signed the ship's papers, mounted a cockade, and was in my own estimation already more than a half a sailor...

About the last of February the ship was ready to receive her crew, and was hauled off into the channel, that the sailors might have no opportunity to run away after they were got on board.

Upwards of three hundred and thirty men were carried, dragged, and driven on board, of all kinds, ages, and descriptions, in all the various stages of intoxication....

The wind being fair, we weighed anchor and dropped down to Nantasket roads, where we lay till about the first of April; and then set sail for a cruise of six months.

After sailing for some time, some indications of tempestuous weather appearing, our captain judged it expedient to steer for the banks of Newfoundland, that he might have more sea room in case of a gale. We arrived off the banks, where we cruised for nearly eight weeks, most of the time in a dense fog, without meeting friend or foe.

On the morning of June 9, 1780, the fog began to clear away. The man at the mast-head gave notice that he saw a ship to the westward of us. We perceived her to be a large ship under English colors to the windward, standing athwart our starboard bow....

As she came down upon us, she appeared as large as a seventy-four; and we were not deceived respecting her size, for it afterwards proved

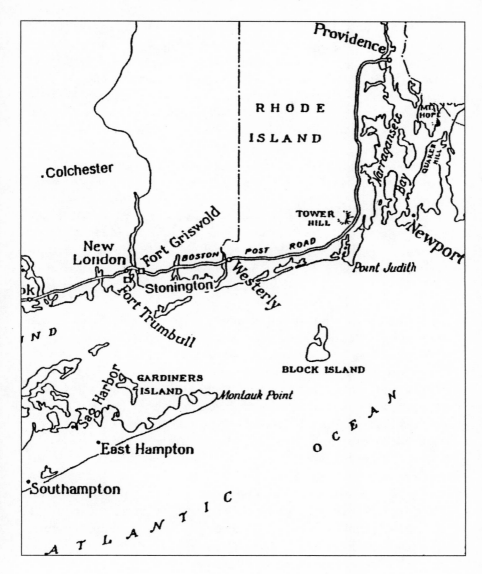

New London to Providence (From *Atlas of American History,* by Kenneth T. Jackson, Charles Scribner's Sons, © 1984, Charles Scribner's Sons. Reprinted by permission of the Gale Group).

that she was an old East-Indian, fitted out as a letter-of-marque for the West-India trade, mounted with thirty-two guns, and furnished with a complement of one hundred and fifty men. She was called the *Admiral Duff* ... laden with sugar and tobacco, and bound to London. I was standing near our first lieutenant, Mr. Little, who was calmly examining the enemy, as she approached, with his spy-glass, when Captain Williams stepped up and asked his opinion of her. The lieutenant applied the glass to his eye again and took a deliberate look in silence and replied, "I think she is a heavy ship, and that we shall have some hard fighting; but of one thing I am certain, she is not a frigate. If she were, she would not keep yawing, and showing her broad sides as she does; she would show nothing but her head and stern; we shall have the advantage of her, and the quicker we get alongside the better." Our captain ordered English colors to be hoisted, and the ship cleared for action. The shrill pipe of the boatswain summoned all hands to their duty. The bedding and hammocks of the sailors were brought up from between decks. The bedding was placed in the hammocks and lashed up in the nettings; our courses hauled up; the top-gallant sails clewed down; and every preparation was made which a skillful officer could suggest or active sailors perform.

The enemy approached till within musket shot of us. The two ships were so near to each other that we could distinguish the officers from the men; and I particularly noticed the captain on the gangway, a noble-looking man, having a large gold-laced cocked hat on his head and a speaking trumpet in his hand. Lieutenant Little possessed a powerful voice, and he was directed to hail the enemy; at the same time the quarter-master was ordered to stand ready to haul down the English flag and to hoist up the American. Our Lieutenant took his station on the after part of the starboard gangway, and elevating the trumpet, exclaimed, "Halloo! Whence come you?"—"From Jamaica, bound to London," was the answer. "What is the ship's name?" inquired the lieutenant. "The Admiral Duff," was the reply.

The English captain then thought it his turn to interrogate, and asked the name of our ship. Lieutenant Little, in order to gain time, put the trumpet to his ear, pretending not to hear the question. During the short interval thus gained, Captain Williams called upon the gunner to ascertain how many guns could be brought to bear upon the enemy. "Five," was the answer. "Then fire, and shift the colors," were the orders. The cannons poured forth their deadly contents, and with the first flash, the American flag took the place of the British ensign at our mast-head.

The compliment was returned in the form of a full broadside, and the action commenced. I was stationed on the edge of the quarter-deck, to sponge and load a six pounder. This position gave me a fine opportunity to see the whole action. Broadsides were exchanged with great rapidity for nearly an hour; our fire, as we afterwards ascertained, produced a terrible slaughter among the enemy; while our loss was as yet trifling.

I happened to be looking for a moment towards the main deck, when a large shot came through our ship's side and killed Mr. Benjamin Scaly who was, I think, a midshipman. At this moment a shot from one of our marines killed the man at the wheel of the enemy's ship; and his place not being immediately supplied, she was brought alongside of us in such a manner as to bring her bowsprit directly across our forecastle. Not knowing the cause of this movement, we supposed it to be the intention of the enemy to board us. Our boarders were ordered to be ready with their pikes to resist any such attempt, while our guns on the main deck were sending death and destruction among the crew of the enemy. Their principal object now seemed to be to get liberated from us, and by cutting away some of their rigging, they were soon clear, and at the distance of a pistol shot.

The action was then renewed with additional fury; broadside for broadside continued with unabated vigor; at times so near to each other that the muzzles of our guns came almost in contact, then again at such a distance as to allow of taking deliberate aim. The contest was obstinately continued by the enemy, although we could perceive that great havoc was made among them, and that it was with much difficulty that their men were compelled to remain at their quarters.

A charge of grape shot came in at one of the port-holes, which dangerously wounded four or five of our men, among whom was our third lieutenant, Mr. Little, brother to the first. His life was despaired of, but by the kind attention he received from his brother, and the surgeon, he finally recovered, though he bore evidence of the severity of his wounds thro' life.

While Captain Williams was walking the quarterdeck, which he did during the whole action, a shot from the enemy struck the speaking trumpet from his hand, and sent it to a considerable distance from him. He picked it up with great calmness of manner, and resumed his walk, without appearing to have been at all disturbed by the circumstance.

The battle still continued with unabated vigor on both sides, till our marksmen had killed or wounded all the men in fore, main, and mizzen tops of the enemy. The action had now lasted about an hour and a half, and the fire from the enemy began to slacken, when we suddenly discovered that all the sails on her mainmast were enveloped in a blaze. The fire spread with amazing rapidity, and, running down the after rigging, it soon communicated with her magazine, when her whole stern was blown off, and her valuable cargo emptied into the sea. All feelings of hostility now ceased, and those of pity were excited in our breasts for the miserable crew that survived the catastrophe.

Our enemy's ship was now a complete wreck, though she still floated, and the survivors were endeavoring to save themselves in the only boat that had escaped the general destruction. The humanity of our captain urged him to make all possible exertion to save the miserable, wounded, and burnt wretches, who were struggling for their lives in the water. The ship of the enemy was greatly our superior in size, and lay much higher out of the water.

Our boats had suffered considerable damage. The carpenters were ordered to repair them with the utmost expedition, and we got them out in season to take up fifty-five men, the greater part of whom had been wounded by our shot or burned when the powder magazine exploded. These men exhibited a spectacle truly heart-rending to behold.... Our surgeon and his assistants had just completed the task of dressing the wounds of our own crew, and then they directed their attention to the wounded of the enemy.... From the survivors we learned that the British commander had frequently expressed a desire to come in contact with a "Yankee frigate," during his voyage, that he might have a prize to carry to London. Poor fellow! He little thought of losing his ship and his life in an engagement with a ship so much inferior to his own—with an enemy upon whom he looked with so much contempt.

3. Ebenezer Fox Runs Away to Sea

After the action was over, I found that I was so deaf as to cause me to fear that I had totally lost the sense of hearing. I attributed this to the noise of the cannon, which I had been employed in loading and sponging for such a period of time. It was nearly a week before my hearing was restored, and then but partially; and, ever since I have experienced great inconvenience from this deafness.

After cruising several more weeks the provisions of the ship began to fail, and there seemed no prospects of making captures soon.

Our captain concluded to steer for Boston. In a few days we came in sight of Boston lighthouse, and anchored in Nantasket roads where we remained a short time, then stood up the harbor, and hauled in at Hancock's wharf. The sails were unbent, the sick landed, the ship unloaded. All hands, who were not disposed to enlist for a second cruise, were paid off and discharged.

Thus ended my first cruise in the *Protector*. And, although I had not added to my wealth, I had gained some knowledge of a sailor's life, and felt disposed to try my fortune a little more by enlisting for a second voyage. During the short interval between my first and second cruise, while I was at home, my father was taken sick and died. The death of a kind parent under any circumstances is a melancholy bereavement, and this was particularly so to my mother and her eight children, some of whom were very young.

Though unwilling to leave her in her affliction, I felt the necessity of exerting myself that I might contribute something to the maintenance of the family, who were left very destitute. I knew of no way in which there was a prospect of my being so useful to them as that of engaging for another cruise....

In the meantime our ship was thoroughly overhauled, her bottom scraped, rigging repaired, and everything done to put her in perfect order. Wood and water, and various kinds of stores necessary for a cruise of six months were taken on board; and having recruited about two hundred men, preparations were made for our immediate departure.

About the last of October, our boats were hoisted on deck and secured, and we dropped down into Nantasket roads, where we remained a few days, and then set sail upon our second cruise.

After sailing to Halifax and then to the West Indies they secured two prizes, a brig and a schooner, near Sandy Hook near New York. They then headed back to Boston and expected to share a considerable sum of prize money.

We continued merrily on our course, without seeing friend or foe, during the next day; but the following morning, the man at mast-head cried out, "Two sail to the leeward." Mr. Little ascended to the main top with his glass, and soon ascertained that they were two large ships, closely hauled upon the wind, in full chase of us. The brig we had in tow was quickly cast off, and she and the schooner were ordered to make the best progress they could. Our yards were braced, and all sail crowded that the ship could carry.

The chase continued, without gaining much upon us till about noon, when, the wind shifting, they fell into our wake, and gained upon us very fast.... It was now nearly sunset, and the enemy were gaining upon us rapidly. They had exchanged their French for English colors, thus ending our hopes and doubts respecting their character. Our capture was now considered no longer problematical...

They proved to be the *Roe-Buck*, a forty-gun ship with a double deck, and the *May-Day [Medea]*, of twenty-eight guns. They had been upon the look-out for us for three or four weeks; having received information from the Tories in Boston that we were expected to return from our cruise about this time. We were ordered to strike our colors, or a broadside would be sent to enforce compliance with the demand....

To attempt resistance against a force so much our superior would have been unjustifiable; and the flag of thirteen stars and stripes, under which we had sailed with much satisfaction and success, was reluctantly pulled down. This was the unfortunate end of our second cruise.

The boats of the enemy were manned, and sent alongside of our ship. Our crew were now permitted by our officers to collect their clothing and their little property together, and secure them in the best manner they could.

By this time the boats had arrived alongside, and the enemy had ascended the deck.

Their first exploit was to strike or kick every sailor that came in their way, bestowing a variety of opprobrious epithets, among which

40

"damned rebels" was of the most frequent recurrence; then they commenced searching in every part of the ship for articles of value.

Our crew were ordered to pass down the side of the ship into the enemy's boats; but were forbidden to carry any thing with them. Some of our crew fastened their bedding upon their backs, and tumbled themselves head foremost down into the boats; and as it was quite dark, they would unperceived get into the cuddy with their bedding, trusting to future circumstances to use or secrete it....

We arrived alongside, and were ordered on to the quarter-deck of our captors ... Our accommodations in the hold were not very desirable, especially to those who had not succeeded in getting their bedding into that place. We found nothing to lie upon softer than the ship's ballast, consisting of stones of all shapes and sizes, with here and there a lump of pig iron by way of variety; and the water casks, which afforded a surface rather uneven for the comfort and convenience of our weary limbs.

Here we spent the first night, and were not allowed to go on deck till the next morning.

The *Roe-Buck* had the charge of the prisoners, while the *May-Day* was sent in pursuit of the two prizes we had in possession at the time of our capture. Greatly to our satisfaction, however, she was unable to over-haul them. They both arrived in safety in Boston a few days later.

Shortly after, we anchored off Sandy Hook, ... we were called up from the hold; ordered to the larboard side of the quarter-deck; thence marched, in single file, past a number of British officers on the starboard side; after that to the gangway, and down again into the hold. The object of thus moving in procession before the officers was, to give them an opportunity to select such as they chose, to serve on board of their ships. With fear and trembling we passed through this examination.... Sailors they wanted, and have them they would, if they set law and gospel at defiance. In this manner was many an American citizen, in the morning of life, dragged from his country, his friends, and his home; forced on board a ship of war; compelled to fight against his own country; and if he lived, to fight in battle with other nations, against whom he had no feelings of hostility. Many a one spent his whole life in foreign service, far from his native land, while his relatives were ignorant of his fate, till worn out with toil and wounds, a shadow of his former self, he dropped into the grave unpitied and unknown.

About a third part of our ship's crew were taken on board their vessels, to serve in the capacity of sailors, without regarding their remonstrances; while the remainder of us were put on board of a wood coaster, to be conveyed on board the noted prison ship called the *Jersey*....

We proceeded slowly up the river towards our dreaded place of confinement, and at doubling a point we came in sight of the gloomy-looking hulk of the old *Jersey*, aptly named by the sailors, "The hell afloat." The *Jersey* was originally a seventy-four gun ship, and at the commencement of the American Revolution, being found in a state of decay and unfit for service at sea, she was dismantled, moored in the East River at New York, and used as a store-ship. In the year 1780 she was converted into a [British] prison-ship, and continued to be used for that purpose during the remainder of the war.

In consequence of the fears that were entertained that the sickness, which prevailed among the prisoners, might spread to the shore, she was removed and moored with chain cables at the Wallabout, a lonely and unfrequented place on the shore of Long Island. Her external appearance was forbidding and gloomy. She was dismantled; her only spars were the bowsprit; a derrick, that looked like a gallows, for hoisting supplies on board; and also flagstaff at the stern. The port-holes were closed and secured. Two tiers of holes were cut through her sides, about two feet square and about ten feet apart, strongly guarded by a grating of iron bars....

The idea of being a prisoner in such a place was sufficient to fill the mind with grief and distress. The heart sickened, the cheek grew pale with the thought. Our destiny was before us, and there was no alternative but to submit.

The sloop anchored at a little distance from the *Jersey*; and two boats were sent alongside to receive us....

After being detained in the boats alongside a little while, we were ordered to ascend to the upper deck of the prison ship. Here our names were registered and the capacity in which we had served previous to our capture. Each of us was permitted to retain whatever clothing and bedding we had brought, after having been examined to ascertain that they contained no weapons nor money; and then we were directed to pass through a strong door, on the starboard side, down a ladder leading to the main hatchway. I now found myself in a loathsome prison, among a collection of the most wretched and disgusting looking objects that I ever beheld in human form. Here was a motley crew, covered with rags and filth, visages palled with disease, emaciated with hunger and anxiety, and retaining hardly a trace of their original appearance. Here were men, who had once enjoyed life while riding over the mountain wave or roaming through pleasant fields, full of health and vigor, now shriveled by a scanty and unwholesome diet, ghastly with inhaling an impure atmosphere, exposed to contagion, in contact with disease, and surrounded with the horrors of sickness and death. Here, thought I, must I linger out the morning of my life, in tedious days and sleepless nights, enduring a weary and degrading captivity, till death shall terminate my sufferings, and no friend will know of my departure. A prisoner on board the "the old *Jersey!*" The very thought was appalling. I could hardly realize my situation.

The first thing we found it necessary to do after our captivity was to form ourselves into small parties, called "messes," consisting of six men each; as, previous to doing this, we could obtain no food. All the prisoners were obliged to fast on the first day of their arrival; and seldom on the second could they procure any food in season for cooking it....

Prisoners on the *Jersey,* by John Trumbull (Charles Allen Munn Collection, Fordham University Library, Bronx, New York).

The various messes of the prisoners were numbered. Nine in the morning was the hour when the steward would deliver from the window in his room, at the after-part of the ship, the allowance granted to each mess. Each mess chose one of their company to be prepared to answer to their number when it was called by the steward, and to receive the allowance as it was handed from the window.... Each prisoner received two-thirds as much as was allowed to a seaman in the British navy.

Our bill of fare was as follows:

On Sunday and Thursday, one pound of biscuit, one pound of pork, and half of a pint of peas. Monday and Friday, one pound of biscuit, one pint of oat-meal, and two ounces of butter. Tuesday and Saturday, one pound of biscuit, and two pounds of salt beef. Wednesday, one and a half pounds of flour, and two ounces of suet.

If this food had been of a good quality and properly cooked, as we had no labor to perform, it would have kept us comfortable, at least from suffering. But this was not the case. All our food appeared damaged.

The bread was mouldy, and filled with worms. It required considerable rapping upon the deck before the worms could be dislodged from their lurking places in a biscuit. As for the pork, we were cheated out of it more than half of the time: and, when it was obtained, one would have judged from its motley hues, exhibiting the consistence and appearance of variegated fancy soap, that it was the flesh of the porpoise, or sea-hog, and had been an inhabitant of the ocean rather than of the sty...

The peas were generally damaged, and, from the imperfect manner in which they were cooked, were about as indigestible as grapeshot.... The flour and the oat-meal were often sour, and when the suet was mixed with it, we should have considered it a blessing to have been destitute of the sense of smelling before we admitted it into our mouths. It might be nosed half the length of the ship.

And last, though not the least item among our staples in the eating line—our beef.... It was so completely saturated with salt, that after having been boiled in water taken from the sea, it was found to be considerably freshened by the process.... It required more skill than we possessed to determine whether the flesh, which we were obliged to devour, had once covered the bones of some luckless bull that had died from starvation; or of some worn-out horse that had been killed for the crime of having outlived his usefulness.

Such was our food. The quality of it was not all that we had reason to complain of. The manner in which it was cooked was more injurious to our health, than the quality of the food; and, in many cases, laid the foundation of diseases, that brought many a sufferer to his grave, years after his liberation.

The cooking for the prisoners was done in a great copper vessel, that contained between two and three hogsheads of water set in brick work. The form of it was square, and it was divided into two compartments by a partition. In one of these, the peas and oatmeal were boiled; this was done in fresh water; in the other, the meat was boiled, in salt water taken up from alongside the ship.

The *Jersey* from her size and lying near the shore, was imbedded in the mud; and I do not recollect seeing her afloat during the whole time I was a prisoner. All the filth that accumulated among upwards of a thousand men was daily thrown overboard, and would remain there till carried away by the tide. The impurity of the water may be easily conceived; and in this water our meat was boiled.

The persons, chosen by each mess to receive their portions of food, were summoned by the cook's bell to receive their allowance, and when it had remained in the boiler a certain time, the bell would again sound, and the allowance must be immediately taken away: whether it was sufficiently cooked, or not, it could remain no longer. The food was generally very imperfectly cooked; yet this sustenance, wretched though it was, and deficient in quantity, was greedily devoured by half-starved prisoners.

No vegetables were allowed us. Many times since, when I have seen in the country, a large kettle of potatoes and pumpkins steaming over the fire to satisfy the appetites of a farmer's swine, I have thought of our destitute and starved condition, and what a luxury we should have considered the contents of that kettle on board the *Jersey*.

The prisoners were confined in the two main decks below. The lowest dungeon was inhabited by those prisoners who were foreigners, and whose treatment was more severe than that of the Americans.

The inhabitants of this lower region were the most miserable and disgusting-looking objects that can be conceived. Daily washing with salt water, together with their extreme emaciation, caused their skin to appear like dried parchment. Many of them remained unwashed for weeks; their hair long and matted, and filled with vermin; their beards never cut, excepting occasionally with a pair of shears, which did not improve their comeliness, though it might add to their comfort. Their clothes were mere rags, secured to their bodies in every way that ingenuity could devise.

Many of these men had been in this lamentable condition for two years, part of the time on board other prison-ships; and, having given up all hope of ever being exchanged, had become resigned to their situation.

In the morning prisoners were permitted to ascend the upper deck, to spend the day, till ordered below at sunset. A certain number, who were for the time called the "Working Party" performed in rotation the duty of bringing up hammocks and bedding for airing, likewise the sick and infirm, and the bodies of those who had died during the night; of these there were generally a number every morning. After these services, it was their duty to wash the decks. Our beds and clothing were allowed to remain on deck till we were ordered below for the night; this was of considerable benefit, as it gave some of the vermin an opportunity to migrate from the quarters they had inhabited....

But little sleep, however, could be enjoyed ... for the vermin were so horribly abundant, that all the personal cleanliness we could practice would not protect us from their attacks, or prevent their effecting a lodgment upon us.

Several attempts were made to escape but most were not successful.

The miseries of our condition were continually increasing: the pestilence on board spread rapidly and every day added to our bill of mortality.... Our privateers captured many British seamen; who, when willing to enlist in our service as was generally the case, were received on board our ships. Those who were brought into port, were suffered to go at large; for in the impoverished condition of the country, no state or town was willing to subject itself to the expense of maintaining prisoners in a state of confinement; they were permitted to provide for themselves. In this way the number of British seamen was far too small for a regular and equal exchange. Thus the British seamen, after their capture, enjoyed the blessings of liberty, the light of the sun and the purity of the atmosphere, while the poor American sailors were compelled to drag out a miserable existence amid want and distress, famine and pestilence.

We had obtained some information in relation to an expected draught that would soon be made upon the prisoners to fill up a complement of men that were wanted for the service of his Majesty's fleet.

One day in the latter part of August, our fears of the dreaded event were realized. A British officer with a number of soldiers came on board. The prisoners were all ordered on deck, were placed on the larboard gangway, and marched in single file round to the quarter-deck, where the officers stood to inspect them and select such ones as suited their fancies, without any reference to the rights of the prisoners, or etc....

Their argument was "Men we want, and men we will have." We continued to march around, in solemn and melancholy procession, till they had selected from among our number about three hundred of the ablest, nearly all of whom were Americans, and they were directed to go below under a guard, to collect together whatever things they wished to take belonging to them. They were then driven into the boats, waiting alongside, and left the prison-ship, not to enjoy their freedom, but to be subjected to the iron despotism, and galling slavery of a British man-of-war; to waste their lives in a foreign service...

In the midst of our distress, perplexities, and troubles at this period, we were not a little puzzled to know how to dispose of the vermin that would accumulate upon our persons, notwithstanding all our attempts at cleanliness. To catch them was a very easy task.... What then was to be done with them? A general consultation was held, and it was determined to deprive them of their liberty.

This being agreed upon, the prisoners went to work immediately, for their comfort and amusement, to make a liberal contribution of those migratory creatures who were compelled to colonize for a time within the boundaries of a large snuff-box appropriated for the purpose. There they lay, snugly ensconced, of all colors, ages, and sizes, to the amount of some thousands, waiting for orders.

British recruiting officers frequently came on board, and held out to the prisoners tempting offers to enlist in his Majesty's service; not to fight against their own country, but to perform garrison duty in the island of Jamaica. One day an Irish officer came on board for this purpose, and, not meeting with much success among the prisoners who happened to be on deck, he descended below to repeat his offers. He was a remarkably tall man, and was obliged to stoop as he passed along between the decks. The prisoners were disposed for a frolic and kept the officer in their company for some time, flattering him with expectations, till he discovered their insincerity, and left them in no very pleasant humor. As he passed along, bending his body, and bringing his broad shoulders to nearly a horizontal position, the idea occurred to our minds to furnish him with some recruits from the colony in the snuff-box. A favorable opportunity presented, the cover of the box was removed, and the whole contents discharged upon the red-coated back of the officer. Three cheers from the prisoners followed the migration, and the officer ascended to the deck, unconscious of the number and variety of recruits he had obtained without the formality of an enlistment. The captain of the ship, suspicious that some joke had been practiced, or some mischief perpetrated, from the noise below, met the officer at the head of the gangway, and seeing the vermin crawling up his shoulders and aiming at his head with the instinct peculiar to them, exclaimed, "Hoot, mon, wha' is the matter with yer bock?" The captain was a Scotchman. By this time many of them, in their wanderings, had travelled around from the rear to the front, and showed themselves, to the astonishment of the officer. He flung off his coat in a paroxysm of rage, which was not allayed by three cheers from the prisoners on the deck. Confinement below, with a short allowance, was our punishment for this gratification....

While prisoners on board of the *Jersey* we could obtain no accurate knowledge of the success of the American cause.... Cold weather was approaching, and we had no comfortable clothing to protect us from the rigors of an inclement season.... In despair of any improvement being in prospect for our liberation, we concluded that we would enlist for soldiers for the West-India service, and trust to Providence for finding an opportunity to leave the British for the American service.

Soon after we had formed this desperate solution, a recruiting officer came on board to enlist men for the eighty-eighth regiment, to be stationed at Kingston, in the island of Jamaica. We had just been trying to satisfy our hunger upon a piece of beef, which was so tough that no teeth could make an impression on it, when the officer descended between decks, and represented to us the immense improvement that we should experience in our condition, if we were in his Majesty's service; an abundance of good food, comfortable clothing, service easy, and in the finest climate in the world; were temptations too great to be resisted by a set of miserable, half-starved, and almost naked wretches as we were....

The recruiting officer presented his papers for our signature. We hesitated, we stared at each other, and felt that we were about to do a deed of which we were ashamed, and which we might regret. Again we heard the tempting offers, and again the assurance that we should not be called upon to fight against our government or country; and with the hope we should find an opportunity to desert ... we signed the papers, and became soldiers in his Majesty's service.

We, shortly after, twelve in number, left the *Jersey* and were landed upon Long Island and marched under guard about a mile to an old barn where we were quartered.

Ebenezer was sent to Jamaica and was able to escape the British and join the crew of the American ship, *Flora*. He sailed on her to France. When the news of the peace came in the spring of 1783, he joined the crew of a brig bound for Boston, arriving in May 1783.

As soon as I could get released from the vessel I visited my brother James, at Mr. Tuckerman's, where he had lived during my absence, to obtain information respecting my good mother and my brothers and sisters. From him I received the pleasing intelligence that the family were all in good health; but that my mother had given up all hope of ever seeing me again on earth.

While walking over Boston Neck to Roxbury, where my mother still resided, my brother and I arranged a plan to introduce me to my mother as a sailor, who had just arrived from a foreign port, where he had seen her son Eben.... We soon arrived at the house, and I was formally introduced in the manner proposed. Time, hardship, and exposure to various climates, produced such an alteration in my personal appearance, that it is no wonder that the eye of maternal love could not recognize me....

After having conversed with her for some time and endeavored to answer a multitude of questions ... I arose to embrace her, "Mother, don't you know your son?" She shed tears of gratitude and joy, and we both blessed God that we were united in a family circle once more...

I returned to the service of Mr. Bosson, and remained with him till I was 21 years of age, when I established myself in business in my native place. I opened a store for the sale of crockery, glass and hardware.

My share of the prize-money was eighty dollars; all of which Mr. Bosson took. As I was his apprentice, and not free, he had a legal right to it. As I remembered his agreement was to give me one-half of the prize money and wages I was to receive. He retained the whole.

Bibliography

Fox, Ebenezer. *The Adventures of Ebenezer Fox of the Revolutionary War.* Boston: Charles Fox, 1847.

4

Abigail Foote Notes Each Day's Tasks on the Home Front

Teen girls were an important part of the war effort as they helped produce the food, make the clothing needed for survival, and care for the wounded. On most farms the family raised sheep for wool and planted flax for linen. Many homes had hand looms to weave cloth for making clothes. Even in cities, nearly all women spun yarn and thread. All could knit. Throughout the war the spinning wheels and looms went to make up for the supply that could no longer come from England.

Fifteen-year-old Abigail Foote of Colchester, Connecticut, recorded her daily activities in her diary for a few months in 1775 and 1776. It was the beginning of the Revolutionary War, when George Washington was elected commander-in-chief. Her entries reflected the average experience of a young girl in the colonies at that time. Only once does she mention the war, when she notes a muster at Mr. Otis' on April 17, 1776.

Most of the entries involved working on clothing, from carding the tow (coarse broken linen flax) to spinning to spooling, to setting a warp and weaving on the loom yards of fabric. Finally, she cut and sewed dresses and shirts and trousers and coats. She even made herself a quilt over several months' time. Each day also involved a choice of other tasks as well. She mentions helping with housework, weeding the garden, and picking strawberries, raspberries, and cherries as they ripened with the change of seasons. She made cheese some days as well. A few of her entries follow. Abigail began her diary in June 1775:

Friday 2. I quilted at Mr. Otis's in the afternoon and Molly went to town and came back to quilting.

Saturday 3. I helped Mol make a Bonnet for Mother and a Bonnet for Ellen and weed in the garden.

Sunday 4. I went to meeting to town and came home at noon to carry Ellen to meeting.

Monday 5. I did housework and wove some. Mother went to Marlborough and Israel and Abraham drove the calves away.

Tuesday 6. I wove and helped Mol do the work and Betty went and brought Eliza and Tiphose Edes here to spin.

Wednesday 7. I carded tow and Betty went to Mr. Pomroy's to work and I carried my camblet for shoes to Noah Foots for him to make.

Thursday 8. I carded tow for Eliza Edes and help Mol do the work. Betty came home at night.

Friday 9. I did housework in the forenoon and I wove in the afternoon and went with Ellen a strawberrying and went to Noah Foots and brought home a pair of shoes.

Sunday 11. I stayed at home and the bees swarmed and Asa Bigelow was here and hived them and they left the hive in the after noon and went down to Captain Wright's lot and settled on a tree as high as....

Monday 19. I carded 4 pound of tow.

Wednesday 21. I carded 4 pound and Molly come here and told us that Sally Wells died this afternoon, very suddenly.

Thursday 22. I carded 1½ and went to the funeral and went home to see David and Ellen married at night. Mol went to town to bring Margaret back.

In April 1776 she wrote:

Sunday 14. I went to meeting to town a foot.

Wednesday 17. I got out a piece of cloth for a [?] gown for Mother and for myself and went to the Widow Wells's in the afternoon and there was a general Muster at Mr. Otis's.

Sunday 21. I went to meeting rid with Sarah Otis and Ann rid Israel's mare and Mr. Little preached from John 6 Chapter 44 verse.

Tuesday 30. I sewed on my quilt run it acrost the bottom and helped Mother make candles.

4. Abigail Foote Notes Each Day's Tasks on the Home Front

In May 1776:

Thursday 16. I wove and picked the geese.
Monday 20. I washed. Mother helped me a little.

And in July 1776:

Friday 12. I did the work and went to lecture in the afternoon and Mr. Lathrop preached from 2 Sam. 15 chap. 25 and 26 verses

Monday 22. I did the work and picked wool. Ruth Root and Rachel Ackley come here and at night Rebeckah and Molly come here and some Marlborough gentlemen.

Bibliography

Abigail Foote diary, 1775–1776. Brainard Family Papers. Library of the Connecticut Historical Society Museum, Hartford, Conn. Used by permission.

5

A Dream Sends Mary Slocumb to the Battle

Mary Slocumb had a different experience near her home in North Carolina in spring 1776. The British royal governor, Josiah Martin, was convinced that the loyalists in the southern provinces could defeat the patriots if they had a few regular British troops. As a result, the British assembled an expedition to sail to North Carolina's Cape Fear. However, the governor did not wait for their arrival. He issued a call for Donald McDonald, Loyalist leader of the Scots clans of the back country, to organize a Tory expedition to go to Wilmington. About 1,500 assembled near Cross Creek (now Fayetteville).

On hearing this news, nearly one thousand patriots of the New Bern and Wilmington districts responded. Colonel Richard Caswell called his neighbors hastily together. They agreed to join Colonel Lillington and General James Moore at a bridge over Moore's Creek to confront the Loyalists on the road they must take to reach the coast. They fought one of the bloodiest battles of the Revolution and a clear victory for the patriots on February 27, 1776. The Americans took 850 prisoners, demonstrating that the southern colonies were not to be easily subdued. These Loyalist troops were not able to join General Clinton when he did arrive on the coast and tried to take Charleston.

Mary Hooks Slocumb was a bride of eighteen when her husband volunteered to help stop the Loyalists. She vividly describes the worry of living at that time and helping the wounded at the end of a battle.

The men all left on Sunday morning. More than eighty went from this house with my husband; I looked at them well, and I could see that every man had mischief in him. I know a coward as soon as I set my eyes upon him. The Tories more than once tried to frighten me, but they always showed coward at the bare insinuation that our troops were about.

Well, they got off in high spirits; every man stepping high and light. And I slept soundly and quietly that night, and worked hard all the next day; but I kept thinking where they had got to—how far; where and how many of the regulars and tories they would meet; and I could not keep myself from the study. I went to bed at the usual time, but still continued to study. As I lay—whether waking or sleeping I know not—I had a dream; yet it was not all a dream. I saw distinctly a body wrapped in my husband's guard-cloak—bloody-dead; and others dead and wounded on the ground about him. I saw them plainly and distinctly. I uttered a cry, and sprang to my feet on the floor; and so strong was the impression on my mind, that I rushed in the direction the vision appeared, and came up against the side of the house. The fire in the room gave little light, and I gazed in every direction to catch another glimpse of the scene. I raised the light; every thing was still and quiet. My child was sleeping, but my woman was awakened by my crying out or jumping on the floor. If ever I felt fear it was at that moment. Seated on the bed, I reflected a few moments—and said aloud: "I must go to him." I told the woman I could not sleep and would ride down the road. She appeared in great alarm; but I merely told her to lock the door after me, and look after the child.

I went to the stable, saddled my mare—as fleet and easy a nag as ever travelled; and in one minute we were tearing down the road at full speed. The cool night seemed after a mile or two's gallop to bring reflection with it; and I asked myself where I was going, and for what purpose. Again and again I was tempted to turn back; but I was soon ten miles from home, and my mind became stronger every mile I rode. I should find my husband dead or dying—was as firmly my presentiment and conviction as any fact of my life. When day broke I was some thirty miles from home. I knew the general route our little army expected to take, and had followed them without hesitation. About sunrise I came upon a group of women and children, standing and sitting by the road-side, each one of them showing the same anxiety of mind I felt. Stopping a few minutes I inquired if the battle had been fought. They knew nothing, but were assembled on the road to catch intelligence. They thought Caswell had taken the right of the Wilmington road and gone towards the northwest (Cape Fear). Again was I skimming over the ground through a country thinly settled, and very poor and swampy; but neither my own spirits nor my beautiful nag's failed in the least. We followed the well-marked trail of the troops.

The sun must have been well up, say eight or nine o'clock, when I heard a sound like thunder, which I knew must be cannon. It was the first time I ever heard a cannon. I stopped still; when presently the cannon thundered again. The battle was then fighting. What a fool! My husband could not be dead last night, and the battle only fighting now! Still, as I am so near, I will go on and see how they come out. So away we went again, faster than ever; and I soon found by the noise of guns that I was near the fight. Again I stopped. I could hear muskets, I could hear rifles, and I could hear shouting. I spoke to my mare and dashed on in the direction of the firing and the shouts, now louder than ever. The blind path I had been following brought me into the Wilmington road leading to Moore's Creek Bridge, a few hundred yards below the bridge. A few yards from the road, under a cluster of trees were lying perhaps twenty men. They were the wounded. I knew the spot; the very trees; and the position of the men I knew as if I had seen it a thousand times. I had seen it all night! I saw all at once; but in an instant my whole soul was centered in one spot; for there, wrapped in his bloody guard-cloak, was my husband's body! How I passed the few yards from my saddle to the place I never knew. I remember uncovering his head and seeing a face clothed with gore from a dreadful wound across the temple. I put my hand on the bloody face; 'twas warm; and an unknown voice begged for water. A small camp-kettle was lying near, and a stream of water was close by. I brought it; poured some in his mouth; washed his face, and behold—it was Frank Cogdell. He soon revived and could speak. I was washing the wound in his head. Said he, "It is not that; it is that hole in my leg that is killing me." A puddle of blood was standing on the ground about his feet. I took his knife, cut away his trousers and stocking, and found the blood came from a shot-hole through and through the fleshy part of his leg. I looked about and could see nothing that looked as if it would do for dressing wounds but some heart-leaves. I gathered a handful and bound them tight to the holes; and the bleeding stopped. I then went to the others; and—Doctor! I dressed the wounds of many a brave fellow who did good fighting long after that day! I had not inquired for my husband; but while I was busy Caswell came up. He appeared very much surprised to see me; and was with his hat in hand about to pay some compliment; but I interrupted him by asking—"Where is my husband?"

"Where he ought to be, madam; in pursuit of the enemy. But pray," said he, "how came you here?" "Oh, I thought," replied I, "you would need nurses as well as soldiers. See! I have already dressed many of these good fellows; and here is one"—going to Frank and lifting him up with my arm under his head so that he could drink some more water—"would have died before any of you men could have helped him."

"I believe you," said Frank. Just then I looked up, and my husband, as bloody as a butcher, as muddy as a ditcher, stood before me.

"Why, Mary!" he exclaimed, "What are you doing there? Hugging Frank Cogdell, the greatest reprobate in the army?"

"I don't care," I cried. "Frank is a brave fellow, a good soldier, and a true friend of Congress."

"True, true! every word of it!" said Caswell. "You are right, madam!" with the lowest possible bow.

I would not tell my husband what brought me there. I was so happy; and so were all! It was a glorious victory; I came just at the height of the enjoyment. I knew my husband was surprised, but I could see he was not displeased with me. It was night again before our excitement had at all subsided. Many prisoners were brought in, and among them some very obnoxious; but the worst of the tories were not taken prisoners. They were for the most part, left in the woods and swamps wherever they were overtaken. I begged for some of the poor prisoners, and Caswell readily told me none should be hurt, but such as had been guilty of murder and house-burning. In the middle of the night I again mounted my mare and started for home. Caswell and my husband wanted me to stay till next morning and they would send a party with me; but no! I wanted to see my child, and I told them they could send no party who could keep up with me. What a happy ride I had back! and with what joy did I embrace my child as he ran to meet me!

Bibliography

Ellet, Elizabeth. *The Women of the American Revolution.* New York: Baker & Scribner, 1848.

6

Michael Smith Meets a British Ship Up the Kills

As the British were about to retreat from Boston, Washington held a council of war with his staff at Roxbury, Massachusetts, on March 13, 1776. He predicted the next move of the British would be "to evacuate [Boston]; that in all probability they were destin'd for New York. [They] would attempt to possess themselves of that City ... They would command the Navigation of Hudson's River—open a communication with Canada—and cut off all intercourse between the colonies."

He was right.

By the middle of 1776 the British admiralty had assigned 87 warships carrying more than 6,500 sailors to the North American station. The 30 enemy warships operating out of New York harbor alone carried 824 cannon. Such a navy paralyzed Revolutionary coastal trade. It also caused major shortages and great suffering ashore.

To protect those living along the New Jersey coast, Washington organized a shore patrol. Michael Smith tells the following story of events after he began serving in the militia in April 1775 in New York City. The following spring, when the British fleet lay at the Narrows near Staten Island, his whole regiment volunteered to serve in the regular Continental army. His brief account illustrates the important part played by teenagers as they independently fight for the freedom from British rule.

In the month of April 1776, General George Washington ordered a detachment from our regiment under command of Lt. Ralph Thurman with a boat and fieldpiece and twenty-four men to keep guard and prevent the enemy from harassing the inhabitants on the Jersey shore. I was orderly sergeant of the company, and one of the detachment, John Garret, was also along. We were stationed up the Kills at Smith's Ferry near Bergen Point.

We had been cruising about this place three days when an enemy's vessel was seen to approach us under a press of sail. It was an armed, square-rigged vessel and full of men and seemed to be particularly desirous of a more intimate acquaintance. As we did not feel ourselves honored by their visit, we run our boat, which was flat, on the shore in order to give them a better reception. No sooner had the boat landed than Lieutenant Thurman and all the party, except John Garret, one Cannon, one Young and myself ran off to their quarters treating our

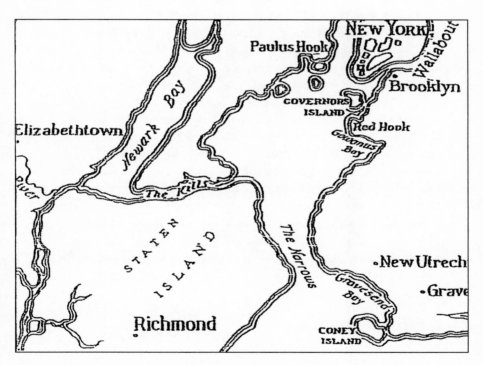

Michael Smith meets a British ship up the Kills. (From *Atlas of American History,* by Kenneth T. Jackson, Charles Scribner's Sons, © 1984, Charles Scribner's Sons. Reprinted by permission of the Gale Group).

visitors with the utmost neglect. As I was now commander-in-chief, I ordered my company of three men to assist me in throwing over our six-pounder [cannon] and the carriage. We had just got it placed in a conspicuous situation on the bank when the enemy approached within speaking distance and commenced firing at us without effect. We had plenty of shot, both round and grape, and fired several times with round shot, but they passed over them. The enemy seemed to tantalize us for our random shots, and we resolved to give them an assortment, so we loaded our piece with grape. She had anchored. Just at the instant she had swung round so as to present her whole length to us, we gave her a raking fire which swept the deck from stem to stern. The enemy immediately slipped her cable and made off with as much speed as possible. They seemed to be in great hurry and confusion. No sooner had they got under way than Lieutenant Thurman and his party made their appearance. We drew our piece [cannon] about three miles.

Next morning I returned with the three men before named, against the remonstrance of the lieutenant, to endeavor to secure our boat. We found two British tenders lying near her. Whilst we were near them, we saw three British soldiers approaching us, and on halting them, they said they were friends to Congress. They proved to be deserters from the party who had landed in the night for the purpose of cutting off our retreat. They informed us that our last shot had killed the captain and six men and wounded nine others.We dragged our cannon to Paulus Hook and crossed, but the news of our victory preceded us and occasioned considerable excitement in the city. Lieutenant Thurman immediately resigned, and Congress, without my solicitation, sent me a captain's commission; but having a grandmother, mother, and sister to support, who lived in the city, I, at their earnest solicitation, declined accepting it.

Bibliography

Smith, Michael. *1832 Revolutionary War Pension Application*. Washington, D.C.: Veterans Administration Archives in the National Archives, Record Group 15, Microcopy 805.

7

British Soldier John Enys Sees Service in Canada

The Americans undertook a campaign to remove the British from Canada. On June 27, 1775, Congress voted that "if General Schuyler finds it practicable and that it will not be disagreeable to the Canadians, he shall immediately take possession of St. Johns, Montreal, and any other parts of the country." General Richard Montgomery replaced the ill General Schuyler. St. Johns fell after a two-month siege, followed by Montreal. Benedict Arnold was at the same time marching north through Maine to Quebec to join their forces. In their joint attack, Montgomery was killed, and Arnold wounded. The troops were seriously ill with smallpox and other diseases. In the following account John Enys follows the retreat of the Americans along the St. Lawrence River to Lake Champlain and describes the action at Valcour Island.

The journal of John Enys captures the experience of the British and German soldiers who were sent to quell the rebellion of the colonists in America. As a 19-year-old ensign in the British army, John Enys embarked from Plymouth, England, for Canada on 18 March 1776. He relates the difficulties of travel on a sailing ship across the Atlantic, depending on the vagaries of the wind and confronting icebergs in the North Atlantic.

It was impossible to have had better weather than we had all this Month but on the first of April it began to blow very hard & continued so to do for two days the greatest part of which time we were obliged to lay to. On the eighth we struck Soundings on the outer bank of Newfoundland, and on the same day saw some Islands of Ice, one of which we Supposed to be Near a Quarter of a Mile Square and about Sixty feet perpendicular hight. This must have been an Imence body of Ice, As According to some experiments Made on board of our Ship we found that Ice floated only one eighth out of the Water...

On the Ninth we had a very thick fog which Froze to our Ropes as it fell, by which means the Ship Appeared as if Rigged with Ropes of Cristal Near four times their usual diameter, which formed a Sight both new and strange. However Agreable this might be to the eye yet the Situation was far from a pleasant one, as not a Rope in the waul run until by dint of beating them we had got them Clear of the encrustation of Ice which had formed Round them, which was not until near 12 OClock in the day, when we again got in Sailing trim Meeting every Now and then with Small Islands of Ice.

On the twelfth about noon we made land which proved to be the Island of St. Peters [St. Pierre].... On the 13th in the Morning we made Sail again, & as our pilot imagined could we once get thro the Strait we Should find no more Ice.... Instead of getting rid of the Ice we came to a peice so long that we could not see the end of it.... Anxious to proceed it was determined to attempt to force a passage thro it, which was done with very little difficulty it being extremely rotten. After having passed this we again began to imagin our difficulty's over as we could see no more Ice, but in the evening were convinced of our Mistake by finding a peice of Ice ahead of us to which we could See no End. At first we attempted to force our way thro this as we did the former one ... but in the course of the night it closed upon us so firm that we could get Nither backwards or forwards. On Morning of the 14th the fog which had been very thick the day before Cleared off and we found our selves within Sight of cape Ray [Cape Race?] distance about four Leagues, This afternoon the Ice being perfectly firm all round us, I and some others took a walk about a Quarter of a Mile round the Ship which you may suppose was very Agreeable after our being on board Ship so long.

From this until the twentieth we were sometimes making Saill and pressing thro the Ice and sometimes laying quite steady in it to all appearance, tho it is plain we altered our situation every day tho sometimes it was without any attempt on our part and even without our knowledge. On the 20th in the Morning we Saw an immense Number of Seals and as the Ship was Still fast i[n] the Ice, we amused ourselves by killing them, one of which was brought on board, and I was quite surprised to see the quantity of blood there was in it.... On the 21st, the Ice began to be Rotten and lesser than usual, and on the 22nd a breze getting up broke up the Ice so much as to let the ship Make way through it, and about one OClock to our great joy we got quite Clear, and having sailed a few leagues toward evening we saw the Island of Anticosti which is Situated in the Mouth of the River St. Lawrence...

At daylight on the 6th we got underway once more. And just as we were turning Point Levi we saw a Canoe with two Men in her put off and make toward the Ship. When they had got Near enough to know who we were they would have willingly have returned but it was then too late as they were within Shot of us, which obliged them to come on board, tho much aginst their wills. As soon as they were on board they were seperated and examined one after the other, When they gave nearly the following intelligence. That the Garrison of Quebec was Still in the possession of General Carleton consisting of about 1500 men for the most part the Militia and Merchants of the town who had taken Armes on the Occasion, as did also the Judges and the rest of the Civil Mages-trates. The remainder were partly regulars and Sailors with McLeans new Regt (then very Weak). On the part of the Rebels they had between 2 and 3000 Men before the town great part of which were Ill of the Small pox which at that time raged in their Army. Secondly, that they expected a very large reinforcement that day or next from above. On the Arrival of which they had determined to assault the town once more for which purposes they had withdrawn all their force from Point Levi and the Isle of Orleans on the preceeding Night. (The last boat from the Isle of Orleans was seen by us about the time of the examination of the two men which appeared to go towards the falls of Montmorency). On these men being Asked why they wanted to return Said they were afraid to come on board, but it seems since that the Rebels had per-suaded them they would have a large french fleet to their assistance early in the Spring and as we had the St. Georges Ensign hoisted they took it for the french Colours, there not being wind Sufficient at that time to Blow out the flag they could not see the Red cross in it, and that it was on the Discovery of that they wanted to turn....

Orders were sent on board for us and the Marines on board to dis-embark Immediately which was very soon done as we had everything ready before we rec'd the Order.... We were no sooner on shore than we received Orders to March out of the Garrison as soon as our Men had refreshed themselves a little. Accordingly About twelve OClock every thing being ready we left the town with about, as I have since been told, 850 Men for the most part English When to our great Surprize the Rebels abandoned the place and that with so great precipitation that they even left a feild peice Loaded in the field with only a Nail put into the Vent which was easyly drawn from thence. At first they seem'd as if they would form in a Smal wood at the end of the hights of Abram [Heights—or Plains—of Abraham], but it was very soon known they had decamped for good....

[We] proceeded 20 Miles Up the River to a place called point au Tremble [Pointe aux Trembles], All the rest remaining in the garrison of Quebec until the 21st in the Evening when we were ordered on board Small transports to go up the River in.... Early on the 22nd we saild and ... proceeded as far as three Rivers [Trois Rivières].... Soon after our Arrival here the remainder of the Army from England and Ireland came up to three Rivers where they lay....

On the 14th about four in the afternoon we Arrived at Sorel which we found abandoned as usual. Sorel is situated at the mouth of River Richelieu tho it is more commonly called the River Sorel which forms a Communication between the River St. Lawrence and Lake Champlain Navigable for Small scooners as far as Chambly which is no more than 19 Miles from St. Johns where the Lake commences in which there is plenty of water. This evening the Grenadiers & Light Infantry of the Army Landed and Next Morning great part of the Army did the Same in order to pursue the Rebels by Route of that River and our Regt and some others continued our Route towards Montreal. Before we had got within 30 Miles of the town an express Arrived to let the Generl know that the Rebels had abandoned the town, on which our Regt was ordered to Land and March thither. The Wind being foul it was the 16th in the After Noon when we landed about 30 Miles from Montreal and that Night reached point au Tremble a place about Nine miles from town and Next Morning about Nine OClock we Marched into it to the great joy of some of the Inhabitants....

The remainder of the Army having as before Mentioned pursued the Rebels by way of the River Sorel who at their approach abandoned and burnt the forts of Chambly and St. Johns after which having boats Ready at the latter place they embarked and got over the Lake without our Army being able to overtake them tho I am told some of their Rear boats were Still within Sight of St. Johns when our people Arrived at that place.

The Rebels being now entirely drove out [of] the Province the Army encamped at Isle aux Noix, St. Johns, Chambly, and on the Roads leading to Sorel and Montreal at which place our Regt remained. No time was lost in preparing a Naval force Sufficient to cope with the Rebel fleet on Lake Champlain. Accordingly Scooners were Bought and being taken to peices at Chambly were transported over the Carring place [carrying place or portage] between that and St. Johns where they were rebuilt for the lake Service. A great many Gun boats the frames of which came from England were rebuilt as was also a Ship Large enough to carry 20 Guns the frame of which was built at Quebec....

In the beginning of Octr our fleet being ready consisting of one Ship of 20 Guns, a Scooner of 14, another of 10, a Gondola with 7, a Radeau with 10 Guns all Brass Battering peices and four Howitzers and about 20 Gun Boats with one Gun in each. After having rendevous'd at point au Fer we all set Sail in quest of the Rebels. On the 10th in the evening we got intelligence where they were, and on the 11th about 12 OClock we saw [them] and some of our headmost Ships fired at them. They were lieng at an Anchor behind the Island of Valcore [Valcour], so that our fleet had passed them before they knew it and were obliged to tack in order to get into the Bay. This rendered the Vessel I was on board totaly useless she being flat bottomed and consequently could not work to Windward. We fired some few Shot at the time we first Saw their fleet but believe it might have been just well let alone. The Gun boats bore the brunt of their whole fire the Greatest part of that day until at length the Carleton Schooner got in tho She was of very little Service to them being very Soon in such a Shattered Condition as to be towed out of the bay by the boats of the fleet for fear of her being taken. The Inflexible and Maria fired also some Shot in the course of the day but I believe with as little effect as Radeau, both being so far off. The firing continued until evening when the boats withdrew leaving the Rebel fleet formed in a line in the Bay whilst our fleet formed in a Semicircle round the Mouth of it, in Such Manner that it might well be thought they could not have escaped, which however they did in the course of the Night by passing between us and the shore unperceived by any one....

Early next Morn it was found the Rebels were escaped and at daylight some of their fleet were Seen at a distance. Our fleet attempted to pursue them but the wind was so hard against us we were obliged put back again....

In the evening one of our tenders discovered their fleet a second time and on the 13 early in the Morning a Breeze Springing up in our favour we all made Sail once more in pursuit of them, when the two Schooners and the Ship overtook and came to Action with them the rest of our fleet not being able to get up. This force however proved Sufficient as in a very short time, one of their Gallies Named the Washinton [Washington] Commanded by one Brigadier Genl. Waterbury [David Waterbury] Struck her Colours and Seven others of their fleet under command of General [Benedict] Arnold ran on Shore in a bay Named Ferries's Bay [Buttonmould Bay] where having burnt their Shiping they took to the Woods and returned to Ticonderoga.... So out of all the 14 Sail of Vessels they had on the lake only four got off Clear and one of them was Not with their fleet being at Ticonderoga changing her guns as I am informed. On our Arrival at Crown Point General Waterbury and his Crew were Suffered to return on their Parole.

A day or two after our Arrival here the Army came up, where they all Stood without doing anything Material untill the 1st of November when we reimbarked to return to Canada as did all the rest of the Army.

James Hadden, a British lieutenant of the Royal Artillery, wrote in his journal that "the remaining American ships muffled their oars as they escaped in the night. Three struck their coulors and the crews taken prisoner; Arnold ran his own vessel and 5 others on shore and set fire to them. The three foremost only escaped to Tyconderoga; as did Gen. Arnold with most of the crews of the burnt vessels." The rebel attempt to take possession of Canada failed.

John Enys remained in Canada and took part in raids that ravaged the Vermont frontier in 1778 and the New York frontier in 1780 before being reassigned to England. After the war he did garrison duty in what is now eastern Ontario. In 1788 he traveled through the United States, visiting homes of prominent citizens. The highlight was the day spent at Mount Vernon with General Washington and his family.

Bibliography

Enys, John. *The American Journals of Lt. John Enys*. Ed. Elizabeth Cometti. Syracuse, N.Y.: Syracuse University Press, 1976. Used by permission.
Hadden, James E. *A Journal Kept in Canada and upon Burgoyne's Campaign in 1776 and 1777*. Albany: Joel Munsell's Sons, 1884.
Journals of the Continental Congress, II, 109–110

8

Sixteen-year-old Walter Bates Arrested as a Tory

Many families living in the Darien, Connecticut, area were supporters of the king. In September 1776, Washington left the New York area and led his troops into the country as far as White Plains, about 12 miles from Stamford. The British fortified Lloyd's Neck with a garrison, opposite the islands and coves lying between Norwalk and Stamford.

Walter Bates' brother, William, joined the British army and served until Yorktown. His sister married a Loyalist, Thomas Gilbert. Walter recalls a time when he, as a suspected Tory, was threatened by local patriots.

At length the thing I greatly feared came upon me. A small boat was discovered by the American guard, in one of these coves, by night. They suspected that one of my brothers, with some others, had come from the British. They supposed them concealed in the neighborhood and that I must be acquainted with it.

At this time I had just entered my sixteenth year. I was taken and confined in the Guard House. Next day I was examined before a Committee and threatened with sundry deaths if I did not confess what I knew not of. They threatened among other things to confine me at low water and let the tide drown me if I did not expose these honest farmers. At length I was sent back to the Guard House until ten o'clock at night. I was taken out by an armed mob, conveyed through the field gate one mile from the town to back Creek.

Having been stripped, my body was exposed to the mosquitoes, my hands and feet being confined to a tree near the Salt Marsh. In two hours time every drop of blood would be drawn from my body. Soon

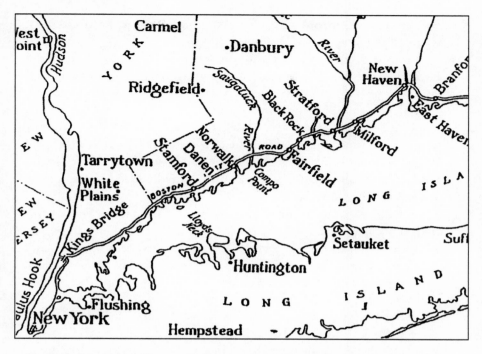

New York to New Haven (From *Atlas of American History,* by Kenneth T. Jackson, Charles Scribner's Sons, © 1984, Charles Scribner's Sons. Reprinted by permission of the Gale Group).

after, two of the committee said that if I would tell them all I knew, they would release me, if not, they would leave me to these men who, perhaps, would kill me.

I told them that I knew nothing that would save my life.

They left me, and the Guard came to me and said they were ordered to give me, if I did not confess, one hundred stripes [lashes]. If that did not kill me, I would be sentenced to be hanged. Twenty stripes was then executed with severity, after which they sent me again to the Guard House. No "Tory" was allowed to speak to me. I was insulted and abused by all.

The next day the committee proposed many means to extort a confession from me. The most terrifying was that of confining me to a log on the carriage in the Saw mill and let the saw cut me in two if I did not expose "those Tories." Finally they sentenced me to appear before

Col. Davenport, in order that he should send me to head quarters, where all the Torys he sent were surely hanged.

Accordingly, next day I was brought before Davenport—one of the descendants of the old apostate Davenport, who fled from old England-who, after he had examined me, said with great severity of countenance, "I think you could have exposed those Tories."

I said to him "You might rather think I would have exposed my own father sooner than suffer what I have suffered." Upon which the old judge could not help acknowledging he never knew any one who had withstood more without exposing confederates. He finally discharged me the third day.

It was a grievous misfortune to be in such a situation, but the fear of God animated me not to fear man. My resolution compelled mine enemies to show their pity that I had been so causelessly afflicted, and my life was spared. I was, however obliged to seek refuge from the malice of my persecutors in the mountains and forests until their frenzy might be somewhat abated.

After two year's absence, on my return home, I found my father down with the smallpox. It was suspected to be given him by design, consequently the family were all in inoculation. I also had to endure it, after which I could not by any means think of leaving my father until I had assisted him in his wheat harvest.

The first night after, I was summoned with a draft for the Continental Service with three day's notice. Consequently, I was compelled to flee for refuge. I knew not where [to go], but providentially found myself next morning in the immediate neighborhood of a British garrison. Here I was informed I must go through the regular process, be reported, and take the oath of allegiance.

I was provided with the necessary pass from the commanding officer to General DeLancey at Jamaica (Long Island). He furnished me with a pass directed to General Smith at Brooklin, who furnished me with a pass to Colonel Axtell at Flat Bush, who administered the oath and also furnished me with a pass to General DeLancey again at Jamaica.

Here, not being acquainted with customs of the army, exposed me to great inconvenience. I just only prudently knocked at the same door where I had received my pass the day before. This I was informed was considered an offense. The old General was apt to be very severe after drinking wine all night. At length the old General came down from his chamber, and surely his face looked to me as red as his coat.

"Where is that damned rascal who has disturbed my quarters this morning? Send him to the guard house!" roared he. This subjected me to great difficulties too unpleasant to mention.

Yet kind providence seemed to prepare ways and means, unforeseen by me, for my escape and preservation amidst all troubles, afflictions and dangers by land and sea. During that unhappy war there were many instances of God's mercy for which I can never be sufficiently grateful.

The account of this Loyalist reveals the sacrifices of the families of those who chose to remain loyal to the king. If they did not swear to the oath of allegiance to the United States of America they were viewed as against the rebel cause. They were threatened with ostracism and their property confiscated. Some were tarred and feathered and subjected to other punishments. Walter Bates was one of those who left for Nova Scotia at the end of the war.

Bibliography

Bates, Walter. Kingston and the Loyalists of the "Spring Fleet" of 1783. With Reminiscences of Early Days in Connecticut. Ed. W.O. Raymond. 1889. Reprint, Fredericton, New Brunswick: Non Entity Press, 1980.

9

Sybil Ludington Rides to Warn the Militia "the British Are Coming"

On April 25, 1777, 26 British ships, carrying about 2,000 troops, appeared off the Connecticut shore at the site of the Saugatuck River near the present city of Fairfield. They were sent to destroy American stores and ammunition held in Danbury, about 20 miles away. The storehouses were filled with thousands of barrels of beef, pork, and flour; several hundred cases of rum and wine; hundreds of barrels of sugar, molasses and coffee; quantities of rice, wheat, oats and corn in bulk; considerable camp equipment including 1,020 tents, 500 hospital cots, and 5,000 pairs of shoes and socks, together with kits of tools and cooking utensils.

The intoxicating liquor, however, almost brought about the downfall of the British regulars who chose to consume it rather than dispose of it otherwise. The result was a disgraceful drunken event during which a number of buildings were set on fire. So much New England rum rendered army discipline woefully ineffective; squads of intoxicated Redcoats staggered up and down Main Street singing army songs, cursing, shouting insults and, in general, conducting themselves in a very offensive manner. Local members of the patriot militia immediately sent expresses to alarm the countryside and collect the militia.

In nearby Fredericksburg, on the night of April 26, 1777, there was a great banging on the front door of the home of Sybil Ludington about 9. Sybil's father was a colonel in the 400 strong New York militia. When he opened the door, he beheld a breathless, rain-soaked, mud-spattered messenger bringing news of the burning and sacking of Danbury only 17 miles away.

Prompt decision and action were imperative. He must gather

his militiamen and prevent the enemy from passing through this territory to the Hudson River; but Danbury needed help at once. Local families had to be alerted to the danger of impending attack. The women and children must pack their possessions, clothing and bedding into horse-drawn wagons or ox carts, and, driving their livestock before them, abandon their homes and flee northward.

The messenger and his horse were spent. They could go no farther that night. Who was there to spread the alarm and to muster the men of Colonel Ludington's command? "I'll go, Daddy," spoke Sybil, his 16-year-old daughter. As to the Colonel's attitude in granting permission for the young girl to undertake the hazardous mission on such a stormy night through an enemy-infested region, some sources say he asked her to go and had planned the course she was to take; others, that he gave his consent with great reluctance.

Sybil immediately went to the barn to rouse a strapping, year-ling colt, recently broken to bit and saddle by Sybil herself. She led him from his comfortable stall and threw a saddle on his back. Sybil, dressed in her father's ill-fitting trousers, mounted astride, seized the rope rein, and suddenly horse and rider vanished into the night. (The statue by Anna Huntington, however, shows her wearing a skirt and riding sidesaddle.)

Accounts differ as to the exact route taken by this young Paul(ine) Revere (it had been almost exactly two years since another famous ride had been made under similar circumstances). It is probable that she proceeded southward along a trail parallel to the middle branch of Croton River. She followed what is approxi-mately Route 52 to Carmel, where, upon her alarm, "the village bell pealed forth its muster call."

Here, we are told, a horseman offered to accompany her, but she asked him instead to spread the news eastward toward the present village of Brewster. Galloping along the shore of Lake Gleneida over essentially the present Route 6, she continued rous-ing the sleeping and defenseless farmers and fishermen as she sped on through the darkness. She shouted as she rode, "The British are burning Danbury, meet at Ludington's!" They were to join the rest of the units at Ridgefield to stop the enemy.

She then rode over Barret Hill to Kent Cliffs through the lonely, heavily forested and most dangerous stretch of her entire journey. It being late at night, lights in the scattered farmhouses had been extinguished, rendering it difficult for her to identify those old familiar landmarks.

An historic marker in Stormville reveals that she passed that point. Upon entering the town, she was surprised to see numerous lights in the houses and people carrying lanterns scurrying to and fro. Suddenly she heard a sharp clanging sound. They were sounding the call to arms by striking with a hammer the big iron ring that was suspended on the village green. It seems another rider dispatched by her father had arrived from the opposite direction. It was only a matter of about four more miles and her mission would be complete. She accordingly followed the direct route through Pecksville back to her Ludington home.

It was well past midnight when, dripping wet from the rain, mud-spattered from head to foot and thoroughly exhausted from her strenuous experience, Sybil reined her steed through the farmyard gate. She had made the journey safely. The rain was slackening. A crowd of militiamen began gathering at the Ludington farm. Some were poorly clad and lacking in arms and ammunition, but all were determined to avenge the fate of their stricken countrymen across the state border.

At dawn, Colonel Ludington was ready to lead his men through Franklin (now Patterson) and out the Haviland Hollow road into Connecticut. The British learned that an American force of 700 men under General Wooster had gathered at Bethel. Fearing attacks from the east and the west, the enemy resumed its work of destruction, before withdrawal. In all 19 private shops, a meeting house, and several other storage buildings were burned.

After burning Danbury, the British had marched on to Ridgefield. The militia was ready, after heeding the warnings of Sybil and others. A skirmish there left 27 British killed, 15 officers and 104 men wounded. Twenty-nine men were missing. The battered British troops retreated to Long Island Sound. They boarded their ships and returned to New York City. In appreciation for her daring escapade, the town of Fredericksburg changed its name to Ludingtonville.

Statue of Sybil Ludington by Anna Hyatt Huntington (photograph by Joanne Mascia).

I Was a Teenager in the American Revolution

In 1961 Anna Hyatt Huntington, the famous sculptress, donated her life-size statue of Sybil on her horse to the Daughters of the American Revolution. It was erected on the shore of nearby Gleneida Lake. There is a replica of this statue in Memorial Continental Hall of the National Society of the Daughters of the American Revolution at 1776 D Street NW, Washington, D.C. The statue shows Sybil Ludington mounted on a horse and has the following inscription:

Sybil Ludington
Revolutionary War Heroine
April 26, 1777
Called out the volunteer militia by riding through the
night alone on horseback at the age of 16 alerting the
countryside to the burning of Danbury, Connecticut by
the British.
Placed by Enoch Crosby Chapter DAR
Presented by Anna Hyatt Huntington
1961

To further honor Sybil, a commemorative stamp was issued at Carmel on March 25, 1975. As noted on the map, there are seven roadside markers along the route she followed:

Sybil Ludington
rode horseback over this road
the night of April 26, 1777 to
call out Colonel Ludington's
regiment to repel the British
at Danbury, Conn.

Bibliography

Courier. Cold Spring, N.Y.: Putnam County Historical Society.

10

Ebenezer Fletcher Is Captured by the British at Hubbardton

    In the spring and summer of 1777, the British launched a three-pronged attack to crush the rebellion. Over 8,000 British troops led by General John Burgoyne invaded New York from the north along Lake Champlain on the way to Albany. Another army of 1,800, including nearly 1,000 Iroquois, under Lieutenant Colonel Barry St. Leger proceeded along the St. Lawrence River and the Oswego River with plans to attack Fort Stanwix (renamed Fort Schuyler). After defeating the rebels, they would follow the Mohawk Valley to Albany to meet General Burgoyne. General William Howe was to ascend the Hudson. All three were expected to meet in Albany and thus divide the colonies, cutting off New England.

    In the third week of June 1777, General Burgoyne was approaching the Americans' Fort Ticonderoga at the southern end of Lake Champlain. He noticed that a high hill overlooking the fort had been left unfortified. The British immediately carried cannon up the steep slope. On the morning of July 5, 1777, the American General St. Clair, commander of Ticonderoga, was shocked to view the British atop the nearby Sugar Loaf hill with two brass cannon. The Americans had considered it inaccessible. Knowing the British could thus demolish Fort Ticonderoga, St. Clair ordered a retreat for that night. Sixteen-year-old Ebenezer Fletcher, from New Ipswich, New Hampshire, was a fifer in the Continental army in Col. Nathan Hale's regiment. In the following account he relates his experiences in the retreat from the fort. Wounded and captured by the British, he vividly describes his escape and survival in the forest.

Ebenezer Fletcher enlisted into the Continental Army, in Capt. Carr's company in Colonel Nathan Hale's Regiment as a fifer, and joined the Army at Ticonderoga under the command of Gen. St. Clair, in the spring of 1777 at which place I was stationed till the retreat of the Army on the 6th of July following.

Early on the morning of the same day, orders came to strike our tents and swing our packs. It was generally conjectured that we were going to battle; but orders came immediately to march. We marched some distance before light. By sunrise the enemy had landed from their boats, and pursued us so closely as to fire on our rear. A large body of the enemy followed us all day, but kept so far behind as not to be wholly discovered. Their aim was to attack us suddenly next morning, as they did.

Having just recovered from the measles, and not being able to march with the main body, I fell in the rear. The morning after our retreat, orders came very early for the troops to refresh and be ready for marching. Some were eating, some were cooking, and all in a very unfit posture for battle. Just as the sun rose, there was a cry, "The enemy are upon us."

Looking round I saw the enemy in line of battle. Orders came to lay down our packs and be ready for action. The fire instantly began. We were but few in number compared to the enemy. At the commencement of the battle, many of our party retreated back into the woods. Capt. Carr came up and says, "My lads advance, we shall beat them yet."

A few of us followed him in view of the enemy. Every man was trying to secure himself behind girdled trees, which were standing on the place of action. I made shelter for myself and discharged my piece. Having loaded again and taken aim, my piece missed fire. I brought the same a second time to my face; but before I had time to discharge it, I received a musket ball in the small of my back, and fell with my gun cocked. My uncle, Daniel Foster, was standing but little distance from me. I made out to crawl to him and spoke to him. He and another man lifted me and carried me back some distance and laid me down behind a large tree where was another man crying out most bitterly with a grievous wound. By this time I had bled so freely, I was very weak and faint. I observed the enemy were like to gain the ground. Our men began to retreat and the enemy to advance. Having no friend to afford me any

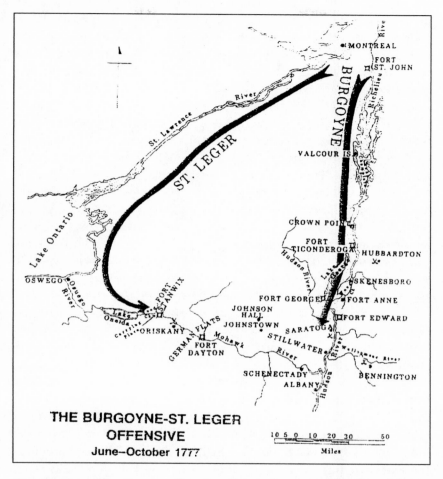

The Burgoyne-St. Leger offensive, June–October 1777 (From *Atlas of American History,* by Kenneth T. Jackson, Charles Scribner's Sons, © 1984, Charles Scribner's Sons. Reprinted by permission of the Gale Group).

relief, every one taking care of himself, all things looked very shocking to me. To remain where I was and fall into the hands of the enemy, especially in the condition I was in, expecting to receive no mercy, it came into my mind to conceal myself from them if possible. I made use of my hands and knees, as well as I could, and crawled about two rods among some small brush, and got under a log. Here I lay concealed from the enemy, who came instantly to the place I lay wounded at. What became of my distressed partner I know not. The enemy pursued our men in great haste. Some of them came over the log where I lay. Some came so near I could almost touch them. I was not discovered by the enemy till the battle was over. When they were picking up the dead and wounded among the brush and logs, I heard them coming toward me. I began to be much terrified, lest I should be found. I flattered myself that our men would come back after the battle was over and take me off; but to my great surprise, two of the enemy came so nigh, I heard one of them say, "Here is one of the rebels." I lay flat on my face across my hands, rolled in my blood. I dared not stir, being afraid they meant me, by saying, "here is one of the rebels." They soon came to me, and pulled off my shoes, supposing me to be dead. I looked up and spoke, telling them I was their prisoner, and begged to be used well. "Damn you," says one, "you deserve to be used well, don't you? What's such a young rebel as you fighting for?" One of these men was an officer, who appeared to be a pretty sort of a man. He spoke to the soldier, who had taken my shoes, and says, "Give back the shoes and help the man into camp." My shoes were given back by the soldier according to order. The soldier then raised me upon my feet, and conducted me to the British camp. Here I found a number of my brother soldiers in the same situation as myself. I was laid on the ground and remained in this posture till the afternoon, before my wound was dressed. Two Doctors came to my assistance. They raised me up, and examined my back. One of them said, "My lad, you stood a narrow chance; had the ball gone in or out half its bigness, you must have been killed instantly." I asked him if he thought there was any prospect of my getting well again. He answered, "There is some prospect." I concluded by his reply, he considered my case hazardous. The Doctors appeared to be very kind and faithful. They pulled several pieces of my clothes from my wound, which were forced in by the ball I received.

Some of the enemy were very kind; while others were very spiteful and malicious. One of them came and took my silver shoe-buckles and left me an old pair of brass ones, and said "exchange was no robbery"; but I thought it robbery at a high rate. Another came and took off my neck handkerchief. An old negro came and took my fife, which I considered as the greatest insult I had received while with the enemy. The

Indians often came and abused me with their language; calling us Yankees and rebels; but they were not allowed to injure us. I was stripped of everything valuable about me.

The enemy soon marched back to Ticonderoga, and left only a few to take care of the wounded. I was treated as well as I could expect. Doctor Haze was the head doctor, and he took true care that the prisoners were well treated. Doctor Blocksom, an under surgeon, appeared to be very kind indeed; he was the one who had the care of me; he never gave me any insulting or abusive language; he sometimes would say, "Well, my lad, think you'll be willing to list in the King's service, if you should get well?" My answer was always "no." The officers would flatter me to list in their service; telling me they were very sure to conquer the country, since they had got our strongest post. I told them I should not list.

But among all the troubles I met with, I received particular favors from two of the British. This conduct appeared to me very remarkable; why or wherefore it should be I knew not; but He who hath the hearts of all men in his hands, gave me favor in their sight. They would often visit me, and asked me if I wanted anything to eat or drink. If I did, I had it. The first time one of these friends came to me, was soon after I was brought to the camp.

As I lay on the ground, he asked me if I did not want a bed to lie on; I told him I did; he went and got a large hemlock bark and finding many old coats and overalls, taken from the dead and wounded, he put them in the bark, made me a bed and laid me into it. He built a shelter over me with barks, to keep the rain from me; which was a great kindness, as it rained exceedingly hard the next night. He went to a spring, and brought me water as often as I wanted, which was very often being very dry; my loss of blood occasioning much thirst. He asked me, also if I wanted to eat. I answered yes; for having eat but little that day, I was very faint and hungry. He told me he did not know as it was in his power to procure anything for me, but would go and try. After an absence of considerable time (certainly the time seemed long) he returned with a piece of broiled pork and broiled liver, telling me this was all the food he could get; I thanked him, and told him it was very good.

The next day he came and told me he had orders to march, and must therefore leave me; was very sorry he could stay no longer with me, but hoped somebody would take care of me; taking me by the hand, he wished me well and left me.

The loss of so good a friend grieved me exceedingly; but I soon heard that my other friend was ordered to stay behind to help take care of the wounded. My spirits, which before were much depressed, when I heard of this, were much exhilarated; and once more I felt tolerably happy. The difference in mankind never struck me more sensibly than while a prisoner. Some would do everything in their power to make me comfortable and cheerful; while others abused me with the vilest language; telling me that the prisoners would all be hanged; that they wou'd drive all the damned rebels into the sea, and that their next winter quarters would be in Boston. They certainly wintered in Boston; but to their great disappointment and chagrin, as "prisoners of war."

But to return. My wound being now a little better, I began to think of escaping from the enemy. Two of my fellow-prisoners agreed to accompany me; one of them being well acquainted with the way to Otter Creek. This plan, however, failed; for before we had an opportunity for making our escape, Doctor Haze called upon my companions to be ready to march for Ticonderoga; telling them that the next morning they must leave this place. Thus, I found, that as soon as the prisoners were able to ride, they were ordered to Ticonderoga. Being thus disappointed I begged of the Doctor to let me go with them. Says he, "You are very dangerously wounded, and it is improper for you to ride so far yet; but as soon as you are able, you shall go." Being thus defeated, I again resolved to run away, even if I went alone, and it was not long before I had an opportunity. As all the prisoners were sent off except such as were badly wounded, they thought it unnecessary to guard us very closely. I soon was able to go to the spring, which was at a little distance from the camp. Thither I often went for water for myself and the Hessians who, by the way, appeared to be pleased with me. I often waited upon them, brought them water, made their beds, &c., and found my fare the better for it.

I often walked out into the woods where the battle was fought. I went to the tree where I was shot down, observed the trees which were very much marked with the balls. Looking around one day I found some leaves of a Bible. I carried them to the camp, and diverted myself by reading them. I felt much more contented when I had something to read. My friend, whom I have before mentioned, one day brought me a very good book, which he told me to keep as a present from him. This I heartily thanked him for, and whenever I was tired by walking, I would lay down and read.

On the 22nd of July, a number of men came down from Ticonderoga, with horses and litters sufficient to carry off the remainder of the wounded. Doctor Haze came to us and told us, that tomorrow we should all be carried where we should have better care.

Says he, "I will send the orderly sergeant, who will see that your bloody clothes are well washed." This, he thought, would be very agreeable news to us. I pretended to be very much pleased, though I was determined never to go. I told the person who lay next to me that I intended to run away; I desired him to make them believe I had taken the north road, if they inclined to pursue me, for I should take the south. Says he, "I will do all in my power to assist you, and wish it was possible for me to go with you."

I made it my business that day to procure provisions sufficient for my journey. I had spared a little bread from my daily allowance, and although dry and mouldy, yet it was the best to be had. I had a large jack-knife left, of which the enemy had not robbed me; I sold this for a pint of wine, thinking it would do me more good on my march than the knife, as the event proved. The wine I put in a bottle, and carefully stowed it in my pocket.

I was hard put to it to get my shirt washed and dried before evening. However, agreeing with some to make their beds if they would dry my shirt, it was ready to put on by dark. I then went to my tent, took off my coat and jacket, and put on my clean shirt over my dirty one. Having filled my pockets with the little provision I had saved, I began to march homeward shoeless.... It came to my mind that one Jonathan Lambart had died of his wound a day or two before and left a good pair of shoes. Supposing my right to them equal to any other person, I took them and put them on.

It being dark, I went out undiscovered, and steering to the woods. After going a little way, I turned into the road and made a halt. The night being very dark, everything before me appeared gloomy and discouraging. My wound was far from being healed. My strength was much reduced by the loss of blood, pain and poor living....

To travel alone, I knew not where, having no knowledge of the way, I thought would be highly presumptuous. How far I should have to travel before I could reach any inhabitants I could not tell. Indians I supposed, were lurking about and probably I might be beset by them and murdered or carried back; and if I avoided them, perhaps I might perish in the wilderness.

Reflecting upon these things, my resolution began to flag, and I thought it most prudent to return and take my fate. I turned about and went back a few rods, when the following words struck me as if whispered in my ear: "Put not your hands to the plough and look back." I immediately turned about again, fully resolved to pursue my journey through the woods. Before morning, had I been possessed of millions of gold, I would freely have given the whole to have been once more with the enemy.

The road which I had to travel, was newly opened, leading from Hubbardton to Otter-Creek. The night being dark and the road very crooked, I found it very difficult to keep it while often running against trees and rocks, before I knew I was out of it. Then it was with much trouble that I found it again, which sometimes I was obliged to do upon my hands and knees and often up to my knees in mire.

About 12 o'clock I heard something coming towards me; what it could be I knew not. I halted and looked back; it was so dark I was at a loss to determine what it was; but thought it looked like a dog. That a dog should be so far from inhabitants, I thought very strange. I at once concluded that he belonged to the Indians, and that they were not far off. I, however, ventured to speak to him, and he immediately came to me. I gave him a piece of mouldy bread, which he eat and soon appeared fond of me. At first I was afraid he would betray me to the Indians; but soon found him of service; for I had not gone far before I heard the noise of some wild beast. I had just set down to rest me, with my back against a tree, my wound being very painful. As the beast approached, my dog appeared very much frighted; laid close down by me and trembled, as if he expected to be torn in pieces. I now began to be much terrified; I however set very still, knowing it would do no good to run. He came within two rods of me, and stopped. I was unable to determine what it was, but supposed it was a wolf. I soon found I was not mistaken. After looking at me some time, he turned about and went off; but before long returned with a large reinforcement. In his absence I exerted myself to the utmost to get forward, fearing he would be after me again. After traveling about half an hour, I was alarmed with the most horrible howling, which I supposed to be near the tree which I rested by. Judge what my feelings were, when I found these beasts of prey were pursuing me, and expected every minute to be devoured by them. But in the midst of this trouble, to my infinite joy, I discovered fires but a little way before me, which, from several circumstances, I was sure were not built by Indians; I, therefore, at once concluded they were fires of some scouting party of Americans and I made great haste to get to them, lest I should be overtaken by the wolves, which were now but a little behind. I approached so near the fires as to hear men talk when I immediately discovered them to be enemies. Thus disappointed I knew not what course to take; if I continued in the woods, I should be devoured by wild beasts; for having eat of the bodies which were left on the field of battle, they continued lurking for more. If I gave myself up to the enemy, I should certainly be carried back to Ticonderoga, and to Canada, and probably fare no better for attempting to run away. Which way to escape I knew not; I turned a little out of the path and lay down on the ground to hear what was said by the enemy, expecting every moment they would discover me; the darkness of the night, however, prevented. These howling beasts approached as near the fires as they dared, when they halted and continued their horrid yell for some time, being afraid to come so nigh as I was. After the howling had ceased, I began to think of getting round the enemy's camp; being pretty certain that, as yet, I was not discovered, I arose from the ground and took a course, which I thought would carry me round the enemy's camp. After travelling a little way, I came to the foot of a high mountain; to go round it I thought would carry me too much out of my course; I resolved therefore to ascend it; with much difficulty I arrived to the top, then took a tack to the right; travelling that course some time I found I was bewildered and lost, and which way to go to find the road again I knew not, having neither moon nor stars to direct me; so I wandered about in this wilderness till almost day, when I became so fatigued and worried, that I was obliged to lay down again. Judge what a person's feeling must be in such a situation.

I now repented of my ever leaving the enemy. Here I was lost in the woods, with but very little provision, my wounds extremely painful, and little or no prospect of ever seeing human beings again. Thus I lay and reflected, my dog walking round me like a faithful sentinel, till I fell asleep; but was soon alarmed with the noise of cannon, which I concluded by the direction must be at Ticonderoga. Never was sound more grateful to my ears than this cannon. I thought I might possibly live to reach the place, and though an enemy's camp, I would have given anything to be with them again.

Soon after the morning gun was fired, I heard the drums beat in the camp which I had visited in the night: this noise was still more grateful, for I was sure they were not a great distance. With much difficulty I got upon my legs again, with a determination to go to their camp. I found, however, that I could scarcely stand; for having laid down when I was very sweaty, I had taken cold, and was so stiff and sore, that I could hardly move. I now had recourse to my little bottle of wine, which relieved me very much, and then began to march towards the drums, which still continued beating.

After travelling a little way, I heard a cock crow, which appeared near the drums. I thought it of little consequence which object to pursue, both being in nearly the same direction. But the noise of the drums soon ceased, and I steered for the other object, which soon brought me into open land and in sight of a house. I got to the door just as the man arose from his bed. After the usual compliments, I asked him how far it was to the British encampments? He answered about fifty rods. "Do you want to go to them?" says he. I never was more at a stand what reply to make. As none of the enemy appeared about the house, I thought if I could persuade the man to befriend me, I possibly might avoid them. If he should prove to be a Tory, and know from whence I came, he would certainly betray me. I stood perhaps a minute without saying a word. He, seeing my confusion, spoke again to me: "Come," said he, "come into the house." I went in and sat down. "I will tell you," said I, "what I want, if you will promise not to hurt me." He replied, "I will not injure you, if you do not injure us." This answer did not satisfy me, for as yet I could not tell whether he would be a friend or foe. I sat and viewed him for some minutes, and at last resolved to tell him from whence I came and where I wished to go, let the event be what it would. I was a soldier, said I, in the Continental army, was dangerously wounded and taken prisoner, had made my escape from the enemy, and after much fatigue and peril, had got through the woods, being directed to this house by the crowing of a cock. He smiled and said, "You have been rightly directed, for had you gone to either of my neighbors, you undoubtedly would have been carried to the enemy again; you have now found a friend, who will if possible protect you. It is true they have forced me to take the oath of allegiance to the king; but I sincerely hope the Americans will finally prevail, for I believe their cause to be just and equitable. Should they know of my harboring rebels, as they call us, I certainly should suffer for it. Anything I can do for you without exposing my own life, I will do." I thanked him for his kindness, and desired him not to expose himself on my account.

After giving me something to eat and drink, he concealed me in a chamber, where he said I might stay till the dew was off and then go out into some secret place in the bushes, there to continue till night; this he said was necessary, as the enemy were often plundering about his house, and if I continued in it, I should probably be discovered, which would ruin him. A little boy was set as a sentinel at the door, who was to give notice if the enemy came near. I had not been in the house half an hour, before a number of them came in, but with no other design than to buy some rum and milk, and to borrow a pot for cooking.

As soon as they were gone, the woman came into the chamber to dress my wound. She washed it with rum, applied dressings, and bound it up as well as she could. She showed every mark of kindness to me but her husband, whose name was Moulton, in a day or two after I got to his house, was pressed by the enemy to bring stores from Skeenborough with his team, and I never saw the good old man anymore. His wife was in much trouble, lest the enemy should find me in the house and be so enraged as to kill all the family. She permitted her little boy to guide me to the bushes, where I might secrete myself; she gave me a blanket to lie on. The boy went with me to my lurking place, that I might be easily found, so as to receive refreshment. When night came on, I was called by the boy to the house again, and took my old stand in the chamber; the woman feared I should receive injury by lodging out of doors. She informed me that a man would lodge there that night, who was brother-in-law to her husband; and who had actually taken up arms against his country. I told her I apprehended danger from tarrying in the house; she said there would not be any. I then lay snug in my straw.

In a short time the Tory came for some drink; the indiscreet woman told him she had an American in the chamber, who had been taken prisoner by the British and had escaped. He asked her what kind of a man I was. She told him I was a young fellow and wanted much to get home, and begged that I might not be taken back to the enemy or betrayed. His answer was very rough, and I began to think I was gone for it. I expected to be forced back; but the woman interceding so hard for me, softened the ferocity of my Tory enemy. Knowing I was discovered, I crawled from my hiding place, and began a conversation with the man. He asked me if I belonged to the rebel service? I told him I belonged to the Continental service. "What is that," says he, "but the rebel service?" He addressed me in very insolent language, and said he was very sorry to have me leave the king's troops in the manner I had done, and he would have me to know I was in his hands. I was patient and mild in my situation, telling him I was at his disposal. My good mistress often put in a word on my behalf.

After some time spent in this way, the man asked me if he should chance to be taken, and in my power as I was in his, whether I should let him escape? I told him I should. "Then," says he, "if you will promise this, I will not detain you. If you are retaken before you reach home, you will not inform, that you have seen me, or have been at my brother's." I gave him my promise. His advice to me was immediately to set out, for if I should stay long I might be picked up by some person. "And," says he, "I advise you to travel in the night, and hide in the day, for many volunteers are reconnoitering up and down the country." I concluded to travel; but my feeling landlady thought it best to stay a few days longer. My friend tory said it was best for me to travel as soon as possible. "If you are determined to go tonight," said the woman, "I will dress your wound and give you food for your journey." I told her I would go as soon as possible. She then dressed my wound for the last time, and filled my pockets with good provision. After thanking her for her kindness, it being all the compensation I could make, and I believe all that she desired, I left her.

But before I proceed on my journey, I must tell you, that my dog, who had accompanied me through many dangers, I was obliged to drive from me; when in the chamber, he would commonly lay at the foot of the stairs. Mrs. Moulton often told me, she was afraid he would betray me, for as the enemy were often in, should they see the dog, might suspect that somebody was in the chamber. I told her, with much regret, to drive him away; she with her little boy tried all in their power to get rid of him, but in vain; the dog would stay about the house; at length she called me to drive him away; I came down, and after much difficulty, effected it.

But to return. After being told the course I must take, I began my journey in the night, which was dark and cloudy, through the woods. I had not travelled more than two hours, before I got lost. I concluded that I had missed the road, and having reached the end of one I was then in, began to think of going back. My wound began to be very painful, and I was so sore, I could scarcely go. While I was seeking for the road again, there came up a thunder shower, and rained fast. I crawled into an old forsaken hovel, which was near, and lay till the shower was over; then went back half a mile, and found the road once more. The road being newly opened through the woods was very bad, and it was with much difficulty I could get along, often tumbling over roots and stones and sometimes up to my knees in mire. I once fell and was obliged to lay several minutes before I could recover myself.

About 12 o'clock at night as I was walking in this wilderness, I was surprised by two large wild animals, which lay close by the road, and started up as soon as they saw me; ran a few rods and turned about towards me; whether they were bears or wolves, I could not tell; I was, however, exceedingly terrified, and would have given any thing for my dog again. One of them followed me for a long time; sometimes would come close to me, and at others, kept at a considerable distance. At last he got discouraged and left me, and certainly I did not regret his absence.

At daylight, I came to open land, and discovered a house belonging to Col. Mead. I was not a little rejoiced to see his house, as I knew he would be a friend to me; but my joy was of short continuance, for as soon as I looked into the door, I saw marks of the enemy; every thing belonging to the house being carried off or destroyed. I thought it not prudent to go into the house lest some of the enemy might be within; so I passed on as fast as possible; it now began to grow light; and what to do with myself I could not tell. My friends had advised me to lay concealed in the day time and travel in the night.

When I viewed the depredations the enemy had made on the inhabitants, and many of whom had fled; not knowing how far I must travel to find friends, and my wound being very troublesome, I reflected long, whether to tarry and be made prisoner, or push forward through a dreary wilderness; death seemed to threaten me on all sides; however, I collected resolution sufficient to make to the east; I conceived myself exposed by my uniform and bloody clothes; to prevent a discovery by any who should be an enemy, I took off my shirt and put it over my coat, by which my uniform was covered; in this line I marched; it being the orders of the British for all tories, who came to join them, to appear in this dress, I considered myself protected...

I travelled till the middle of the day, before I saw any person. I then met a man driving cattle, as I supposed to the enemy. He examined me closely, and enquired if I was furnished with a pass. I gave him plausible answers to all his questions, and so far satisfied him as to proceed unmolested. I enquired of him, if he knew one Joshua Priest; he told me he did, and very readily directed me to the place where he lived. Leaving this man, I had not travelled far, before I met a number more, armed; being within about fifty rods of them, I thought to hide myself, but found I could not; I then made towards them, without any apparent fear. Coming up to them, I expected a strict examination; but they only asked me how far it was to such a town; I informed them as well as I could, and pushed on my way.

Being within a mile and a half of said Priest's, I saw two men making towards me; they came to a fence and stopped; I heard them say, "Let's examine this fellow, and know what his business is." One of them asked me where I was going. I told him to Joshua Priest's; he asked me my business there: I answered him upon no bad errand: He says you are a spy: I told him I was no spy. I did not like the fellow's looks, therefore dropped the conversation with him, believing he was one of the enemy. I resolved not to converse with anyone, till I had arrived at Priest's, unless compelled to. Being almost overcome with fatigue, I wished for rest; however, these men seemed determined to stop me or do me some mischief, for when I walked on, they followed me upon the run, and in great rage told me, I should go no further, until I had made known to them who and what I was; saying they had asked me a civil question, and they required a civil answer. I told them if they would go to Priest's, I would tell them all the truth and satisfy them entirely; repeating to them I was no spy. They said they did not mean to leave me till they were satisfied respecting me. I then, in short, told them what I had before in the whole, and added, that I was well acquainted with Priest, and intended to tarry with him some time.

We all arrived at Priest's, who at first did not recollect me. After some pause, he told me he was surprised to see me, as my father had informed him I was slain at Hubbardton. I told him I was yet alive, but had received a bad wound. His family soon dressed my wound and made me comfortable.

I then in the presence and hearing of my tory followers, told Priest the story of my captivity and escape; also repeated the insolent language used by the tories towards our people, when prisoners with the enemy, finding Priest my friend, I said many severe things against the tories, and fixed my countenance sternly on those fellows, who had pretended to lord it over me and stop me on the way. They bore all without saying a word, but looked *as surly as bulls.*

I soon found these tory gentry had premeditated carrying me back, and were seeking help to prosecute their design. My friend Priest loaded his gun, and said he would give them a grist if they dared come after me; but failing of getting any persons to join them, I was not molested.

I could often hear my tory followers' threatenings against me, to take me back, saying I should be able to fight again, and do injury to the enemy. I feared these tories would do hurt, but my fears were quieted by finding the neighbors were my friends, and would afford me their protection.... At my old friend's, I remained six weeks; in the mean time, my wound almost healed. I was hospitably entertained by him.

Having heard that one Mr. Atwell belonging to New-Marlborough, was in the neighborhood with a team to move a family, I agreed with him for a horse to ride. After a journey of a few days, I safely arrived at New-Ipswich, and once more participated in the pleasure of seeing and enjoying my friends, and *no enemy to make me afraid.*

Not long afterwards, an officer from the army hearing of my return ordered me to be arrested and returned to the main body of the American army, although my wound was scarcely healed. In a few weeks, I joined my corps, then stationed in Pennsylvania; having yet two years to serve my country in the tented field.

We afterwards went on an expedition against the Indians, to the Genesee Country, a long and tedious march, commanded by Gen. Sullivan, where we drove the Indians before us, burnt their huts, destroyed their corn. The first Indian settlement we came to was called Tiauger [Tioga] where they lay in ambush, in a thick wood, on a hill, where they fired on our men and killed seven; after that we were ordered to march in the following order: the army was divided into four columns and the head of each column had a horn or trumpet, and each of these divisions marched as far apart as they could hear each other sound; we marched in this line all the way afterward. If we had not they undoubtedly would have waylaid and killed us all. There were two men that left their place and went out from the main body and were taken by the Indians, and tortured to death in the most cruel manner.

Our provision was like to fail. We had to go on half allowance a long time, or we should have starved. Finding few enemies to contend with in that quarter, as they were not disposed to meet us in the open field, we received the gladly obeyed orders to return to New England, where we remain the ensuing autumn. Nothing more of importance, to me or the reader, occurred, until the three long years rolled away, except when in Pennsylvania, I had the honor of being acquainted with Gen. Washington and Gen. Lafayette and then I received my discharge (March 20, 1780).

And now, kind reader, wishing that you may forever remain ignorant of the real sufferings of the veteran soldier, from hunger and cold, from sickness and captivity, I bid you a cordial adieu.

Ebenezer Fletcher
New-Ipswich, Jan. 1813.

The British had taken Fort Ticonderoga, but in pursuing the retreating Americans they had lost a significant part of their army. The American army, on the other hand, escaped from the fort and, despite some losses, was able to fight again in the continuing action against the British as they marched to their surrender at Saratoga.

Bibliography

Fletcher, Ebenezer. *The Narrative of the Captivity and Sufferings of Ebenezer Fletcher of New Ipswich.* New Ipswich, N.H.: S. Wilder, 1827. (This autobiographical narrative of his adventures during the Revolutionary War was originally published in 1813. The present issue has been taken from one of the original imprints of 1827, that being the author's last revised and most improved edition.)

11

David Holbrook at Bennington Heard "Boys Follow Me"

As the British expedition continued its invasion journey the German Brunswick dragoons accompanying Burgoyne on his expedition from Canada to Albany were suffering in the August heat of 1777. They were wearing high boots, stiff leather breeches, and huge gauntlets. Each man was carrying a 12-pound broadsword, a canteen for water, a hatchet, a knapsack, a heavy carbine and ammunition. Obviously they wished to find horses. Hearing that ammunition, supplies and mounts were nearby, Burgoyne sent the Germans as part of an 800-man troop on a side trip to Bennington, Vermont.

Seventeen-year-old David Holbrook, whose home was in East Hoosac (now Adams, Mass.), had become ill during his second tour of duty with the militia and was home on furlough on August 14. He recalls:

In the morning, having regained my health I heard the alarm that the enemy were about to attack Bennington. I started immediately and got to Bennington the same night. The next morning I joined a unit and went to the lines of the enemy. I remained there watching their movements that day.

The next day, being the sixteenth of August, Capt. Enos Parker and Lieutenants Kilborn and Cook of the Mass. Militia, selected a company of sixty or seventy men from the men who had come together, of which I was one. We marched across the river by a circuitous route of five or six miles, mostly through woods, with all possible silence. We came up in a piece of woods at the enemy's rear. A line was formed on the right. There, pursuant to orders, we sat in silence until a signal [the firing of two muskets] was given. The American army, upon three sides of the British encampment, made a simultaneous attack.

The American army made a rush upon the British entrenchments. They were received by the British with boldness. The battle became general and desperate immediately and continued about two hours close combat without form or regularity. Each American was fighting according to his own discretion until the entrenchments were completely routed. Those who had not been killed and had not escaped surrendered at discretion. General Baum, being wounded, was among the prisoners.

About the time of the general rout of the British army, Colonel Herrick of the Green Mountain Rangers rode along near where I was and cried out, "Boys, follow me." With one other I ran after him about two miles to Ramplar Mills. He stopped his horse, and drew up his piece, and fired. He then wheeled his horse and said there was a reinforcement of British coming.

It was soon discovered to be from nine hundred to twelve hundred British soldiers with a nine- and six-pounder and a band of music [playing in the forest trail]. Colonel Herrick ran his horse to give intelligence to General Stark. My companion and I, having got out of breath, ran behind a haystack and rested till the British army came along. We then went out from behind the stack and discharged our pieces at the enemy and ran. The enemy returned the fire by the discharge of a six-pounder, which gave general alarm.

The American militia then ran together and formed about a mile southwesterly from the entrenchments which had been occupied by General Baum. However, the Americans, in pursuing those who escaped from the entrenchments, had got scattered and fatigued. Few assembled at first. They kept falling in continually until a line was formed along a fence on the northeast side of the meadow where the haystack was in the edge of a piece of woods. And the British army formed a line in the same meadow and extended across the road.

The firing commenced as soon as they came within musket shot. The Americans, not being sufficiently strong to keep the ground, retreated from tree to tree. They fired as they left the trees, until they came to a ravine where there was a long fence. They made a halt, and held the ground. The British came up within about sixteen rods and stood. The firing then continued some time with out cessation.

Colonel Warner, with the remains of his regiment, came up. Some of his men, understanding the artillery exercise, took one of the field-pieces taken in the first engagement and formed at the right of the party where I was.

And, about the same time, an old man, with an old Queen Anne's iron sword and mounted upon a old black mare, with about ninety robust men following him in files two deep, came up. They filed in front of the company where I then was. And just as the old man had got his men to the spot and halted, his mare fell. He jumped upon a large white oak stump and gave the command.

Captain Parker, seeing the old man's company between him and the enemy, ordered his men to file in between their files, which were some distance apart. This was immediately done, and the battle then became desperate.

I heard a tremendous crash up in the woods at the right wing of the American troops, which was seconded by a yell, the most terrible that I ever heard. Then I heard the voice of Colonel Warner's like thunder, "Fix bayonets. Charge."

Then the old man on the stump cried out, "Charge, boys," and jumped from the stump and ran towards the enemy. His men, some with, and some without bayonets, followed suit and rushed upon the enemy with all their might, who seeing us coming, took to their heels and were completely routed.

As we came up to the enemy's lines, their fieldpieces being charged, a Sergeant Luttington knocked down the man with the port fire and caught hold of the limber and whirled about the piece and fired it at the enemy. The blaze overtook them before they had got ten rods and mowed down a large number of them. Those of the Americans, who had not got too much fatigued, pursued and killed and took a number of the enemy. The Indians that survived the slaughter escaped.

When I was scaling the breastwork of the enemy in the first engagement, I put my right hand upon the top of the breastwork. I threw my feet over, but my right leg was met by a British bayonet which held it fast. I pitched headfirst in the entrenchment, and a British soldier hit me a thump upon the head. But the enemy was dispatched by the next man that came up, and I was thereby relieved. In the heat of feeling I forgot my wounds.

Painting by John Trumbull shows the surrender of the British at Saratoga. Burgoyne is offering his sword to General Gates, who returned it and invited his opponent to dine with him in his tent. Daniel Morgan is in white and Philip Schuyler is in mufti (National Archives).

But when the enemy fled in the second engagement, I found myself exhausted and could not pursue, the blow upon my head and the wound in my leg having occasioned the loss of considerable blood, I found myself unable to walk and was put upon a horse and carried back to Bennington.

I remained there ten or twelve days, until sufficiently recovered from my wounds to march. When Lieutenant White, with whom I enlisted, came on, I went with him to Manchester. Soon after I was taken with a fever and was sent home, where I remained sick a number of months.

On the twelfth February, 1778, Lieutenant White came to my father and gave me a discharge. Being then very sick and not expected to recover, I was not able to do duty during the whole of the year 1778.

The action at Bennington on August 16, 1777, was a serious setback for Burgoyne. It did not produce the horses, the ammunition, the supplies he had hoped to find there. It also cost him almost 1,000 men, reducing his forces to 6,000. The American losses were 30 killed and 40 wounded. It demonstrated that American farmers, inexperienced in warfare, could defeat two forces of trained, professional soldiers. At Freeman's farm, Burgoyne faced another battle on September 19, 1777. Daniel Morgan's riflemen picked off key officers and soldiers in a confrontation of the American Indian fighting tactics of the New World against the Old World's traditional volleys fired by lines of soldiers. By October 14, the British asked for a cessation of hostilities to consider terms. Their three-pronged attack had been defeated. This turning point of the war brought the French into an alliance with the Americans and was the stepping stone to a free and independent America.

Bibliography

Holbrook, David. *1832 Revolutionary War Pension Application.* Washington, D.C.: Veterans Administration Archives in the National Archives, Record Group 15, Microcopy 805.

12

Lafayette Buys a Ship to Join the Americans

The French government's support for the American rebels was crucial to the victory at Yorktown. By sending ships, supplies and military personnel they provided for the essential needs the American colonists required to defeat their enemy. A French teenager played an important role in promoting that alliance. He was a wealthy 19-year-old French orphan—the Marquis de Lafayette—with an incredibly long name: Marie-Joseph-Paul-Yves-Roch-Gilbert du Motier.

From his birth on September 6, 1757, he grew up at his family's Chateau Chavaniac in the remote hills of Auvergne in central France. When he was only two years old, his father was killed in the battle of Minden during the Seven Years' War. In his memoirs he says:

I can recall no time in my life when I did not love stories of glorious deeds, or have dreams of traveling the world in search of fame. At the age of eight, my heart pounded when I heard of a hyena that had done some mischief in our neighborhood. The hope of meeting it made my walks exciting. When I went to school.... I like to recall that in Rhetoric class, when I described the perfect horse, I sacrificed a chance of pleasing the teacher to the pleasure of depicting a horse, that, on perceiving the whip, threw his rider.

In 1768, at the age of 11, he joined his mother in Paris in her family's apartments in the Palais du Luxembourg. He enrolled in the Collège du Plessis, next to the Sorbonne and operated under its direction. The students were the sons of the greatest families of France.

The courses emphasized the Latin classical writings of Cicero and Seneca on stern precepts of duty and the moralizing biographies of Plutarch. They portrayed the Roman Republic as a society in which there was equality before the law; one whose leaders were always on the alert to preserve their liberty.

Lafayette's mother died of a fever on April 3, 1770, in his 13th year. A few weeks later her father, the Marquis de La Rivière, died of the same. The orphaned Lafayette inherited his grandfather's estates, providing an increase in his annual income from 25,000 livres to 120,000.

At that time, marriages were decided by parents and families. Thanks to Lafayette's noble birth and handsome income, the powerful and influential Noailles family arranged for his marriage (at 16), to their daughter Adrienne, 14. At the same time he joined the Noailles Dragoons. It was expected that he would be a courtier at Louis XVI's court at Versailles.

Republican anecdotes delighted me. When my wife's family obtained a place for me at court, I did not hesitate to be disagreeable to preserve my independence. It was while I was in that frame of mind that I first learned of the troubles in America. They were not well known in Europe until 1776, and the memorable declaration of July fourth arrived there toward the end of the same year....

When I first learned of that quarrel, my heart was enlisted, and I thought only of joining the colors. Some circumstances, which it is not necessary to relate, had taught me to expect from my family only obstacles to the attainment of my goal. I therefore relied upon myself .

He contacted Silas Deane, the American representative in Paris, and signed an agreement for receiving a rank of major general in the Continental army:

When I presented myself to Mr. Deane I was just nineteen years old, and I spoke more of my enthusiasm than of my experience. I dwelt upon the minor sensation my departure would raise, and he signed the agreement. The secrecy of those negotiations and of my preparations was truly miraculous. Family, friends, ministers, French spies, English spies, all were blind to them....

12. *Lafayette Buys a Ship to Join the Americans*

Paris, December 7, 1776

The desire which Mr. The Marquis de la Fayette shows of serving among the Troops of the United States of North America, and the Interest which he takes in the Justice of their Cause making him wish to distinguish himself in this war and to render himself as useful as he possibly can; but not thinking that he can obtain leave of his Family to pass the seas and serve in a foreign Country till he can go as a General Officer; I have thought I could not better serve my Country and those who have entrusted me than by granting to him in the name of the very honorable Congress the Rank of Major General which I beg the States to confirm to him, to ratify and deliver to him the Commission to hold and take rank, to count from this Day, with the General Officers of the same degree. His high Birth, his Alliances, the Great Dignities which his Family holds at this Court, his considerable Estates in this Realm, his personal merit, his reputation, his disinterestedness, and above all his Zeal for the Liberty of our Provinces, have only been able to engage me to promise him the Rank of Major General in the name of the United States. In witness of which I have signed the present 7th of December 1776.

Silas Deane
Agent for the United States of N. America

Lafayette added the following:

On the conditions here explained I offer myself and promise to depart when and how Mr. Deane shall judge proper, to serve the United States with all possible Zeal, without any Pension or particular allowance, reserving to myself the Liberty of returning to Europe when my family or my King shall recall me. Done at Paris this 7th of December 1776.

The Marqs. De La Fayette

He continues his account:

A ship was being prepared for America when very bad news arrived: New York, Long Island, White Plains, Fort Washington, and the Jerseys had been the scene of successive destructions of the American forces by thirty-three thousand British or German troops. Only three thousand troops remained in arms and General Howe was pursuing them.

From that moment the insurgents' credit vanished; it became impossible to dispatch a ship. The envoys themselves thought it their duty to admit their discouragement to me, and to dissuade me from my project. I called upon Mr. Deane and thanked him for his frankness.

"Before this," I added, "you have only seen my enthusiasm, perhaps it will now become useful: I shall buy a ship to transport your officers. Be confident. I want to share your fortune in this time of danger." My idea was well received, but then it was necessary to find the money to buy and arm a ship in secrecy. All that was soon accomplished with great dispatch.

Soon he was able to contact William Carmichael, secretary to Silas Deane, as indicated in the following letter describing the secrecy necessary to arrange for his departure for America:

To William Carmichael

[Paris, February 11, 1777]
Tuesday, three o'clock

I do not leave for England until Sunday, Sir, so I shall have the time to see Mr. Franklin and Mr. Deane. It is impossible for me to keep today's rendezvous because the queen is giving a ball which I am obliged to attend.

If I could see you tomorrow between six and seven o'clock, I would come and take you in my carriage, as I did the other day, and we could talk of our affairs. I announce to you with great pleasure, Sir, that I have just purchased my ship, and that, in a month at the latest, I hope to be able to take to your country the zeal that animates me for their happiness, their glory, and their liberty. All your fellow citizens are dear to me, but I shall never find any of them to whom I can be more affectionately attached than to you.

THE MARQUIS DE LAFAYETTE

If you do not reply, that will be a sign that you will expect me tomorrow.

Lafayette continues in his memoir:

We came, however, to the time for a trip to England, which had been planned for a long while. I could not refuse to go without compromising my secret; whereas, by accepting, I concealed my preparations. This last measure was strongly supported by MM. Franklin and Deane. The Doctor himself was then in France, and although I did not go to his home for fear of being seen there, we corresponded through Mr. Carmichael, an American less well known.

Thus I arrived at London with the Prince de Poix, and saw Bancroft, the American, and then His Britannic Majesty. At nineteen, one may take too much pleasure in mocking the tyrant whom he is about to fight, in dancing at the home of Lord Germain, minister for American affairs, and at the home of Lord Rawdon, who had just arrived from New York, and in meeting at the opera that Clinton whom I would meet again at Monmouth. But, while hiding my intentions, I displayed my sentiments. I often defended the Americans; I rejoiced at their success at Trenton, and my spirit of opposition earned me an invitation to breakfast with Lord Shelburne. I ... declined offers to inspect the seaports and the vessels that were being sent out against the "rebels," and avoided everything that I believed to be a breach of confidence.

Toward the end of his visit, he gleefully informed his father-in-law of his plans in a letter from London dated March 9, 1777:

I have found a unique opportunity to distinguish myself, and to learn my profession. I am a general officer in the army of the United States of America ... at this very moment I am in London, awaiting news from my friends. As soon as I receive it, I shall leave here and without stopping in Paris, board a ship that I have equipped, and which belongs to me.

My traveling companions are M. Le Baron de Kalb, an officer of the highest distinction, a brigadier general in the king's army and a major general in the service of the United States like myself, and a few excellent officers who are willing to share my adventures. I am overjoyed at having found such a fine opportunity to do something and to improve myself. I know very well that I am making enormous sacrifices, and that it will be more painful for me than anyone to leave my family, my friends, and you, my dear Papa, because I love them more dearly than anyone has ever loved. But this voyage is not such a long one. People undertake longer ones every day for pleasure. Moreover, I hope to return more worthy of all who will have the goodness to miss me.

At the end of three weeks he returned to Paris but stopped at M. De Kalb's house as he feared the opposition of his family. He then hid for three days at Chaillot, where he was visited by the Americans and a few friends. To Adrienne on his last day, March 16, 1777, he wrote:

I am too guilty to vindicate myself, but I have been too cruelly punished not to deserve a pardon. If I had expected to feel my sacrifices in such a frightful manner, I would not be at present the unhappiest of men. But I have given my word, and I would die rather than go back on it.... Do not be angry with me. Believe that I am sorely distressed. I had never realized how much I loved you—but I shall return soon, as soon as my obligations are fulfilled. Good-bye, good-bye, write to me often, every day.

When his ship was ready at Bordeaux, they set sail, stopping in Los Pasajes, a Spanish port. Learning of his plans at last, his family tried to stop him. He relates that letters from his family were terrifying, and the lettre de cachet was peremptory: "you are forbidden to go to the American continent, under penalty of disobedience, and enjoined to go to Marseilles to await further orders." Lafayette decided to ignore the threats. With nearly a dozen French officers he set sail on April 20, 1777, on *La Victoire* for a 56-day voyage ending near Georgetown, South Carolina, on June 13, 1777.

To Adrienne de Noailles de Lafayette

On board *La Victoire*, May 30 [1777]

I am writing to you from very far away, dear heart.... So many fears and so many worries are added to the intense grief of leaving everything that is most dear to me.... Have you forgiven me? ... Since my last letter I have been in the most tedious of regions; the sea is so dismal, and I believe we sadden each other, she and I. I should have landed by now, but the winds have cruelly opposed me, and I shall not see Charleston for eight or ten more days. That is where I expect to land.... I was very ill during the first part of the voyage.... I treated myself in my own way, and I recovered sooner than the others. Now I feel almost as if I were on land....

12. Lafayette Buys a Ship to Join the Americans

June 7

I am still on this dreary plain, dear heart, and it is so dismal that one cannot make any comparison with it.... As the defender of that liberty which I idolize, freer than anyone else, coming as a friend to offer my services to this most interesting republic, I bring there only my sincerity and my goodwill, and no personal ambition or selfish interest. In striving for my own glory, I work for their happiness. I trust that, for my sake, you will become a good American. Besides, it is a sentiment made for virtuous hearts. The welfare of America is intimately connected with the happiness of all mankind; she will become the respectable and safe asylum of virtue, integrity, tolerance, equality, and a peaceful liberty.

We have from time to time some minor alerts, but, with a little skill and good luck, I am quite certain of getting through without trouble.... Today we have seen several types of birds that indicate that we are not far from land.... I divide my time between military books and English books. I have made some progress in that language, which will soon be so necessary. Farewell, my dear, I cannot continue because night is falling, and I have forbidden all lights on my vessel for several days now.

June 15, at Major Huger's house

I have arrived, dear heart, in very good health, at the house of an American officer....

Nine accompanied him ashore here and the rest remained on board to sail to Charleston.

Charleston, June 19 [1777]

I landed after sailing for several days along a coast that swarmed with enemy vessels. When I arrived here, everyone told me that my vessel had surely been taken, because two English frigates blockaded the port. I even sent orders, by land and sea, for the captain to put the men ashore and burn the ship, if there was still time.

Well, by inconceivable good fortune, a squall had momentarily driven off the frigates, and my vessel arrived in broad daylight without encountering either friend or foe.... I cannot help being pleased with the reception I have had here, even though I have not judged it proper to enter into any details about either my arrangements or my plans. I want to see the Congress first. I hope to leave in two days for Philadelphia, an overland journey of more than two hundred and fifty leagues. We will separate into small parties; I have already purchased some horses and small carriages for transportation.

For myself I have received the most pleasant reception possible from everyone.... I have just spent five hours at a grand dinner given in my honor by a resident of this city.... We drank toasts and conversed in broken English—at present I am just beginning to speak a little of it. Tomorrow I shall take all those gentlemen with me when I call upon the president of the assembly, and I shall work on the arrangements for my departure.

After a month of traveling by carriage, on horseback, boat, and foot he finally arrived in Philadelphia. Upon receiving a cool reception from Congress as being just one more of too many French officers, Lafayette sent them the following message:

After the sacrifices I have made, I have the right to exact two favors: one is to serve at my own expense, and the other is to begin to serve as a volunteer. [In France a young noble was often attached to a general officer who taught him the art of war as he performed the duties of an aide-de-camp.]

After considering letters from American representatives in Paris, and other information, Congress passed the following resolution:

Resolution of Congress: July 31, 1777

Whereas the Marquis de la Fayette, out of his great zeal to the cause of liberty in which the United States are engaged, has left his family & connexions & at his own expence come over to offer his service to the United States without pension or particular allowance, and is anxious to risque his life in our cause:

Resolved That his service be accepted and that in consideration of his zeal, illustrious family and connexions, he have the rank and commission of major-general in the army of the United States.

Within a week, on July 31, General Washington was having a late dinner in Philadelphia with some members of Congress, and

Lafayette was presented to him. This young man was about five feet nine inches tall, broad of shoulder, prominent eyebrows, reddish hair. He seemed timid and spoke halting English. Washington learned his story and invited him to sit at his own table for the whole of the campaign. The next day he asked the young Frenchman to join him in an inspection of the fortifications around Philadelphia.

Shortly thereafter letters arrived from Silas Deane to Robert Morris, and another from Deane and Benjamin Franklin, praising Lafayette and urging that "a generous reception of him will do us infinite service." Morris was asked to be a banker.

Washington and Congress were not ready to give Lafayette a command of troops. However, Washington assured him of his friendly regard and said he would be pleased to have his confidence as a friend and father. This friendship between them became an important anchor in the life of this young man who had known no father. In a subsequent letter to Washington dated October 14, 1777, Lafayette refers to this special relationship:

Give me leave, dear General, to speack to you about my own business with all the confidence of a son, of a friend, as you favoured me with those two so precious titles.

British General Howe planned to occupy Philadelphia, the largest city in America and the seat of government. Fifteen thousand soldiers were sent aboard ships to the Chesapeake Bay, and then to Philadelphia.

Washington waited with his 11,000 men, poorly armed and even more poorly clothed, according to Lafayette's memoirs. In that motley and often naked array, the best garments were hunting shirts, large jackets of gray linen commonly worn in Carolina. On the way to meet the British troops landing in the Head of Elk Bay on Sunday, August 24, 1777, the patriot army passed through Philadelphia with their heads adorned with green branches and marching to the sound of drums and fifes. These soldiers (they wore whatever clothes they had, not proper uniforms) presented a pleasing spectacle to the eyes of all the citizens. The general showed at the head, and Lafayette was at his side.

When the British troops disembarked at the Head of Elk, they greatly outnumbered Washington's army as they began marching northward. Washington waited 26 miles from Philadelphia, at Brandywine Creek, hoping to halt the enemy.

Lafayette learned that Cornwallis and Howe were really leading a larger force across the upper branches of the creek. Receiving permission from Washington, he and his aide galloped off. They joined a brigade that included some French officers. On September 11, 1777, he met the British and Hessians in one of the few large-scale battles of the war. It was Lafayette's first battle of the American Revolution. He described his experiences in a letter to Adrienne:

Philadelphia September 12, [1777]

I send you a few lines, dear heart, by some French officers, my friends, who came here with me but have not obtained positions and are returning to France. I shall begin by telling you that I am well, because I must end by telling you that we fought in earnest yesterday, and we were not the victors.

Our Americans, after holding firm for a considerable time, were finally routed. While I was trying to rally them, the English honored me with a musket shot, which wounded me slightly in the leg. But the wound is nothing, dear heart; the ball hit neither bone nor nerve, and all I have to do, for it to heal, is to lie on my back for a while—which puts me in very bad humor.

I hope, dear heart, that you will not worry; on the contrary, you should be even less worried than before, because I shall now be out of action for some time. I intend to take good care of myself; you may be sure of that, dear heart. This battle will, I fear, have unpleasant consequences for America; we must try to repair the damage, if we can.

You must have received many letters from me, unless the English are as hostile to my letters as to my legs. I have received only one from you so far, and I long for news. Farewell. They won't let me write longer than this. For several days I have not had time to sleep. Last night was spent in our retreat and in my journey here, where I am very well cared for.... Good night, dear heart, I love you more than ever.

When he was hit in his left leg below the calf, the ball went clear through. He did not notice it until the blood began to run

Lafayette wounded at Brandywine while trying to rally troops (Emmet Collection, Miriam and Ira Wallach Division of Art, Prints and Photographs, The New York Public Library, Astor, Lenox and Tilden Foundations).

outside his boot. His aide Gimat helped him remount, and they retreated to the woods.

Washington, leading some troops, then came by at a gallop, followed shortly after by General Greene and Weedon's brigade. Lafayette started to join them, but he felt weak with the loss of blood. He stopped to have Dr. John Cochran, Washington's personal physician, attend to his wound; but men, wagons, and cannon rushed by so fast that they feared capture and hastened on. There was time only for a hasty bandage.

The Hessian General Knyphausen had meanwhile crossed Chadd's Ford, and the American rout was complete. Lafayette joined the troops hastening to the shelter of Chester, 12 miles away. Night fell as they neared the town.

Lafayette came to a stone bridge across Chester Creek. Here

he tried to stop the fugitives, reformed some of them behind the creek, and succeeded in re-establishing a little order.

Finally Washington and his generals arrived, and Lafayette was at last able to have his wound bandaged. When the other generals entered the house where he had been carried, they found him on a table having his wound dressed. He joked that "they all looked so hungry that he begged them not to eat him up though he was the only dish set out for them."

That night Lafayette was sent by boat to Philadelphia to have his wound dressed. He stayed for several days. As the British troops moved closer, Washington informed Congress he could no longer assure the city against capture. Congress moved to Lancaster and then to York. On September 16, a boat had been found to take Lafayette to Bristol. On September 19, Henry Laurens, president of the Congress, arrived in Bristol with his coach. He took in Lafayette and brought him by easy stages to Bethlehem on September 19. Here the Moravian Brethren, who would not engage in actual fighting, were serving the American cause by taking care of the wounded. Finally able to leave on October 18, Lafayette wrote Henry Laurens:

At length I go to camp, and I see the end of my so tedious confinement. My wound (tho' the skin is not yet quite over) seems to me in so fine a way of recovery that I judge myself able to play my part in our first engagement.

Lafayette was the best known foreigner serving the American cause. As a field officer he fought at Brandywine, Gloucester, and Monmouth. He held important commands at Albany, Barren Hill, and Rhode Island. His last military assignment in America was as commander of the Continental forces in Virginia during the spring and summer of 1781. Until he was joined by the allied armies before Yorktown, Lafayette proved himself as a field commander and won the confidence of Washington, his fellow officers, and his men.

Lafayette also had a significant part in the creation and maintenance of the French alliance. During his service in America, from 1777 to 1782 (and while on leave in France in 1779), he maintained an extensive correspondence with family, friends, and officials in France and America. In France he was the steady representative of the American cause; he reported American prospects, strengths, and needs, and he proposed ways in which the French government could increase its support for the "insurgents."

In America he was the principal advocate of the alliance. He reassured the Americans about the French, and the French about the Americans. He soothed wounded sensibilities on both sides. He supported Washington's proposals for the military coordination that ultimately won the war. He also served as interpreter between the French and the Americans, particularly for generals Washington and Rochambeau.

After the war he returned to France. He assisted the American commissioners in the peace negotiations. Later he aided in developing trade concessions in Europe. After his experiences in America, he espoused liberal causes for the rest of his life: the abolition of slavery, the emancipation of French Protestants and Jews, the establishment of constitutional government in France.

Bibliography

Lafayette in the Age of the American Revolution: Selected Letters and Papers 1776–1790, Vol. I, by Marquis de Lafayette. Copyright (c) 1977 Cornell University. Used by permission of publisher, Cornell University Press.

13

Henry Yeager: "You Are to Be Hanged Until You Are Dead! Dead! Dead!"

British General Howe did not meet General Burgoyne at Albany as part of the British plan to gain control over the Hudson River and Lake Champlain waterway and cut off New England. Instead, General Howe sent his army by land and by sea to occupy Philadelphia, the largest city in America and the place where Congress was meeting. At this time the militias and the army under General Washington were retreating from New York. The opposing troops met in several battles. The American victory at Trenton on December 26, 1776, was their high point before going into winter quarters at Morristown.

Thirteen-year-old Henry Yeager first volunteered as a drummer in the fall of 1776. He served several short tours of duty around Philadelphia. When his regiment went up the Delaware River in boats from Philadelphia, they encamped near Trenton.

General Washington, with the army, went on toward Princeton. Henry's regiment drew three days' provisions and struck their tents to follow according to orders. Henry recalls the following:

General Washington retreated. He learned a large force of British under Cornwallis was marching upon him from New Brunswick. The Americans crossed the Delaware from New Jersey. Destroying the bridges, they also removed all boats to prevent the British from following. We returned to Philadelphia in some of the boats. We encamped in the district of Kensington for ten days until dismissed in December 1776.

13. Henry Yeager

In February, as a drummer, he joined the company going to the fort at Billingsport in New Jersey. When the fort was attacked by a superior British force, his regiment retreated. First they spiked the cannon. They went over to Fort Mifflin but did not stay there. They then crossed to Red Bank in Gloucester County, New Jersey. From there they marched up through New Jersey as far as Burlington, where they encamped.

They had been there a short time when they heard of the hostilities at Germantown. They immediately marched to join the army there. On their way they met some scattered American troops who told them of the defeat at that battle. They moved up farther into New Jersey, encamping at White Marsh until his term expired and he was dismissed. (Washington went into winter quarters at Valley Forge.)

Upon being discharged, Henry returned to Philadelphia with another young man, George Lechler. By this time the British were in control of the city. The boys were at home but a few days when they were both arrested by British officers. They were taken to General Howe's quarters on Second Street below Spruce, opposite Little Dock Street.

I was accompanied by my mother. When we arrived at the General's headquarters, a Major Bedford asked if I were her son. Being answered "yes," he remarked that I would be hanged.

I was put in a guardhouse at the corner of Second and Little Dock Street. Lechler was confined separately in another at Little Dock Street. The next day we were taken to the house at the northwest corner of Second and Spruce Streets for trial. I was taken before the judges first.

I was charged with having brought letters from the American Army. Asked if it was true, I answered in the negative.

I was asked if I belonged to the rebel army.

I answered that I belonged to Washington's army. I was then charged with having come to the city as a spy. I was asked if such was not the fact. I answered "no." I came to see my parents.

I was examined for a length of time upon similar matters. After a short conference, one of the judges asked me my name. Upon giving it, the former said to me "You are to be hanged by the neck until you are dead, dead, dead." I was then conducted from the room.

In the entry or hall, I met Lechler. He inquired what had taken place. I told him that I was to be hanged.

Lechler was then conducted before the judges. I was afterwards told by him a like sentence was pronounced on him.

We were then both taken to the Walnut Street prison. Soon after we had been there, Provost Marshal Cunningham, directed the "spies" to be brought before him.

Lechler and I were accordingly conducted to him. He said "I'll give you half an hour and no longer," and ordered us to be confined in separate dungeons.

At the expiration of the half hour (to me a very short one), we were again taken before Provost Marshal Cunningham. He ordered two halters to be brought.

The marshal asked who was the oldest. Lechler answered he was the youngest. The marshal then directed that all the other prisoners should quit the yard and the gates be closed. He directed an orderly to place one halter on Lechler's neck and the other on mine. He was to back both of us against the gate. Next he was to draw the ropes through the top of it.

At this moment, a man came in and gave a paper to the marshal. He read it. He then ordered the ropes to be loosed from the gate and wound round prisoners' bodies. Lechler and I were then ordered to the dungeons, where we were taken.

The next morning we were brought to the marshal's room. The ropes were taken off. We were put into the yard among the other prisoners. After this, I remained in prison eight weeks and three days. Then I was released.

The British evacuated Philadelphia on June 18, 1778. Henry volunteered again as a private in an artillery regiment. He served two years at Fort Mifflin and on relief duty in Philadelphia. Henry, from age 13 to 20, served in the Revolutionary War. As a drummer he signaled orders to the men of his regiment with the taps of his drumsticks on the drum. He also served aboard a privateer capturing British ships. However, he was captured again and had to serve two years in a prison in Plymouth, England.

Bibliography

Yeager, Henry. *1832 Revolutionary War Pension Application.* Washington, D.C.: Veterans Administration Archives in the National Archives. Record Group 15, Microcopy 805.

14

Sally Wister: "My Teeth Rattled and My Hand Shook Like an Aspen Leaf"

Before the British troops occupied Philadelphia, Sally Wister's Quaker family fled to a farm in nearby Gwynedd (North Wales) northeast of Valley Forge. They shared a farmhouse belonging to the family of Hannah Foulke, Mrs. Wister's sister. Sally's cousins Jesse, Priscilla, and Lydia occupied one side of the house with their mother and the five Wister children and their parents the other.

From the fall of 1777 until the spring of 1778, Sally expected there would be no chance to exchange letters with her friends who stayed in the city. In a journal she vividly describes her experiences and feelings as British and American troops skirmished nearby—as American officers shared her home.

To Deborah Norris:

Tho' I have not the least shadow of an opportunity to send a letter, if I do write, I will keep a sort of journal of the time that may expire before I see thee; the perusal of it may some time hence give pleasure in a solitary hour to thee and our Sally Jones.

Yesterday, which was the 24th of September, two Virginia officers call'd at our house, and inform'd us that the British Army had cross'd the Schuylkill. Presently after, another person stopp'd and confirm'd what they had said, and that Gen'l Washington and Army were near Pottsgrove. Well, thee may be sure we were sufficiently scared; however, the road was very still till evening.

About seven o'clock we heard a great noise. To the door we all went. A large number of waggons with about three hundred of the

116

Philadelphia Militia were coming. They begged for drink, and several push'd into the house. One of those that entered was a little tipsy, and had a mind to be saucy.

I then thought it time for me to retreat; so figure me (mightily scar'd, as not having presence of mind enough to face so many of the military), running in at one door, and out another, all in a shake with fear; but after a while, seeing the officers appear gentlemanly, and the soldiers civil, I call'd reason to my aid. My fears were in some measure dispell'd, tho' my teeth rattled, and my hand shook like an aspen leaf. They did not offer to take their quarters with us; so, with many blessings, and as many adieus, they marched off.

I have given thee the most material occurrences of yesterday faithfully.

Fourth Day, September 25th

This day, till twelve o'clock, the road was mighty quiet, when Hobson Jones came riding along. About that time he made a stop at our door, and said the British were at Skippack road; that we should soon see their light horse, and [that] a party of Hessians had actually turn'd into our lane. My Dadda and Mamma gave it the credit it deserv'd, for he does not keep strictly to the truth in all respects; but the delicate, chicken-hearted Liddy and I were wretchedly scar'd. We cou'd say nothing but "Oh! what shall we do? What will become of us?" These questions only augmented the terror we were in.

Well, the fright went off. We saw no light horse or Hessians. O. Foulke came here in the evening, and told us that Gen'l Washington had come down as far as the Trappe, and that Gen'l McDougle's brigade was stationed at Montgomery, consisting of about 16 hundred men. This he had from Dr. Edward's, Lord Stirling's aid-de-camp; so we expected to be in the midst of one army or t'other.

Fourth Day Night.

We were not alarm'd.

Fifth Day, September 26th

We were unusually silent all the morning; no passengers came by the house, except to the Mill, and we don't place much dependence on Mill news.

I Was a Teenager in the American Revolution

About twelve o'clock, cousin Jesse heard that Gen. Howe's army had moved down towards Philadelphia. Then, my dear, our hopes & fears were engaged for you. However, my advice is, summon up all your resolution; call Fortitude to your aid and don't suffer your spirits to sink, my dear; there's nothing like courage; 'tis what I stand in need of myself, but unfortunately have little of it in my composition.

I was standing in the kitchen about 12 [the kitchen was a small distance from the house], when somebody came to me in a hurry, screaming, "Sally, Sally, here are the light horse!" This was by far the greatest fright I had endured; fear tack'd wings to my feet; I was at the house in a moment; at the porch I stopt, and it really was the light horse.

I ran immediately to the western door, where the family were assembled, anxiously waiting for the event. They [soldiers] rode up to the door and halted, and enquired if we had horses to sell; he was answer'd negatively.

"Have not you, sir," to my father, "two black horses?"

"Yes, but have no mind to dispose of them."

My terror had by this time nearly subsided. The officer and men behav'd perfectly civil; the first drank two glasses of wine, rode away, bidding his men follow; which after adieus in number, they did. The officer was Lieutenant Lindsay, of Bland's regiment, Lee's troop. The men, to our great joy, were Americans, and but four in all. What made us imagine them British, they wore blue and red, which with us is not common.

It has rained all this afternoon, and to present appearances, will all night. In all probability the English will take possession of the city tomorrow or next day. What a change will it be!

> "May heaven's guardian arm protect my absent friends,
> From danger guard them, and from want defend."

Forgive, my dear, the repetition of those lines, but they just darted into my mind.

Nothing worth relating has occurred this afternoon. Now for trifles. I have set a stocking on the needles, and intend to be mighty industrious. This evening some of our folks heard a very heavy cannon. We supposed it to be fir'd by the English. The report seem'd to come from Philad. We heard the American army will be within five miles of us tonight.

The uncertainty of our position engrosses me quite. Perhaps to be in the midst of war, and ruin, and the clang of arms. But we must hope the best.

Here, my dear, passes an interval of several weeks in which nothing happened worth the time and paper it would take to write it. The English, however, in the interim had taken possession of the city.

Second day, October the 19th, 1777

Now for new and uncommon scenes. As I was lying in bed, and ruminating on past and present events, and thinking how happy I shou'd be if I cou'd see you, Liddy came running into the room, and said there was the greatest drumming, fifing, and rattling of waggons that ever she had heard. What to make of this we were at a loss. We dress'd and downstairs in a hurry. Our wonder ceas'd.

The British had left Germantown, and our Army was marching to take possession. It was the general opinion that they wou'd evacuate the capital. Sister Betsy and myself and G. E. [George Emlen, family friend] went about half a mile from home, where we cou'd see the army pass. Thee will stare at my going, but no impropriety in my opine, or I wou'd not have gone. We made no great stay, but returned with excellent appetites for our breakfast.

Several officers call'd to get some refreshment, but none of consequence till the afternoon. Cousin Prissa and myself were sitting at the door; I in a green skirt, dark short gown, &c. Two genteel men of the military order rode up to the door: "Your servant, ladies," &c; ask'd if they cou'd have quarters for Genl. Smallwood. Aunt Foulke thought she cou'd accommodate them as well as most of her neighbors [and] said they could. One of the officers dismounted and wrote

Smallwood's Quarters

over the door, which secured us from straggling soldiers. After this he mounted his steed and rode away.

When we were alone our dress and lips were put in order for conquest, and the hopes of adventures gave brightness to each before passive countenance.

Thee must be told of a Dr. Gould who, by accident, had made acquaintance with my father; a sensible, conversible man, a Carolinian,—

and had come to bid us adieu on his going to that state. Daddy had prevailed upon him to stay a day or two with us.

In the evening his Generalship came with six attendants—which compos'd his family—a large guard of soldiers, a number of horses and baggage-waggons. The yard and house was in confusion, and glitter'd with military equipment.

Gould was intimate with Smallwood, and had gone into Jesse's to see him. While he was there, there was great running up and down stairs, so I had an opportunity of seeing and being seen, the former the most agreeable, to be sure. One person in particular attracted my notice. He appeared cross and reserved; but thee shall see how agreeably disappointed I was.

Dr. Gould ushered the gentlemen into our parlor, and introduced them. General Smallwood, Captain Furnival, Major Stodard, Mr. Prig, Captain Finley, and Mr. Clagan, Colonel Wood, and Colonel Line. These last two did not come with the general. They are Virginians and both indisposed. The general and suite are Marylanders.

Be assur'd I did not stay long with so many men, but secur'd a good retreat, heart-safe, so far. Some sup'd with us, others at Jesse's. They retired about ten, in good order.

How new is our situation! I feel in good spirits, though surrounded by an army; the house full of officers, yard alive with soldiers—very peaceable sort of men, tho.' They eat like other folks, talk like them, and behave themselves with elegance; so I will not be afraid of them; that I won't.

Adieu. I am going to my chamber to dream, I suppose, of bayonets and swords, sashes, guns, and epaulets....

Third day, Morn., October 20th

Nothing of any moment today; no acquaintance with the officers. Col. Wood and Line and Gould din'd with us. I was dressed in my chintz, and look'd smarter than night before.

Fourth Day, Oct. 21st

I just now met the Major, very reserv'd; nothing but "Good morning," or "Your servant, madam," but Furnival is most agreeable; he chats every opportunity; but luckily has a wife!

I have heard strange things of the Major. Worth a fortune of thirty thousand pounds, independent of anybody; the Major, moreover, is vastly bashful; so much so he can hardly look at the ladies. (Excuse me, good sir; I really thought you were not clever; if 'tis bashfulness only, we will drive that away.)

Fifth-day, Sixth-day, and Seventh-day pass'd. The Gen'l still here; the Major still bashful.

Second Day Afternoon

The General and officers drank tea with us, and stay'd part of the evening. After supper I went into aunt's where sat the Gen'l, Col. Line, and Major Stodard. So Liddy and I seated ourselves at the table in order to read a verse-book.

The Major was holding a candle for the Gen'l, who was reading a newspaper. He look'd at us, turn'd away his eyes, look'd again, put the candlestick down; up he jump'd, out of the door he went.

"Well," said I to Liddy, "he will join us when he comes in."

Presently he returned, and seated himself on the table.

"Pray, ladies, is there any songs in that book?"

"Yes, many."

"Can't you favor me with a sight of it?"

"No, Major, 'tis a borrow'd book."

"Miss Sally, can't you sing?"

"No."

Thee may be sure I told the truth there. Liddy, saucy girl, told him I cou'd. He beg'd and I deny'd; for my voice is not much better than the voice of a raven. We talk'd and laugh'd for an hour. He is very clever, amiable and polite. He has the softest voice, never pronounces the R at all....

Dr. Diggs came Second-Day; a mighty disagreeable man. We were oblig'd to ask him to tea. He must needs prop himself between the Major and me, for which I did not thank him. After I had drank tea, I jump'd from the table, and seated myself at the fire. The M_____ followed my example, drew his chair close to mine, and entertain'd me very agreeably.

Oh, Debby; I have a thousand things to tell thee. I shall give thee so droll an account of my adventures that thee will smile. "No occasion of that, Sally," methinks I hear thee say, "for thee tells me every trifle."

But child, thee is mistaken, for I have not told thee half the civil things that are said of us sweet creatures at "General Smallwood's Quarters." I think I might have sent the gentlemen to their chambers, I made my adieus and home I went.

Third Day Eve., October 27th

We had again the pleasure of the Gen'l and suite at afternoon tea. He (the Gen'l, I mean) is most agreeable; so lively, so free, and chats so gaily, that I have quite an esteem for him. I must steel my heart! Capt. Furnival is gone to Baltimore, the residence of his belov'd wife.

The Major and I had a little chat to ourselves this eve. No harm, I assure thee; he and I are friends....

Seventh Day, October 31st

A most charming day. I walk'd to the door and received the salutation of the morn from Stodard and other officers. As often as I go to the door, so often have I seen the Major. We chat passingly, as "A fine day, Miss Sally." "Yes, very fine, Major...."

First Day Morn.

The Army had orders to march today; the regulars accordingly did. Gen'l Smallwood had the command of Militia at that time, and they being in the rear, were not to leave their encampment until Second-Day.

Observe how militarish I talk. No wonder, when I am surrounded by people of that order....

Smallwood, Wood, and Stodard drank tea with us and spent the greater part of the evening.

I declare this Gen'l is very, very entertaining, so good natur'd, so good humour'd yet so sensible I wonder he is not married. Are there no ladies formed to his taste?

Some people, my dear think that there's no difference between good nature and good humour; but, according to my opinion, they differ widely. Good nature consists in a naturally amiable and even disposition, free from all peevishness and fretting. It is accomplished by a natural gracefulness—a manner of doing and saying everything agreeably; in short, it steals the senses and captivates the heart. Good humour consists in being pleas'd, and who wou'd thank a person for being cheerful, if they had nothing to make them otherways. Good humour is a very agreeable companion for an afternoon; but give me good nature for life.

Adieu.

Second Day Morn, November 1st

Today the Militia marches, and the Gen'l and officers leave us. Heigh ho! I am very sorry; for when you have been with agreeable people, 'tis impossible not to feel regret when they bid you adieu, perhaps forever. When they leave us we shall be immur'd in solitude.

The Major looks dull.

Second day Noon

About two o'clock the Gen'l and Major came to bid us adieu. With daddy and mammy they shook hands very friendly; to us they bow'd politely.

Our hearts were full. I thought Major was affected.

"Good-bye, Miss Sally," spoken very low. He walk'd hastily and mounted his horse. They promised to visit us soon.

We stood at the door to take a last look, all of us very sober.

The Major turn'd his horse's head, and rode back, dismounted.

"I have forgot my pistols," pass'd us, and ran upstairs.

He came swiftly back to us, as if wishing, through inclination, to stay; by duty compell'd to go. He remounted his horse.

"Farewell, ladies, till I see you again," and canter'd away.

We looked at him till the turn in the road hid him from our sight. "Amiable major," "Clever fellow," "Good young man" was echo'd from one to the other. I wonder whether we shall ever see him again. He has our wishes for his safety....

Second Day Even

Jesse, who went with the Gen'l return'd. I had by him a letter from my dear Polly Fishbourne. She is at George Emlen's. Headquarters is at their house. We had compliments from the Gen'l and Major. They are very well disposed of at Evan Meredith's, six miles from here. I wrote to Polly by Uncle Miles, who waited upon Gen'l Washington next morn.

Third Day Morn, November 2d

It seems strange not to see our house as it used to be. We are very still. No rattling of waggons, glittering of muskets. The beating of the distant drum is all we hear.

Here I skip a week or two, nothing of consequence occurring....

December 5th, Sixth Day

Oh, gracious! Debby, I am all alive with fear. The English have come out to attack (as we imagine) our army. They are on Chestnut Hill, our army three miles this side. What will become of us, only six miles distant?

We are in hourly expectation of an engagement. I fear we shall be in the midst of it. Heaven defend us from so dreadful a sight. The battle of Germantown, and the horrors of that day, are recent in my mind. It will be sufficiently dreadful if we are only in hearing of the firing. To think how many of our fellow-creatures are plung'd into the boundless ocean of eternity, few of them prepar'd to meet their fate. But they are summon'd before an all-merciful Judge, from whom they have a great deal to hope....

Seventh Day; 4 o'clock

I was much alarm'd just now, sitting in the parlour, indulging melancholy reflections, when somebody burst open the door, "Sally, here's Major Stodard!"

I jumped. Our conjectures were various concerning his coming. The poor fellow, from great fatigue and want of rest, together with being expos'd to the night air, had caught cold, which brought on a fever. He could scarcely walk, and I went into aunt's to see him.

I was surpris'd. Instead of the lively, alert, blooming Stodard, who was on his feet the instant we enter'd, he look'd pale, thin, and dejected, too weak to rise. A bow, and "How are you Miss Sally?"

"How does thee do, Major?"

I seated myself near him, inquir'd the cause of his indisposition, ask'd for the Gen'l, received his compliments. Not willing to fatigue him with too much chat, I bid him adieu.

To-night Aunt Hannah Foulke, Sen.ʳ administer'd something. Jesse assisted him to his chamber. He had not lain down five minutes before he was fast asleep. Adieu. I hope he shall enjoy a good night's rest.

First Day Morn, December 7th

I trip'd into aunt's. There sat the Major, rather more like himself. How natural it was to see him.

"Good Morning, Miss Sally."

"Good morrow, Major, how does thee do today?"

Major: "I feel quite recover'd."

Sally: "Well, I fancy this indisposition has sav'd thy head this time."

Major: "No, ma'am; for if I hear a firing, I shall soon be with them." That was heroic.

About eleven, I dress'd myself, silk and cotton gown. It is made without an apron. I feel

quite awkwardish, and prefer the girlish dress.

First Day Afternoon

A Mr. Seaton and Stodard drank tea with us. He and I had a little private chat after tea.

[When the gentlemen left, Liddy and Sally] laugh'd and chatted at a noisy rate, till a summons for Liddy parted us. I sat negligently on my chair, and thought brought on thought, and I got so low spirited that I cou'd hardly speak. The dread of an engagement, our dreadful situation (if a battle shou'd ensue) we should be in, join'd to my anxiety for P. Fishbourn and family, who would be in the midst of the scene, was the occasion.

And yet I did not feel half so frighten'd as I expected to be. 'Tis amazing how we get reconciled to such things. Six months ago the bare idea of being within ten, aye twenty miles, of a battle, wou'd almost have distracted me. And now, tho' two such large armies are within six miles of us, we can be cheerful and converse calmly of it. It verifies the old proverb, that "Use is second nature"...

In the afternoon we distinctly heard platoon firing. Everybody was at the door; I in the horrors. The armies, as we judg'd, were engag'd.

Very compos'dly says the Major to our servant, "Will you be kind enough to saddle my horse? I shall go!"

Accordingly, the horse was taken from the hospitable quiet barn to plunge into the thickest ranks of war. Cruel change!

Seaton insisted to the Major that the armies were still; "nothing but skirmishing with the flanking parties; do not go."

We happen'd, (we girls, I mean) to be standing in the kitchen, the Maj. passing thro' in a hurry, and I, forsooth, discover'd a strong partiality by saying, "Oh! Major, thee is not going!"

He turn'd around, "Yes, I am, Miss Sally," bow'd and went into the road; we all pitied him.

The firing rather decreas'd; and after persuasions innumerable from my father and Seaton, and the firing over, he reluctantly agreed to stay. Ill as he was, he would have gone. It show'd his bravery, of which we all believe him possess'd of a large share.

Second Day, December 8th

Rejoice with us, my dear. The British have return'd to the city. Charming news this. May we ever be thankful to the Almighty Disposer of events for his care and protection of us while surrounded with dangers.

Major went to the army. Nothing for him to do; so returned.

Third- or Fourth-day, I forget which, he was very ill; kept his chamber most of the day. In the evening I saw him. He has a violent sore mouth. I pity him mightily, but pity is a poor remedy...

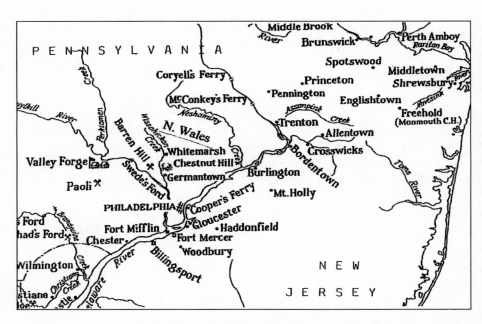

The British occupied Philadelphia from winter 1777 to spring 1778. The Americans endured Valley Forge (From *Atlas of American History*, by Kenneth T. Jackson, Charles Scribner's Sons, © 1984, Charles Scribner's Sons. Reprinted by permission of the Gale Group).

Seventh Day, December 20th.

General Washington's army have gone into winter quarters at the Valley Forge. We shall not see many of the military now. We shall be very intimate with solitude. I am afraid stupidity will be a frequent guest. After so much company, I can't relish the idea of sequestration.

First day Night

A dull round of the same thing over again. I shall hang up my pen till something offers worth relating....

Sixth Day, June 5th, Morn, 11 o'clock

Last night we were a little alarm'd. I was awaken'd about 12 o'clock with somebody's opening the chamber door. I observ'd Cousin Prissa talking to Mamma. I asked what was the matter.

"Only a party of light horse."

"Are they Americans?" I quickly said.

She answer'd in the affirmative (which dispell'd my fears).... This morn I rose by or near seven, dress'd in my light chintz, which is made gown-fashion, kenting handkerchief, and linen apron.

"Sufficiently smart for a country girl, Sally."

Don't call me a country girl, Debby Norris. Please to observe that I pride myself upon being a Philadelphian, and that a residence of 20 months has not at all diminished the love I have for that dear place. As soon as one very capital alteration takes place (which is very much talk'd of at present), I expect to return to it with a double pleasure.

Dress'd as above, down I came, and went down to our kitchen, which is a small distance from the house....

Fifth Day Night, June 18th

Rose at half-past four this morning. Iron'd industriously till one o'clock, din'd, went up stairs, threw myself on the bed, and fell asleep. About four sister Hannah waked me, and said uncle and Foulke were down stairs; so I decorated myself, and went down. Felt quite lackadaisical. However, I jump'd about a little, and the stupid fit went off.

We have had strange reports about the British being about leaving Philad. I can't believe it.

Adieu.

Sixth Day Morn, June 19th

We have heard an astonishing piece of news!—that the English have entirely left the city! It is almost impossible! Stay, I shall hear further.

Sixth Day Eve.

A light horseman has just confirm'd the above intelligence! This is charmante! They decamp'd yesterday. He (the horseman) was in Philad. It is true. They have gone. Past a doubt. I can't help forbear exclaiming to the girls,

"Now are you sure the news is true? Now are you sure they have gone?"

"Yes, yes, yes!" they all cry, "and may they never, never return."

Dr. Gould came here tonight. Our army are about six miles off, on their march to the Jerseys.

Seventh Day Morn.

O.F. [Owen Foulke] arrived just now, and relateth as followeth: The Army began their march at six this morn by their house. Our worthy Gen'l Smallwood breakfasted at Uncle Caleb's. He ask'd how Mr. And Mrs. Wister and the young ladies were, and sent his respects to us.

Our brave, our heroic General Washington was escorted by fifty of the Life Guard, with drawn swords. Each day he acquires an addition to his goodness.... I now think of nothing but returning to Philadelphia.

So shall now conclude this journal with humbly hoping that the Great Disposer of events, who has graciously vouchsaf'd to protect us to this day through many dangers, will still be pleas'd to continue his protection.

Sally Wister
North Wales, June 20th, 1778.

Bibliography

Wister, Sally. *Sally Wister's Journal.* Ed. Albert Cook Myers. 1902. Reprint, New York: Arno Press, 1969.

15

African-American James Forten Was a Rebel

The American Revolution touched everyone in the country. The memorable phrases of the Declaration of Independence—All men are created equal—had to be examined against the existence of slavery. During the war itself, the abolition movement bore its first fruits, and within two decades after the war's end, all the northern states were emancipating their slaves. In 1783 Massachusetts Judge C.J. Cushing ruled in *Commonwealth v. Nathaniel Jennison* that "all men are born free and equal," thus abolishing slavery in the state. At the time of the Revolution, nearly half a million of the two-and-one-half million colonists were African-Americans, a few free, the rest slaves. Nearly 5,000 served in the military of the Americans. In some cases they served as part of local militias and the Continental army. Some colonies, like Connecticut, formed a corps of African-American soldiers. A battalion was soon enlisted. Rhode Island also enlisted a special unit of African-Americans. They also served at sea and on ships along the coast. In most cases the owners of slaves were paid to give them their freedom if they served.

Twenty thousand went with the British. A proclamation by John Murray, Earl of Dunmore and royal governor of Virginia, offered them freedom. On November 7, 1775, on board the *William* in the harbor at Norfolk, he declared martial law. Colonists who refused "to resort to his Majesty's standard" were to be adjudged traitors. And "I do hereby further declare all indentured servants, Negroes, or others, free, that are able and willing to bear arms, they joining His Majesty's Troops, as soon as may be, for the more speedily reducing the Colony to a proper sense of their duty, to His Majesty's crown and dignity." This policy of recruiting black slaves to fight against the colonists, and particularly plantation owners, aroused a great deal of animosity against the British.

African-Americans served from earliest times on the waterways of the Atlantic coast. Even in colonial times service at sea opened the door to freedom for many a slave. Many were pilots. On the American ships, some, like James Forten, carried powder to the guns. Born free on the second day of September, 1766, James was the son of Thomas Forten, who died when James was but seven years old. He attended a racially mixed school operated by the antislavery Quaker Anthony Benezet in Philadelphia.

In the year 1775, James left school to work in a grocery store and at home. In 1781, then in his fifteenth year, as part of a crew of 200, he joined twenty black seamen aboard a newly commissioned ship for the colony of Pennsylvania—the *Royal Louis*. He embarked as a "powder boy" under the command of Stephen Decatur, Sr. Their ship was soon brought into action with an English vessel, the *Lawrence*. After a severe fight, many were killed or wounded on each ship. James recalled that every man except himself on board the *Louis* was wounded. However, they succeeded in capturing the brig-of-war and brought her into port amid the loud huzzas and cheering of the crowds watching on the shore.

Forten shared in the excitement of the battle and their success. With fresh courage and a desire to continue with his fellow patriots, he signed on in the same vessel for another cruise. However, this time they were attacked by three of the enemy's vessels, the *Amphyon, Nymph,* and *Pomona,* and became prisoners of war. It was a special worry to James. Even though he was a free man, rarely, if ever, did the British exchange black prisoners. They sold them in the West Indies to a life of slavery.

But Forten was lucky. After he was placed on board the *Amphyon,* Captain Beasly made him the companion of his son. During quiet periods on the ship, young Beasly and Forten played marbles. When Forten won every game with great skill, young Beasly was surprised and called his father's attention to it. Upon being questioned, Forten assured the captain that nothing was easier for him. The marbles were again placed in the ring, and in rapid succession he redeemed his word. A fresh and deeper interest was from that moment taken in his behalf. Captain Beasly offered him a passage to England and life on a large family estate. James would have many advantages.

James replied "No, No! I am here a prisoner for the liberties of my country; I never, never, shall prove a traitor to her!" After the ship was captured, with other prisoners he was sent to that floating and pestilential hell, the frigate *Jersey*. A thousand prisoners crowded the hold of the old East India merchantman anchored in New York harbor. An estimated 10,000 died during the war on that rotting hulk.

However, the captain gave him, as a token of his regard and friendship, a letter commending him to the commander of the prison-ship. He also requested that Forten should not be forgotten on the list of exchanges. Thus (as he frequently remarked in later life) did a game of marbles save him from a life of West Indies slavery.

While James was a prisoner, an officer of the American Navy was about to be exchanged for a British prisoner. Forten conceived the idea of an easy escape for himself in the officer's chest. When about to avail himself of this opportunity, he thought first of a young fellow-prisoner, Daniel Brewton. He immediately urged him to hop into the chest. The offer was accepted. Forten assisted in taking down the "chest of old clothes" from the side of the prison ship. (Many years later, in 1837, the two former prisoners met again and recalled the incident. Daniel had become a captain in the U.S. Navy.)

After remaining seven months on board this prison ship, young Forten was released in a general exchange of prisoners. Without shoes upon his feet, he walked from New York to Trenton. There, he found a sympathetic person who provided shoes for the remainder of the journey. He arrived home in a wretchedly bad condition.

His mother, thinking that her son had been shot from the foretop of the *Royal Louis,* was relieved when he appeared after an absence of nearly eight months. In a short time he joined his brother-in-law and sailed in the ship *Commerce* for London.

After the war he became an apprentice to a sail-maker in Philadelphia and later took over the business. He eventually amassed a fortune, a portion of which came from his invention of a device for handling sails. He became associated with William Lloyd Garrison in the abolition of slavery movement.

When urged to apply for a pension as a veteran of the Revolutionary War, he declined, saying, "I was a volunteer, sir!"

Bibliography

Fleming, Thomas. *Liberty! The American Revolution*. New York: Viking Penguin, 1997.

Kaplan, Sidney, and Emma Nogrady Kaplan. *Black Presence in the Era of the American Revolution*. Amherst: University of Massachusetts Press, 1989.

Massachusetts Historical Society. Proceeding.s 1873–1875.

Nell, William C. *The Colored Patriots of the American Revolution*. 1855. Reprint, New York: Arno Press, 1968.

Quarles, Benjamin. *The Negro in the American Revolution*. Chapel Hill, N.C.: University of North Carolina Press, 1961.

16

Eliza Faces the Enemy When They Invade Her Home

The British occupied Savannah on December 20, 1778. Fort Sunbury and Augusta were next. With the fall of Charleston on May 12, 1780, and the capture of the entire southern American army, the British then controlled the two largest southern ports. British General Clinton then established a string of outposts across South Carolina to extend his reach over the interior and win the war in the South. He hoped to obtain the cooperation of a large body of Loyalists who would join him in securing control of the country.

As the British and Tories moved through the country, they quickly became known for pillage, looting, and disrespect toward women. Patriot women whose husbands were prisoners of war or were away with the partisan bands showed great courage.

Eliza Yonge Wilkinson was 19 the first time the British had tried to take Charleston, South Carolina, in June of 1776. When three of their ships ran aground on the Middle Ground and fire from the Americans disabled others, the British were forced to withdraw to New York. They did not return until four years later when they entered the city on May 12, 1780. In the following letters Eliza describes what it was like to live with enemy troops nearby and be subjected to a visit from them.

To Miss M_____ P._____   Yonge's Island, 1782

As I mean never to forget the *loving-kindness and tender mercies* of the renowned Britons while among us, in the ever-memorable year 1779, I shall transmit you a brief account of their *polite* behavior to my Father and family, where you will find me sufficiently punished for being something of an unbeliever heretofore. You know we had always heard most terrible accounts of the actions of the British troops at the northward; but (fool that I was) I thought they must be exaggerated, for I could not believe that a nation so famed for humanity, and many other virtues, should, in so short a time, divest themselves of even the least trace of what they once were.

Surely, said I, they can't, in so short a time, have commenced savages, and lost those virtues which have distinguished them from other nations. Yet, sometimes, when I heard fresh accounts of their cruelty to our Northern brethren when in their power, I could not repress my indignation against the barbarous, hard-hearted Britons, (how changed their character!) and believed, or almost believed, what I had heard of them. I say almost, for I was so infatuated with what I had formerly heard and read of Englishmen, that I thought humanity, and every manly sentiment, were their inherent qualities—though I cannot but say that, much as I had admired the former lustre of the British character, my soul shrunk from the thought of having any communication with a people who had left their homes with a direct intention to imbrue their hands in the blood of my beloved countrymen, or deprive them of their birthright, Liberty and property. The thought alarmed me, shocked me. I began to look on the Britons in earnest as enemies.

At length I heard they had got possession of the Georgia State, and used the inhabitants cruelly, paying no respect to age or sex; but then again, I heard to the contrary, that their behavior to the ladies was unexceptionable. I did not know what to think, much less what to do, should they invade our State, which was daily expected.

Thousands would I have given to have been in any part of the globe where I might not see them, or to have been secure from the impending evils, which were ready to burst over our heads.

I was in Charlestown when we heard that a large party of them had landed somewhere near Beaufort. I saw several detachments of our Southern troops leave town to oppose the invaders of their country. They marched with the greatest alacrity imaginable, not regarding the weather, though the rain poured down incessantly upon them. I cannot describe my feelings upon this sight—gratitude, affection, and pity for my country-men filled my heart and my eyes, which pursued them until out of sight, and then every good wish attended them. However, it was not long before our little band of patriots returned to their homes in triumph, excepting a few, who had sealed the cause with their blood. Peace to their ashes, and everlasting happiness to their immortal part.

"Well have they perished—for in fight they fell." I think old Priam says this of his sons, who fell at the siege of Troy. But who can forbear the tear of sympathy for the distressed families, who are left behind to mourn the fall of those they highly valued, and from whom they derived their support? Pitiable reflection! "How seldom do the rich feel the distresses of the poor, and in the midst of conquest and acclamation, who regardeth the tears and afflictions of those who have lost their friends in the public?"

Now the time drew near when this State was to have her day of suffering in sympathy with her sister States. Oh, how I dreaded the approaching enemy! I had thoughts (with my other friends), to go higher up the country to avoid them; but as my Father, with many others of my relations, had not conveniences ready to carry off their effects with them, and as the enemy approached rapidly, they agreed to stay. It was a melancholy sight to see such crowds of helpless, distressed women, weeping for husbands, brothers, or other near relations and friends, who were they knew not where, whether dead or alive....

Surely, if the British knew the misery they occasion, they would abate their rigor, and blush to think that the name of Englishman, (once so famous among the Fair,) should now produce terror and dismay in every female breast. I'll now lay by my pen—Farewell....

I will proceed by and bye with my narrative, for the various scenes I've been witness to are so much in my head, that I shall not want subjects to employ my pen for some time.

Once more adieu.

Eliza W.

Letter Two

At last my brothers, with the Willtown hunters, arrived from Charlestown. Judge of our joy, augmented, too, by their assuring us that they had heard from Gen. Lincoln; that he was hurrying to our assistance, and would soon be with us! How we congratulated one another on these tidings; we could now converse with cheerfulness, and take pleasure in each other's company; the gloom, which had so lately darkened every object, seemed dispelled, and hope, smiling hope, succeeded.

Hope seems implanted in us. It is the foundation of happiness. The great Creator, knowing our weak, desponding natures, has endowed us with it to soothe, soften, and heal the wounds of keen distress and anguish, and make us bear with fortitude the many misfortunes which attend humanity.

Farewell! my dear Mary.

Letter Three

All this time we had not seen the face of an enemy, not an open one—for I believe private ones were daily about. One night, however, upwards of sixty dreaded redcoats, commanded by Major Graham, passed our gate in order to surprise Lieut. Morton Wilkinson at his own house, where they understood he had a party of men. A negro wench was their informer, and also their conductor; but (thank heaven) somehow or other they failed in their attempt, and repassed our avenue early in the morning, but made a halt at the head of it, and wanted to come up; but a negro fellow, whom they had got at a neighbor's not far from us to go as far as the Ferry with them, dissuaded them from it, by saying it was not worth while, for it was only a plantation belonging to an old decrepit gentleman, who did not live there; so they took his word for it, and proceeded on. You may think how much we were alarmed when we heard this, which we did the next morning; and how many blessings the negro had from us for his consideration and pity.

Well, now comes the day of terror—the 3rd of June [1780]. (I shall never love the anniversary of that day.) In the morning, fifteen or sixteen horsemen rode up to the house; we were greatly terrified, thinking them the enemy, but from their behavior, were agreeably deceived, and found them friends. They sat a while on their horses, talking to us; and then rode off, except two, who tarried a minute longer and then followed the rest, who had nearly reached the gate. One of the said two must needs jump a ditch—to show his activity I suppose; for he might as well, and better, have gone in the road. However, he got a sad fall; we saw him, and sent a boy to tell him, if he was hurt, to come up to the house, and we would endeavor to do something for him. He and his companion accordingly came up; he looked very pale and bled much; his gun somehow in the fall, had given him a bad wound behind the ear, from whence the blood flowed down his neck and bosom plentifully;

we were greatly alarmed on seeing him in this situation, and had gathered around him, some with one thing, some with another, in order to give him assistance. We were very busy examining the wound when a negro girl ran in, exclaiming "O! The King's people are coming, it must be them, for they are all in red!" Upon this cry, the two men that were with us snatched up their guns, mounted their horses and made off; but had not got many yards from the house before the enemy discharged a pistol at them. Terrified almost to death I was. I was still anxious for my friends' safety; I tremblingly flew to the window, to see if the shot had proved fatal; when seeing them both safe, "Thank heaven," said I, "they've got off without hurt!" I'd hardly uttered this, when I heard the horses of the inhuman Britons coming in such a furious manner, that they seemed to tear up the earth, and the riders at the same time bellowing out the most horrid curses imaginable; oaths and imprecations, which chilled my whole frame. Surely, thought I, such horrid language denotes nothing less than death; but I'd no time for thought—they were up to the house—entered with drawn swords and pistols in their hands; indeed, they rushed in, in the most furious manner, crying out, "Where're these women rebels?" (pretty language to ladies from the *once famed Britons!*) That was the first salutation! The moment they espied us, off went our caps, (I always heard say none but women pulled caps!) And for what, think you? Why, only to get a paltry stone and wax pin, which kept them on our heads; at the same time uttering the most abusive language imaginable, and making as if they'd hew us to pieces with their swords. But it is not in my power to describe the scene; it was terrible to the last degree; and, what augmented it, they had several armed negros with them, who threatened and abused us greatly. They then began to plunder the house of every thing they thought valuable or worth taking; our trunks were split to pieces, and each mean, pitiful wretch, crammed his bosom with the contents, which were our apparel, etc., etc., etc.

I ventured to speak to the inhuman monster who had my clothes. I represented to him the times were such we could not replace what they'd taken from us, and begged him to spare me on a suit or two; but I got nothing but a hearty curse for my pains; nay, so far was his callous heart from relenting, that, casting his eyes towards my shoes, "I want them buckles," said he, and immediately knelt at my feet to take them out, which while he was busy about, a brother villain, whose enormous mouth extended from ear to ear, bawled out, "Shares there, I say, shares!" So they divided my buckles between them. The other wretches were employed in the same manner; they took my sister's ear-rings from her ears; hers and Miss Samuel's buckles; they demanded her ring from her finger; she pleaded for it, told them it was her wedding ring, and begged they'd let her keep it; but they still demanded it, and, presenting a pistol at her, swore if she did not deliver it immediately, they'd fire. She gave it to them, and after bundling up all their booty, they mounted their horses. But such despicable figures! Each wretch's bosom stuffed so full they appeared to be all afflicted with some dropsical disorder; had a party of rebels (as they called us) appeared we should soon have seen their circumference lessen.

They took care to tell us, when they were going away, that they had favored us a great deal—that we might thank our stars it was no worse. But I had forgot to tell you, that, upon their first entering the house, one of them gave my arm such a violent grasp, that he left the print of his thumb and three fingers, in black and blue, which was to be seen, very plainly, for several days after. I showed it to one of our officers, who dined with us, as a specimen of British cruelty. If they call this favor, what must their cruelties be? It must want a name. To be brief; after a few words more, they rode off, and glad was I. "Good riddance of bad rubbish," and indeed such rubbish was I never in company with before. One of them was an officer too! A sergeant, or some such, for he had the badge of honor on his shoulders. After they were gone, I began to be sensible of the danger I'd been in, and the thoughts of the vile men seemed worse (if possible) than their presence; for they came so suddenly up to the house, that I'd no time for thought; and while they staid, I seemed in a maze! Quite stupid! I cannot describe it. But when they were gone, and I had time to consider, I trembled so with terror, that I could not support myself. I went into the room, threw myself on the bed, and gave way to a violent burst of grief, which seemed to be some relief to my full-swollen heart.

For an hour or two I indulged the most melancholy reflections. The whole world appeared to me as a theatre, where nothing was acted but cruelty, bloodshed, and oppression; where neither age nor sex escaped the horrors of injustice and violence; where the lives and property of the innocent and inoffensive were in continual danger, and lawless power ranged at large.

Bibliography

Wilkinson, Eliza. *Letters of Eliza Wilkinson, During the Invasion and Possession of Charlestown, S.C., by the British in the Revolutionary War.* Arranged from the original manuscripts by Caroline Gilman. New York: Samual Colman, 1839. Courtesy of the Charleston Library Society.

17

Dicey Langston: Spy/Courier Threatened by the Enemy

Not far away from Eliza Wilkinson, in the Laurens district of South Carolina, Dicey Langston acted as a spy/courier to pass information about the enemy to the patriots at the risk of her life as she secretly rode through the night. She was confronted by neighboring Tories who threatened her and her family.

Dicey Langston was only sixteen when the war began. As her mother had died when she was very young, she lived with her brothers and her father, Solomon, on a plantation. Like her brothers she could ride a horse, handle a rifle as expertly as they could, and was a patriot. When the war came to the South, her brothers left home and joined a group of soldiers camping several miles away on the river Enoree.

Overall, the South was more Loyalist in sentiment than the North. The planters depended on Britain not only as a market for their tobacco, but also for the ships to get it to market and the naval power to protect the ships' cargoes. The British laws, so oppressive to the commercial North, did not bother some of the planters, yet many resented the British and favored the patriots. The region was thus involved in the Revolution against Great Britain, but also in a civil war among its own people. Both sides formed guerrilla bands that attacked each other, raided plantations and settlements, and destroyed property and crops. Often the Loyalist bands included men who had been malcontents or plain outlaws before the war, and who now found some status and power in fighting for the British.

Some of Dicey's relatives were Loyalists, and she and her brothers were political enemies of the relatives with whom they had Sunday dinner. However, this was a means by which Dicey gained information regarding Loyalist activities. During visits, she simply listened to the

140

conversations for any news of enemy moves, and later she would go off to find her brothers' camp and report the information to them.

Dicey's relatives considered her only a child, and they made no attempt to hide their conversations from her. After a while, though, when they wondered how news of their plans seemed to constantly find

Revolutionary War in the South (From *Atlas of American History*, by Kenneth T. Jackson, Charles Scribner's Sons, © 1984, Charles Scribner's Sons. Reprinted by permission of the Gale Group).

its way to the patriot bands, they became suspicious of her. At first they only threatened. They warned her father to put a stop to Dicey's spying, or else suffer the consequences himself. He had to depend on the restraint of his Loyalist neighbors for the safety of Dicey's life, his own life and his property. He forbade Dicey to pass any more information to her brothers. She promised to stop.

One of the Loyalist bands operating in the Laurens District was called the "Bloody Scouts"; their name describes the ruthless cruelty that marked their raids on defenseless families living on isolated plantations and settlements. Dicey learned that the "Bloody Scouts" were going to attack a small patriot settlement called Little Eden, located near her brothers' camp.

Dicey knew that the settlement would be taken by surprise. The people would not have time to get together a defense, and at least some of them would be murdered. Moreover, in the attack on Little Eden, the "Bloody Scouts" would certainly find her brothers' camp and kill them. Dicey had to get word to them. However, she had to keep the Loyalists from finding out, and she could not let her father find out because of the promise she had made to him. If her brothers and Little Eden were to be saved, she must go herself, at night, on foot. Taking a horse would rouse the household and make her a target for Loyalist gangs on the road.

When everyone in the house was asleep that night, she set off alone, and on foot. Dicey went through woods and fields with only a sense of direction to guide her. She made steady progress until she came to a swollen and rushing creek; there was no bridge or even a log to take her across. She did not know how deep the water was, but to deliver her warning she had to get to the other bank. She decided to ford the creek. The swift current made her lose her footing on the mud bottom, and the water picked her up and spun her around as it carried her downstream. When she finally regained her footing against the current, she could not tell which bank she had stepped from and which she had to get to. Trusting her instinct, she climbed the bank and set off in the direction she thought led to her brothers' camp.

Her instinct had been right! After hours of hiking she arrived. The men had just returned from a mission and they were tired, wet, and hungry. She gave them news of the "Bloody Scouts'" plans, but they were all too exhausted to set off to warn the settlers. She saw that nothing could be done until they had food.

She had them build a fire. Although she, too, was exhausted and wet, she made a hoecake from the flour and cornmeal they had on hand. She spread the dough on a board and laid it in the embers of the fire to bake. In a short time the hoecake was ready and the men made plans. They each took some of the bread in their ammunition pouches to eat on the way and set off to warn the settlers.

The "Bloody Scouts" rode down on Little Eden at the first light of morning and found it completely empty. While the gang boiled with rage over the frustration of their plan, Dicey was back at the plantation, freshly dressed and having breakfast with her family. She had made a twenty-mile trip through the night, and she was so tired she could hardly converse. Her father wondered if she were ill, but he did not suspect her nighttime adventures.

After missing so easy a target as Little Eden, the "Bloody Scouts" decided to make the Langstons their next target. They came ready to kill Dicey's father. The household was defenseless, and considering Solomon's infirm condition, he and Dicey could not escape.

The Loyalist leader demanded to know what part her father had had in raids on members of their group. When he denied having any active part, the leader accused him of lying. The Loyalist leader pointed his pistol at her father's heart and cocked it. Dicey jumped between her father and the pistol and began harshly denouncing the gunman, who became so angry that he nearly shot her instead. One of the guerrillas got his leader under control. He felt that killing Dicey was going too far. The Loyalists got into an argument among themselves. They left as angry as when they had forced their way inside, but with their nerve broken by Dicey's defense.

The raid on the house did not mark the end of the gang's harassment of the Langstons. Not long afterward Dicey ran into the gang as she was heading homeward from the Spartansburg district. They saw her coming and blocked the road; though she was a skillful rider, she had no choice but to halt and face them.

The leader demanded to know what news she had of the patriots. She explained that she had seen none on her visit, and so she had no news to give them even if she were willing to. He held his pistol to her chest and gave her one last chance to tell him what she knew.

To this, Dicey pulled open the front of her riding habit and dared him to "Fire!" The enraged Loyalist was about to pull the trigger when one of his own men reached out and knocked the leader's arm upward, and the bullet sailed off into the sky instead of into Dicey. His attempted murder sabotaged by his own follower, his pistol empty and his nerve rattled, the leader forgot about Dicey and attacked the man who had saved her. The other guerrillas joined in the fight and forgot about Dicey. She gave her horse a lash and took off down the road at a full gallop toward her home.

A short time later a patriot leader learned not to take Dicey for granted. He had arrived at the Langston plantation to pick up a rifle which one of Dicey's brothers had left with her, saying she would recognize the man by a countersign he would give her. Dicey retrieved the rifle from its hiding place, but as she was about to turn it over, she hesitated. The band was suspicious- looking. She thought they might well be Loyalists since she had never seen any of them before. To make sure, she asked the leader for the countersign. The leader laughed and told her that it was too late for that sort of thing since he now had both the rifle and herself in his possession.

His teasing was cut short in a moment. Dicey cocked the rifle and pointed it at him, inviting him to try and take what he thought he had. In a chilling instant he realized she meant it; he gave her the countersign and later bore the laughter of his men for being tripped up by the girl. He and Dicey must have been impressed with each other, though— after the war she married him.

Bibliography

Ellet, Elizabeth. *Women of the American Revolution*. New York: Baker and Scribner, 1848.

18

Grace and Rachel Capture Enemy Documents

In another location in South Carolina, 16-year-old Grace Martin and her sister-in-law, Rachel Martin, wished to take a more active part in the war. Married to brothers who were absent fighting in the war, they were living with their mother-in-law near Fort Ninety-Six, South Carolina. One day when they were at home, they learned that an enemy courier would pass by their house. In a packet he would be carrying important dispatches to British forces nearby.

The two planned to waylay the courier, and at the risk of their lives, to obtain possession of the papers. They could then pass on the information to nearby patriot troops. Dressing in their husbands' clothes and taking pistols, they selected their station at a point on the road which they knew the courier and his two escorts must pass.

On the selected night, they took up their station hidden on the road. It was already late, and they had not waited long before the tramp of horses was heard in the distance. The heroines waited in the silence of the night until the enemy came close to the chosen spot. The disguised women leaped from their cover in the bushes and called on the three of them to halt and "put up your hands!" Grace told the courier, "Hand over the dispatches!"

The men were taken completely by surprise, and, in their alarm at the sudden attack, yielded a prompt submission. Immediately they were paroled and sent on their way. Grace and Rachel hastened home by a shortcut through the woods. No time was lost in sending the documents by a messenger to General Greene. They removed their soldier outfits and quickly resumed their usual attire.

That was fortunate, as there was soon a knock at the door. The paroled officers stopped at the house of Mrs. Martin and asked accommodation for the night. They told her of their experience and showed her their paroles, saying they had been taken prisoners by two rebel lads.

The ladies asked, "Had you no arms?"

The officers answered that they had arms, but had been suddenly taken off their guard, and were allowed no time to use their weapons. They departed the next morning, having no suspicion that they owed their capture to the very women whose hospitality they had claimed.

Bibliography

Ellet, Elizabeth. *Women of the American Revolution.* New York: Bakerand Scribner, 1848.

19

Paul Hamilton: One of Marion's "Swamp Foxes"

Paul Hamilton's narrative reveals a personal side of the Revolutionary War in the South. He was an eyewitness to, and participant in, much of the action after the British successfully attacked Savannah at the end of 1778 and began a drive to control rural Georgia and the Carolinas. Loyalist southerners aided the enemy. Paul was part of the scattered patriots, numbering a few to hundreds, who opposed the British in what became a guerrilla war. Often relatives and friends were fighting each other.

Under leadership of the hit-and-run tactics of Francis Marion (the "Swamp Fox") and others, Paul vividly describes the nearly impossible goal of keeping the cause of independence alive. He was part of the Continental troops until the end, when they united with the French at Yorktown to achieve victory. In this part of his narrative, from December 1778 to October 1781, he traces the change from his education with a tutor to becoming a soldier fighting for his country.

In the month of December, 1778, being then a little over 16 years old, removed from school, just at the time when I had begun to feel a devotedness to my books, and to profit every moment by the instruction of my master, with whom I had acquired a most friendly interest for my success in life. I now left Thomson, but never have I forgotten the inculcations of that best of tutors, and most able guide of inexperienced youth. I left him with sincere regret and often sickened to return to him. Fortunate would it have been for me if the time which I lost at Alexander's had been spent with him, but he had not till the year 1775 arrived from Princeton College, where he had been a teacher of the first reputation.

I Was a Teenager in the American Revolution

Or still more fortunate would it have been for me would my uncle have permitted me to remain with him 12 months longer, but it was otherwise determined, and perhaps the measure of felicity which it has pleased God to allow me to enjoy, has not been the less for that deprivation. Events (wisely) are not placed at our disposal or control. Having left school, I returned to the home of my dear and ever to be respected mother, who received me with all the fondness of which her warm heart was capable, and as far as her means would go in that time of general distress and want, indulged me in every matter suited to my time of Life and Expectations. In the first moments of relaxation from my studies, being of an active temper both of mind and body, the pleasures of Deerhunting attracted me, and as my most particular friends and Relatives were fond of it, I spent most of my time in the Chase, in the course of which I became (I suppose) one of the best riders in the Country. In a few months I was called to join in an avocation of a more serious nature. The British army under General Prevost, having conquered our Sister State, Georgia, made a sudden irruption into So. Carolina, and pushed for Charleston, which it was expected must yield to its Arms. Prevost, however was foiled, but remained in the vicinity. Extraordinary exertions were made to subdue or expel him, for which purpose every man capable of bearing Arms, and every boy of and above 16 years old was called into the field. I, amongst others, shouldered my musket under an eagerness to unite in the defense of my country, & joined the Militia Company of the Neighborhood called the Wiltown Hunters commanded by Captain Osborn, a gentleman of respectable character, and good conduct as a commander. I felt a great anxiety to see the enemy & to hear a shot whistle, the stories of my friends who had seen some service, and could descant upon the merits of our struggle for Independence—and relate the enormities committed by our Enemies, the British, warmed and excited me to a pitch of enthusiastic hatred of them, and I really longed to engage in Battle. In a few days this desire was gratified, for in an attack on a party of the Enemy who were retreating Southwardly by Water, I got into a most tremendous cannonade from their Gallies, and had need of all the Spirit, Honor and I may add shame to enable me to stand it. It was a severe initiation for so young a soldier, and I candidly confess that it was owing wholly at one time to the steadiness of some of my older friends, who had before been repeatedly in battle, and whom I kept my eye on, that I did not at an improper time leave the field, in doing which however I would have incurred no less of credit as upwards of 200 North Carolina regulars had previously broke and fled from the fire of the enemy. I felt my resolution severely tried when a cannon shot cut off a small tree within three feet of my left ear, and when in a few seconds after, a charge of Grape Shot took down on my right about 20 stalks of corn within so short a distance as to send the shattered bits of broken stalks all about me. I had however the satisfaction of being among the last who were driven from the Fields, and of being told by the Commander that his little fellow had behaved well, this was a Major Moore of North Carolina, who as the officer of highest rank commanded, and was wounded in the action. I saw at this time very little blood-shed, and the few who were killed fell not near me, and were buried without my having seen them, a few wounded, however, convinced me that to go into Battle was very different from what I had conjectured it to be and very much abated my ardor for a repetition of the adventure, it so happened, however, that we were frequently involved in some skirmishes while though matters of little consequence, being with small parties not unattended with risk, habituated me to danger, and produced that kind of indifference or insensibility to it that in most men goes by the name of Courage. The British at length left the State, and we had a short space of repose and peace. In the month of September following we were gladdened by the intelligence that a French fleet under Count de Estaing, with a considerable military force, was on the Coast of Georgia intending to unite in the reduction of the British Army then at Savannah, which had been ravaging our State; the militia were immediately called out to join the Continental Troops who were to march to Savannah and unite with the French in the meditated attempt on that place. I repaired with alacrity to my post and proceeded with our regiment, then commanded by Col. Wm. Skerring, to the siege, but previously to my setting out on this expedition, an instance occurred to convince me that the merits of my worthy father would be useful to me in life, it was this—

There lived near my mother, an old Gentleman named James Stobo, who had been well acquainted with my father and much attached to him; he was a man of wonderful understanding and great experience, he had been in his youth a Libertine, and possessed of ample means had gratified all his propensities and desires and drunk deep at the fountain of pleasure even to satisfy and to satiety, and had at last made conclusions somewhat similar to those of King Solomon as to the pleasures of this world, and could give lectures and admonitions to young men in terms not less indicative of Wisdom, but far more pleasant than those used by the Israelitish King. This old man hearing that I was going to the siege of Savannah, on the day before my departure sent for me. I accordingly waited on him, and found him seated as usual in his Elbow Chair, to which he had for years been confined by the effects of Palsy, and a fall by which he had fractured his thigh. Having taken breakfast with him, he was wheeled into his parlor, whither at his desire I accompanied him. Having ordered his servant to withdraw, and shut the door, he drew a parcel from his bosom, and observed that he had always had a sincere regard for my Father, whom he considered as one of the best of men, and wished to pay a tribute to his Memory, by making a present to his son; he then offered me the parcel he had drawn from his bosom, which contained in paper money of that day 500 pounds, equal nominally to somewhat more than seventy pounds present currency, but as it was depreciated, less intrinsically worth, but still a handsome present, and added that as I was going far from home and the time of my stay would be uncertain, I might find this sum useful to me. Although I always esteemed the old gentleman, not being a connection [relative] made me unwilling to incur the obligation. I therefore informed him that my mother had already furnished me with as much money as I should need and thanked him heartily for his goodness, requesting that he would excuse me from pocketing his present. He persisted and desired that I would accept it as a token of his regard for my father—I did so. He then proceeded to inform me, that this was not the most valuable present he intended to make me, as he had some advice to give me, to which he requested my most serious attention. He then began and in language never to be forgotten gave me such a picture of the unwariness of youth and the designs of the Artful to entrap them, of the blessings of a quiet Conscience and the curse of an uneasy one, and closed the whole with such a string of useful maxims and such wholesome admonitions as proved indeed that his Money was the least valuable part of his donation—the words with which he concluded took particular hold on me—they were "Remember that you are the son of

19. Paul Hamilton

Aubrey Hamilton"—that I believe I left that old—that wise man in as
virtuous a state of mind as a youth could experience, and that the effects
of his good counsel did not forsake me of this I am certain, that with
respect to one description of youthful irregularities I was ever after most
decidedly determined and fortified. Resuming my detail, I proceeded
to the Siege of Savannah and there partook of all the dangers and ultimately shared in the disgrace of the defeat to which the American Army
was then subjected. The slaughter of my Countrymen generally and of
our Allies, and the loss of some of my particular friends and school fellows, who fell in the Action that terminated the Siege made a deep
impression on my mind. I had before felt a noted antipathy to the British
Cause, founded, as well as I could judge, on claims the most unjust,
but here it forced itself upon my mind, that in support of that iniqui-
tous Cause, Britain had shed in torrents the blood of my Countrymen
and Friends, and a thirst after vengeance was the immediate emotion
and I well recollect that while returning among the shattered forces to
our homes, I often wished that an opportunity might shortly occur of
avenging with Interest the stroke we had received at Savannah. Such as
mine I believe may have been the first sentiments of most of our Youth
who dropped in succession into the struggle for Freedom, reasoning but
little as to the merits of the question that had arrayed in hostile attitude the two Countries, we joined our friends who had at first on principle engaged in the cause. We acted with them because we believed
them to be right, and our Country's laws required that we should act,
but never until some close appeal was made to our feelings have we in
many instances set about informing ourselves what were the causes that
led to the events that we deplored. Certain am I that I had little information and such was the state of my mind until the defeat at Savannah, when sore under the loss which we had there sustained, I set about
enquiring whether the cause in which we had embarked demanded or
admitted of such sacrifices. Conferring with my friends whose superior
experience I respected and whose Integrity I could never doubt, I was
led to believe that the Cause of America was that of Justice, that of
Britain was consequently oppression, and that consequently opposition
at every expense of Blood and Treasure was on our part admissible and
indeed a duty, thenceforward I felt a decided, an unconquerable hatred
to the cause of Britain, and to myself I said that never would I submit

to her power while there remained in America one spot free from her wicked domination. In that spirit I am certain I remained and acted until the year 1783 consolidated our Independence. After my return from Savannah I engaged in such pastimes as the neighborhood afforded.

About this time our Country was again invaded by the British Army under Sir Henry Clinton, who from New York threatened the immediate reduction of Charleston; again all the friends of their Country were in motion for its defence. Through the mistakes and indiscreet conduct of our Captain (Slann) the company of which I was a member was not led to the defence of the Capital, and suffered a miserable defeat by a detailment of the British that advanced from Savannah through the Country to join in the siege of Charleston. In this defeat I had a hairbreadth escape from the British Dragoons who were five times our number; several of my acquaintances were cut down and killed, others severely wounded and made prisoners. After this occurrence the company was disheartened, and little disposed to obey their Commander. The Capital being completely invested by the British Army and their light Troops ranging without control or opposition over the Country; having no rallying point, we disbanded, and every man shifted for himself. Determined not to submit to the Enemy while I could find a party to oppose them, I had in view making my way across the country to a Body of our cavalry which it was said was posted at Monck's Corner, but while I was preparing to set out, information reached me that our Cavalry had been surprised, and defeated by that of the enemy. I then accepted an invitation from Capt. Slann, the brother of my Stepfather, to retire with him to the high hills of Santee, and there to await the arrival of an army from the northward, which it was said was advancing to the relief of Charleston. I therefore took leave of my mother, whom I left in an agony of grief at my departure, to which however she made no objection, for I believe that great as was her affection for me, she would rather have parted with me forever than have seen me forfeit my Honor and duty to my Country, by an unnecessary submission to its oppresssor. I had another trying parting, which must be obvious, yet this also I was equal to, and I set out.

In a short time after, the intelligence reached us at Santee that Charleston had surrendered, and that a large detachment of the British Force was pushing for that quarter, in pursuit of a small body of Virginia

Troops that were posted there. On the retreat of this American party and the approach of the British still determined to persevere in defence of my Country, I wrote my Mother a parting letter expressive of my intention, and retired with Capt. Slann, and some other friends to the number of 7 into North Carolina, where after a small incursion through the upper part of Virginia, we enjoyed the privilege of joining the American Army under the Baron de Kalb, at Hillsborough, in North Carolina, with this army I remained as a volunteer, until August 16, 1779, when it was defeated under General Gates who had superseded the Baron, and being reinforced by bodies of Militia gave battle to the British Army under the Command of Lord Cornwallis, in this defeat I had among the numerous flying troops several hard runs, as I may call them, with the pursuing British Dragoons, for being determined to keep the road as long as possible, and my horse, not one of the best, they were frequently close up, and at times were prevented from coming quite up with me only as it appeared by the plunder, which they found strewed along the road. At the end of twenty-one miles from the field of battle, their pursuit was discontinued and all apprehensions as to personal safety having ceased, I began to reflect seriously on my future prospects, even the recollections of the horrid scenes of bloodshed and devastation, from which I had just escaped was absorbed in anxiety as to the future. I had to look forward, almost, as it seemed to me, without hope. All expectations of ever returning to those attachments which I had left at Wiltown were annihilated, as that Army on which I relied for the recovery of our Country had just been destroyed, it was doubtful whether another adequate to the purpose could ever be raised, and I felt determined never to return at the expense of Political Integrity in a Submission to the enemy.

While ruminating on my misfortunes and travelling slowly along I successively came up with my friends from all of whom I had been separated in the defeat, and who in the retreat had at first got ahead of me. On our collecting the first matter that engaged our attention was the loss of our servants with all of our Baggage; these fellows had been stationed at Rugeley's, from whence we had marched the night before, with directions there to remain till further orders. When the rout became general I looked for them at this place, intending to lead them off, but they were not at the spot. I then concluded that they had taken an early alarm, and gone off with the first of the flying troops and hoped to come up with them, but we afterwards found that they had taken the opportunity to desert us, and return homewards to which the rest of them were overseduced by two of them who had families at the High Hills of Santee about 30 miles below the place of action, thus we were left without a second suit of clothes, and the only consolation was that we hoped our friends would endeavor by some means to relieve our Necessities, of which the arrival of these Villains would give them an adequate idea. They were now six of us in Company all equally destitute as to clothing, possessing each very little money, most that we had having been lodged in our portmanteaux, which our servants had carried off, and the little we had was the depreciated paper Currency then in circulation. After reviewing our situation, we determined to proceed northwardly and unite ourselves with the first camp of our friends that we should find formed, still hoping that we might obtain sight of our servants and Baggage, not knowing at that time what had become of them; we halted for the night in the settlements called Waxhaw's, at about 40 miles distance from the field of Battle which was 20 at least short of Charlotte to which in the same time Gen. Gates had gone. The farmhouse where we stopped being, previous to our reaching it, filled with fugitives, we took up our Quarters in the Barn and obtained a loaf of bread from the owner of the place, in gloomy sadness we broke our fast. We then lay down to rest but such was the state of my spirits and the impression made on my mind by the horrid scenes of the morning that I could not for a long time close my eyes. At one time I would dwell upon the sights I had beheld of my slain and wounded Countrymen, shot, sabred and trampled upon, in my presence by an insulting, triumphant Army that was giving away to all the furious passions of our nature, the roar of Cannon and Musketry, the shouting of victors, the cries and screams of the vanquished, some of whom were trodden down and destroyed by their friends who had not as yet been deprived of the means of flying, and were so fortunate as to be on horseback; and others crushed to death beneath the wheels of the Ammunition Wagons, all crowded on my recollection and drew many a tear of silent sympathy from my eyes, for at that moment, screened by the darkness, I felt not the restraint which my pride imposed when my emotions could be discerned. Again I would call to mind my attachment to that best of

Mothers, whom I figured to myself, indulging all her fears and fondness for my welfare and safety. I remembered all her kindness for me, and contrasted the situation in which I had under her protecting care enjoyed every comfort (called up my fondness for Mary) with the prospect before me, in which, in a strange Country, destitute of friends, but those immediately with me and who were partaking of the general distress, and like me indigent and almost despairing, I could reasonably judge from my presages look forward only to necessity and want.

While thus indulging apprehensions and sorrow most poignant, I perceived that my friend Sanders also was awake. It happened that without design we had placed ourselves in a part of the Barn remote from our associates. I accosted him and in a few words candidly told him the state of my mind, a conversation followed, the result of which was that in the morning we would take leave of our friends and return homewards, throw ourselves in the way of the Enemy and make our submission. We then attempted to sleep, daylight appeared, when Sanders reminded me of my agreement. I told him that on further reflection I had changed my mind, that sooner than submit to the Enemy, I would retire to the utmost extremity of America and endure every hardship. "Well said my friend," was his reply. "This is also my determination, and we can never starve while we have the use of our Limbs and Intellects." I arose, renewed in spirits, and prepared for future enterprise and hardships. We resumed our saddles and proceeded with other fugitives to Hillsboro in N. Carolina, witnessing by the way many scenes of heartrending effect among our wounded brethren. In this ride we one day stopped hungry and faint at a little cabin near the road, the good man of which had a small field of a few Acres, and a Blacksmith's shop on the profits arising from which it appeared that he wholly depended for a subsistence. His wife (his only companion he had not a slave or a child) was far advanced in a state of pregnancy, and still did the dredging of his humble cot. Pressed with hunger we asked him if we could obtain a mouthful, he answered cheerfully, "yes for you, but nothing for your horses." We dismounted and in a very short time his wife presented us with a loaf, fresh baked, and some sour milk, which she told us was a part of the best they had. We eagerly devoured the whole which was by no means a meal. Intent on our journey we asked what we had to pay. "Nothing," said this best of men, "far be it from me to accept of pay for what you have eaten, from men in distress." Inhospitable as we had found the N. Carolinians to be, I could scarcely credit my own ears. A silence ensued, at length he was urged to accept of payment only in indemnification, he obstinately refused. I could perceive his worthy partner, by her smiling countenance as she sat by the side of their only bed, bore testimony to his refusal. "No," said this good man, "never while I have a mouthful to spare, will I accept of pay from men like you, my wife's situation and my poverty have prevented me from sharing in your dangers and defeat, let me then by feeding as far as my means go, and otherwise relieving my unfortunate Countrymen, contribute towards the support of the General Cause; what you have received had been given with good will, and I only wish it had been more and better." We departed and I can scarce describe what was my admiration of these worthy, these truly christian people. I took the man's name, but in my many perigrinations, it was lost, but if Heaven should ever throw him or his the most remote in my way, with a knowledge of this my Charitable Beneficent Entertainer, what a feast to my feelings would it be to express to him my thankfulness and now while Providence affords me the means to remunerate his God-like Benevolence a thousand fold. Separated as perhaps we are for this world, I pray the almighty that if he or his wife or their offspring are on earth his best bounty may alight on them. They fed the hungry, may they never want; they felt for the distressed, may their benevolent hearts receive more abundantly of God's best favors.

Arrived at Hillsborough, we found Gen. Gates, and others of the foremost in the flight who presented something like a rendezvous and rallying point for the fugitives. In a day or two after our arrival in Hillsboro, Gen. John Rutledge of this state came in. I well recollect the equipage of this well tried Patriot. He wore a coat of grey cloth, much the worse for use, rode in a coarse sulky drawn by a poor grey horse, and was attended by a single servant. As soon as he took quarters our distresses were made known to him, and he (Good Man) informing us that his case was scarcely better assured us that he would endeavor to procure from the Military Chest of General Gates for our relief, which he accordingly did, presenting each of us with $500 of depreciated Paper Currency, not worth as times went above $5, for this our notes were respectively given and since faithfully paid at the rate of Depreciation.

With this small supply we were further favored by the Governor with an order for daily rations, which we drew from the Commissary of Gen. Gates at Hillsboro. It next became necessary to seek for quarters on some cheap plan where we were to wait events, we therefore procurred suits to the N. Westward of that town about 4 miles, at the House of two worthy but poor Farmers, Thomas and Laurence Thomson. I stayed with the latter, and the day of my arrival was productive to me of the most poignant feelings I had ever experienced. It was then the fifteenth day after Gates defeat [Camden], during which time I had never changed my clothes, for I had none but those on my back, being very dirty and loathsome, even to myself, I went down into a beautiful rivulet near the house, stripped off half of my dress and washed it in the stream, hung it on the bushes until it was dry enough to be worn then did the same by the other half, thus procuring once more a clean suit. During the while my clothes were drying, I seated myself on a rock, which divided the stream and gave free indulgence to my reflections and feelings. Language cannot express what were my feelings and reflections on this day on calling to mind and contrasting what I had left behind with my situation at that time. I felt no diminution of Political Integrity and Perseverance, and returned to the House & ate a hearty but coarse dinner. Here we remained for nearly three months, and experienced a hospitable treatment during the whole time from this good old man, Laurence Thomson, occasionally amusing ourselves with engaging in the pastimes of the Neighborhood, of which, what then were called Husking Frolics, were the chief which were the stripping of the husk or shuck from the Corn, after it had been all pulled from the Stalk, and drawn down in Waggons to the Corn Crib or House. For this purpose the Neighbors were all assembled and partook of a Treat in the Evening after all the Corn was housed. Dancing closed the Frolic, and this went round in succession during the Harvest Season.... I left this in November of that year, and returned with my friends Jas. Moore & J. Slann, southward to the Camp which General Gates had again formed at a place called New Providence some miles below the town of Charlotte, N.C....

We came on the Camp at New Providence, just in time to see Gen. Gates resign his command to Gen. Greene of immortal memory. Here we remained a few days. Hearing that Gen. [Francis] Marion was carrying

Francis Marion crossing the Peedee River (Emmet Collection, Miriam and Ira Wallach Division of Art, Prints and Photographs, The New York Public Library, Astor, Lenox and Tilden Foundations).

on a desultory warfare on the lower part of the Santee, my friend Moore and I agreed to repair to his camp, under an expectation that we might thence more easily force our way homeward for supplies, of which we were very much in need. We accordingly joined this able Partisan (Marion) and remained with him for three months during which the most active scene of partisan warfare was exhibited that perhaps has occurred in the Annals of Nations. Advancing, retreating, ambuscading and skirmishing were almost our daily fare insomuch that a dear friend of mine (Peter Porcher) one day, very gravely said to me "Hamilton, I do not expect to live to see Saturday night, for General Marion is constantly leading us into some scrape, therefore if I fall, do you take what I leave." The stipulation became reciprocal and mutually binding. In the course of these operations, I had the satisfaction of being one of the 26 under Captain Jno. Postell, who compelled the same number of British Grenadiers under Captain Du Peyster to surrender, in the house of Postell's Father on Pee Dee River, near Georgetown, and was one of the 6 young fellows who applied the fire to the buildings which caused this surrender.

Having remained sometime with Marion, I availed myself of an opportunity that offered of returning homeward with Col. Harden, who had fled from the Parish of Prince William to Marion's camp and assembling about 70 followers, determined to return Southward, and by stirring up his friends who had submitted to the Enemy to cover that part of our country. Him I joined as a volunteer, having previously received, while with Marion, a letter from my good mother with a supply of money and clothes, most wonderfully conveyed to me through the Country then overrun by the enemy. With Harden I approached Jacksonboro, and then hearing that my mother was then at the plantation of my deceased Grandfather Branford, two miles off, I, with leave, quitted the party, galloped off to the plantation opposite (then Dupont's, now Jacob Walter's), where finding a small canoe which I ordered a negro man to enter, I threw thereon my arms, and on my horse swam the river. Arriving near the house I was informed that my grandfather's Widow was then in a most dreadful state with small pox, which I had not had, and that my mother had that morning gone to her house at Wiltown. An express was sent for her and in a very short time she was at Mrs. Slann's, whose husband I had left northwardly, arrived. To avoid the infection of small pox I had remained at the fence of the plantation near the swamp, where I met the best of mothers. What our meeting was I cannot describe. Neither had for minutes the power of utterance, at length a flood of tears on her part enabled her to break silence, when such affectionate expressions were poured out as I can never forget, nor the warmth of that maternal embrace in which I was clasped to her aching bosom, after an absence of 12 months, lacking 6 days, during which she had received but one letter from me and had often heard of my having been killed. I remained with her for two hours. I then left with her blessing on my head, and an assurance that I would shortly again see her. She presented me with some clothing which she had prepared for me, these she had tied up hastily in a pillow case, and I tucked them behind my saddle, a circumstance which had well nigh cost me my life that very night. On regaining my party, we proceeded Southwardly, and at midnight encountered a Body of British Cavalry near Saltketcher Bridge. The onset was in our favor, but Harden being but an indifferent commander, we were defeated and in the rout I suffered a hard pursuit, in which my pursuers were guided by the whiteness of the Pillow Case that contained the clothes behind me. A good horse and some presence of mind at last secured me from pursuit. Our whole party was dispersed, and about 15 severely wounded with the Sabre. In two days we were again collected and retorted this defeat by surprising and making prisoners of part of this cavalry at Pocotaligo, among them their Colonel Fenwicke and other officers. This success led to the surrender of the British Fort Balfour, at the above place, under the ramparts almost of which this surprise was made. I must, as I am writing of myself, be allowed to be somewhat particular as to this little, but handsome military exploit. Colonel Harden, knowing that we had some staunch friends, who had been compelled to enter and garrison the Fort, thought that if he could destroy the Cavalry, he might induce a surrender of the remainder of the Garrison, which were Militia, and perhaps one half of them friendly to the American Cause; some of whom were men of considerable influence and weight. He therefore drew near the fort and, with the effective force he had remaining, formed an Ambuscade. Twelve well-mounted young men, of whom I was one, named as Light Horsemen, were selected and ordered to decoy the Cavalry out. With this view we moved on briskly and openly toward Von Bitter's Tavern, which stood almost a quarter of a mile from the Fort and in full view, while approaching we discovered that some of the enemy were at the Tavern, on which we darted forward and captured as follows: Col. Fenwicke, Lieut. Bond, a sergeant and 15 privates of the Cavalry with Lieut. Col. Lechmere of the British Militia. Lechmere was taken as he ran within 100 yards of the Fort and brought off by one of our young men named Green. Our prisoners had come out on foot to the Tavern to regale themselves [and], having only their swords, made no attempt to resist. They were hurried off to the Ambuscade and delivered. After which, reinforced by eight more swordsmen, we returned, 20 in number, to the Tavern, drew up in the adjoining pasture, offered battle to the British Cavalry whose number we had reduced now to about our standard, a part of their force having been previously detached to Charleston immediately after we had been defeated by them at Saltketchie. The Cavalry made a show of advancing to the charge, but, finding us firm, they turned about and were insulted by us as they retired to the Fort. Col. Harden now came up with the remainder of his force, leaving the Servants and Baggage just partly in view to keep up the appearance of a reserve, Major Harden, the brother of the colonel, was now sent to summon the Fort to surrender with threats of an assault if refused. I accompanied the Major, we were met by Major De Veaux (after Col. De Veaux who took the Bahamas from Spain) at so short a distance from the Fort that we could recognize countenances and exchanged an occasional nod with some of the Garrison.

At first the answer through Major De Veaux was a refusal from Col. Kitsall, who commanded the Fort, to surrender, on which I was desired by Major Harden to communicate to his brother this answer. The Col. inquired of me if we could distinguish any of our friends in the Fort. I replied that Major Harden had recognized Cols. Stafford and Davis and Mr. Thomas Hutson, with none of whom I had any acquaintance, but that I thought that I discovered some confusion and clamour in the Fort. On which the colonel, his countenance brightening, formed his men in column and ordered them to prepare for immediate action. This done, he turned to me and said, "Go to Major Harden and say to him that I allowed ten minutes to Col. Kitsall to consider of a surrender, after which if he refuses, you are both to return immediately to me and, by God, I will be in the Fort!" The major communicated this to Major De Veaux with whom he had been chatting with great familiarity, being acquaintances and closely related by blood. The latter went in and delivered this last message to Col. Kitsall, who having discovered a division among his Militia, agreed to lay down his arms. Thus was Fort Balfour, which had for some months completely bridled that part of the country, surrendered without a shot. The Garrison consisted of 92 Militia, about 25 Regulars, Cavalry well-mounted and equipped and uniformed as Light Dragoons. In the Fort we found an abundance of provisions, some muskets and a six-pound cannon, with a good supply of ammunition for it.

We had just completed this and paroled our prisoners when a body of British composed of Artillery, Cavalry and Infantry appeared within a mile of us, far too strong for us. We, therefore, drew off leaving them Fort Balfour in ruins....

The arrival of General Greene in the lower country in the last of 1781 drove the Enemy into the walls of Charleston, left us free to resume our homes and a safety to which we long had been strangers. I now devoted myself to the company of my friends and the sports of the chase of which I was immoderately fond. My chief delight was to converse with Mary whom I now considered as entirely mine, as soon as prudence would admit of our being united.... Every day appeared an age till the 10th of October 1782, united me to Mary, she then turned 18 and I, short by 6 days, of being 20 years of age.

Paul Hamilton began a public career as a local tax collector, justice of the peace, and district commissioner. Later he was elected to serve in the legislature. In 1804 he became governor of South Carolina, and in 1809 President Madison appointed him as secretary of the navy.

Bibliography

Hamilton, Paul. "Extracts from a Private Manuscript Written by Governor Paul Hamilton, Sr. during the Period of the Revolutionary War, from 1776–1800." In *The Yearbook of Charleston 1898.* Courtesy of the Charleston Library Society.

20

Andrew Jackson: "Take It Altogether, I Saw and Heard a Good Deal of War"

When the British set out to control the interior of the Carolinas, they brought the war near the home of the future president, Andrew Jackson. At Waxhaw Creek on May 29, 1780, their brutal tactics won a victory, but aroused the countryside. Surrounded by the British, the American commander Colonel Abraham Buford hoisted a white flag and ordered his men to ground their arms. But British Lieutenant-Colonel Banastre Tarleton would not stay his troops. They fell upon the unarmed Americans with sword and bayonet. One hundred thirteen were killed, 150 badly wounded and 53 taken prisoner. From that time on, "Tarleton's quarter" became a byword to describe relentless slaughter of surrendered men. In further action on August 16, 1780, the British had also defeated American General Gates at Camden and established a prison there.

The Jackson family had suffered a serious loss. Hugh Jackson, Andrew's 16-year-old brother, enlisted in 1778 in Colonel William R. Davie's regiment. It was sent to reinforce the army of General Lincoln at Charleston. At Stono Ferry, June 20, 1779, he had perished.

Andrew Jackson was born March 15, 1767, a few days after the death of his father. He was only 14 when he took part in the war in the spring of 1781. He told Francis Preston Blair the following account:

I witnessed two battles, Hanging Rock [August 6, 1780] and Hobkirk's Hill [April 25, 1781]. I did not take part in either. I was in one skirmish—that of Sands House—and there, they caught me, along with my brother Robert and my cousin, Tom Crawford. A lieutenant of Tarleton's Light Dragoons tried to make me clean his boots and cut my arm with his sabre when I refused. After that, they kept me in jail at Camden about two months, starved me nearly to death and gave me the small-pox. Finally, my mother persuaded them to release Robert and me on account of our extreme youth and illness. Then Robert died of the small-pox and I barely escaped death. When it left me, I was a skeleton—not quite six feet long and a little over six inches thick! It took me all the rest of that year [1781] to recover my strength and get flesh enough to hide my bones. By that time Cornwallis had surrendered and the war was practically over in our part of the country.

I was never regularly enlisted, being only fourteen when the war practically ended. Whenever I took the field it was with Colonel Davie, who never put me in the ranks, but used me as a mounted orderly or

Andrew Jackson defying a British officer in "The Brave Boy of the Waxhaws" in a Currier and Ives print (permission of North Carolina Historical Commission, Raleigh, NC).

messenger for which I was well fitted, being a good rider and knowing all the roads in that region. The only weapons I had were a pistol that Colonel Davie gave me and a small fowling-piece that my Uncle Crawford lent to me. This was a light gun and would kick like sixty when loaded with a three-quarter-ounce ball or with nine buckshot. But it was a smart little gun and would carry the ball almost as true as a rifle fifteen or twenty rods and threw the buckshot spitefully at close quarters—which was the way I used it in the defence of Captain Sand's house, where I was captured.

I was as sorry about losing the gun there as about the loss of my own liberty because Uncle Crawford set great store by the gun, which he had brought with him from the old country; and besides it was the finest in that whole region. Not long afterward—I was still in the Camden jail or stockade—some of Colonel Davie's men under Lieutenant Curriton captured a squad of Tories, one of them had that gun in his possession, together with my pistol that Colonel Davie had given to me. This Tory's name was Mulford. The gun and pistol cost him his life. Davie's men regarded his possession of them as prima facie evidence that he had been a member of the party that captured Captain Sands's house, sacked and burned it and insulted the womenfolks of his family. He pleaded that he was not there; that he had bought the gun and pistol from another Tory. Davie's men told him it would do him no good to add lying to his other crimes [and] hanged him forthwith and afterward restored the gun and pistol to their proper owners.

The Tories also got the horse I had when captured. He was a three-year-old colt—fine fellow—belonging to Captain Sands himself. He was hid in the woods when they attacked the house, but they [the Tories] found him the next morning. This colt was also retaken about six weeks afterward. The Tory who had him was not hanged because he had been shot through the stomach before he surrendered and was already dying.

Take it altogether, I saw and heard a good deal of war in those days, but did nothing toward it myself worth mention.

After Andy recovered from smallpox, his mother made the 160-mile journey to Charleston Harbor to help care for his cousins. They were among the captured soldiers lying sick and wounded in British prison ships. From the plague-ridden men she caught

cholera and died at the home of distant relatives who lived nearby. Andy received the news, along with a small bundle of her clothing. "I felt utterly alone," he lamented.

When the final treaty was signed in Paris on September 3, 1783, Andrew Jackson had lost both parents and both brothers during the war. He knew the high cost of victory. However, he had also received a legacy of 300 pounds from his grandfather, who had died that spring in Scotland. As a 16-year-old he lost most of it going to the racetrack and gambling. It taught him a hard lesson.

Andrew began a career in politics. In 1796 he served in the convention that drew up the constitution under which Tennessee entered the Union. He was the state's first member of the United States House of Representatives, from December 1796 to March 1797. The state legislature then elected him to the United States Senate. Resigning the next year, he became a superior court judge from 1798 to 1804.

In 1802 he became a leader of the state militia, the beginning of a military career that brought him into prominence. By 1812, when war with Britain was again expected, Andrew was a general in the state militia. He led his men against the Creek Indians and on May 28, 1814, was made a major-general commanding the seventh military district. Winning the battle of New Orleans made him a hero overnight.

The 15th of March 1815 was Jackson's forty-eighth birthday. He was then disbanding the army with which he had won the battle of New Orleans. The day and date filled his mind with reminiscences of his mother. To three members of his military family who happened to be with him—Major John Henry Eaton, Major William Berkeley Lewis and Captain William O. Butler—he said:

How I wish she could, Gentlemen, have lived to see this day.... Almost her last words to me when about to start for Charleston on the errand of mercy that cost her life were: "Andrew, if I should not see you again I wish you to remember and treasure up some things I have already said to you: In this world you will have to make your own way. To do that you must have friends. You can make friends by being honest, and you can keep them by being steadfast. You must keep in mind that friends worth having will in the long run expect as much from you as they give to you. To forget an obligation or be ungrateful for a kindness is a base crime—not merely a fault or a sin, but an actual crime. Men guilty of it sooner or later must suffer the penalty. In personal conduct be always polite, but never obsequious. No one will respect you more than you esteem yourself. Avoid quarrels as long as you can without yielding to imposition. But sustain your manhood always.... Never wound the feelings of others. Never brook wanton outrage upon your own feelings. If ever you have to vindicate your feelings or defend your honor, do it calmly. If angry at first, wait till your wrath cools before you proceed." Gentlemen her last words have been the law of my life.

In later action in Florida he opposed the Seminole Indians. He seized Pensacola and became military governor of the territory of Florida in 1821 following its purchase from Spain. However, he resigned after 11 weeks. In 1823 he was again elected to the U.S. Senate, but he resigned in 1825. Three years later he was elected president of the United States as representative of the New West. In 1832 he was reelected. Four years later he left the White House. He died at his home in Nashville, Tennessee, on June 8, 1845.

Bibliography

Buell, Augustus C. *A History of Andrew Jackson*. New York: Charles Scribner and Sons, 1904.

Jackson, Andrew. *Papers of Andrew Jackson*. Eds. Sam B. Smith and Harriet Chappell Owsley. Knoxville, Tenn.: University of Tennessee Press, 1980.

James, Marquis. *Life of Andrew Jackson*. New York: Bobbs Merrill, 1938.

21

James Armistead: A Spy for Lafayette

Like an estimated 5,000 free and slave African-Americans, James Armistead served the patriot cause. Although a "slave of William Armistead of New Kent County, Virginia," James entered the war, serving under the Marquis de Lafayette from March through October 1781, frequently operating as a spy and courier. At that time the British troops were based on the Virginia coast at Portsmouth. Benedict Arnold had turned traitor and was leading British army troops on raids in the countryside.

Washington had ordered Lafayette, with three regiments of light infantry, to march southward and hopefully capture the traitor. Serving as a spy for Lafayette, James became the servant of Benedict Arnold. He was often present when plans were being made. Armistead sent Lafayette reports on British activity almost daily. Using that information the patriots once staged a raid on the British camp that nearly caught Benedict Arnold himself.

When Arnold was sent north, Armistead signed on with Lord Cornwallis, commander of the British forces in the South. Serving in Cornwallis's tent, he again was able to overhear the staff officers laying out strategies, which he secretly passed to Lafayette.

When the British arrived at Yorktown, Armistead reported to Lafayette that Cornwallis was digging in and fortifying the town. Lafayette forwarded this information to Washington. Having received other similar reports, Washington cooperated with the French army under Rochambeau and the French fleet under Admiral de Grasse to head also for Yorktown. They encircled the British on land and sea.

Cornwallis was trapped and surrendered in what would be the

last major battle of the Revolution. After the surrender Cornwallis paid Lafayette a courtesy call before leaving Yorktown. He was surprised to find at Lafayette's headquarters his servant James, who had been in the pay of the British to spy on the Americans. Now it became obvious that James had really been a counter-spy for the Americans. The British general is said to have shaken his head in surprise that he had been deceived by an African-American spy.

When Lafayette returned to the United States in 1784 to visit Washington and sites of the Revolutionary War, he provided the following testimony of James's exploits:

> This is to certify that the Bearer By the Name of James Has done Essential Service to Me While I Had the Honour to Command in this State. His Intelligence from the Enemy's Camp were Industriously Collected and Most faithfully delivered. He Perfectly Acquitted Himself With Some Important Commissions I Gave Him and Appears to me Entitled to Every Reward His Situation Can Admit of.
> Done Under My Hand, Richmond November 21st 1784.
> Lafayette

James presented this certificate in 1786 to the Virginia legislature in a petition to give him his freedom:

> A petition of James, a negro slave; setting forth, that being impelled by a most earnest desire of gaining that liberty which is so dear to all mankind, and convinced that if he rendered any essential services to the public, that that would be his reward, he often during the invasion of the enemy in the year 1781, at the risk of his life entered into the enemy's camp, and collected such intelligence as he supposed of importance, and which he conveyed in the most expeditious manner to the Marquis de la Fayette, who then commanded the American army in Virginia; and praying that an act may pass for his emancipation; and that a reasonable compensation may be made for him, to his present proprietor.

A law passed in October 1786 ordered the state treasurer to pay to James's master the equivalent of the price the slave would have commanded on the auction block. On January 9, 1787, James was emancipated by the Virginia legislature. In 1816, he was able to purchase 40 acres of land. In 1819 another legislature voted the former spy a $40.00 a year pension.

Bibliography

African-Americans, Voices of Triumph, Perseverance. Alexandria, Virginia: Time-Life, 1993.

Certification of Lafayette, dated Nov. 21, 1784. Reproduced from original in Virginia Historical Society. In Luther P. Jackson, "Virginia Negro Soldiers and Seamen in the American Revolution." *Journal of Negro History* 27, 1942.

Gottschalk, Louis. *Lafayette and the Close of the American Revolution.* Chicago: University of Chicago Press, 1942.

Hening, ed. Statutes of Va., XII, 380–81.

Journal of (Virginia) house of Delegates. October 1784 session, p. 57: December 4, 1784.

Quarles, Benjamin. *The Negro in the American Revolution.* Chapel Hill: University of North Carolina Press, 1961.

Virginia. Acts of the Assembly, Chap. CLXIX, p. 188.

Virginia. State Library. Tax Books (MS) *Land* New Kent County, 1816–24, p. 284

22

Joseph Plumb Martin: At Yorktown "We Thought the More the Merrier"

Serving in the Continental army for seven years, Joseph Plumb Martin fought under Washington, Lafayette, and Steuben. He vividly brings to life the difficulties of living as a soldier fighting against the British for the country's independence as the war moved from the North to the South.

I, the redoubtable hero of this Narrative, first made my appearance in this crooked, fretful world, upon the twenty-first day of November in the year 1760.... I lived with my parents until I was upwards of seven years old, when I went to live with this good old grandsire; for good he was, particularly to me. He was wealthy, and I had everything that was necessary for life and as many superfluities as was consistent with my age and station....

I remember the stir in the country occasioned by the Stamp Act, but I was so young that I did not understand the meaning of it; I likewise remember the disturbances that followed the repeal of the Stamp Act, until the destruction of the tea at Boston and elsewhere. I was then thirteen or fourteen years old and began to understand something of the works going on. I used, about this time, to inquire a deal about the French War, as it was called, which had not been long ended; my grandsire would talk with me about it while working in the fields, perhaps as much to beguile his own time as to gratify my curiosity. I thought then, nothing should induce me to get caught in the toils of an army. "I am well, so I'll keep," was my motto then, and it would have been well for me if I had ever retained it.

Time passed smoothly on with me till the year 1774 arrived. The smell of war began to be pretty strong, but I was determined to have no hand in it, happen when it might; I felt myself to be a real coward. What—venture my carcass where bullets fly! That will never do for me. Stay at home out of harm's way, thought I, it will be as much to your health as credit to do so. But the pinch of the game had not arrived yet; I had seen nothing of war affairs and consequently was but a poor judge in such matters.

The winter of this year passed off without any very frightening alarms, and the spring of 1775 arrived. Expectation of some fatal event seemed to fill the minds of most of the considerate people throughout the country. I was ploughing in the field about half a mile from home, about the twenty-first day of April, when all of a sudden the bells fell to ringing and three guns were repeatedly fired in succession down in the village; what the cause was we could not conjecture. I had some fearful forebodings that something more than the sound of a carriage wheel was in the wind. The regulars [British] are coming in good earnest, thought I. My grandsire sighed, he "smelt the rat." He immediately turned out the team and repaired homeward. I set off to see what the cause of the commotion was. I found most of the male kind of the people together; soldiers for Boston were in requisition.

A dollar deposited upon the drumhead was taken up by someone as soon as placed there, and the holder's name taken, and he enrolled with orders to equip himself as quick as possible. My spirits began to revive at the sight of the money offered; the seeds of courage began to sprout; for, contrary to my knowledge, there was a scattering of them sowed, but they had not as yet germinated; I felt a strong inclination, when I found I had them, to cultivate them. O, thought I, if I were but old enough to put myself forward, I would be the possessor of one dollar, the dangers of war to the contrary notwithstanding; but I durst not put myself up for a soldier for fear of being refused, and that would have quite upset all the courage I had drawn forth.

The men that had engaged "to go to war" went as far as the next town, where they received orders to return; as there was a sufficiency of men already engaged, so that I should have had but a short campaign had I have gone.

This year there were troops raised both for Boston and New York. Some from the back towns were billeted at my grandsire's; their company and conversation began to warm my courage to such a degree that I resolved at all events to "go a sogering." [His grandsire said] he should never give his consent for me to go into the army unless I had the previous consent of my parents.... My parents were too far off to obtain their consent before it would be too late for the present campaign. What was I to do? Why, I must give up the idea, and that was hard; for I was as earnest now to call myself and be called a soldier as I had been a year before not to be called one. I thought over many things and formed many plans, but they all fell through, and poor disconsolate I was forced to set down and gnaw my fingernails in silence.

I said but little more about "soldiering" until the troops raised in and near the town in which I resided came to march off for New York; then I felt bitterly again. I accompanied them as far as the town line, and it was hard parting with them then. Many of my young associates were with them, my heart and soul went with them, but my mortal part must stay behind. By and by, they will come swaggering back, thought I, and tell me of all their exploits, all their "hair-breath escapes," and poor Huff will not have a single sentence to advance. O, that was too much to be borne with by me....

During the winter of 1775–76, by hearing the conversation and disputes of the good old farmer politicians of the times, I collected pretty correct ideas of the contest between this country and the mother country (as it was then called). I thought I was as warm a patriot as the best of them; the war was waged; we had joined issue, and it would not do to "put the hand to the plough and look back." I felt more anxious then ever, if possible to be called a defender of my country....

One evening, very early in the spring of the year [1776] I chanced to overhear my grandm'am telling my grandsire that I had threatened to engage on board a man-of-war.... My grandsire told her that he supposed I was resolved to go into the service in some way or other and he had rather I would engage in the land service if I must engage in any. This I thought to be a sort of tacit consent for me to go, and I determined to take advantage of it as quick as possible.

Soldiers were at this time enlisting for a year's service. I did not like that; it was too long a time for me at the first trial; I wished only to take a priming before I took upon me the whole coat of paint for a soldier. However, the time soon arrived that gratified all my wishes. In the month of June [1776], orders came out for enlisting men for six months from the twenty-fifth of this month.... The troops were styled new levies. They were to go to New York. And notwithstanding, I was told that the British army at that place was reinforced by fifteen thousand men, it made no alteration in my mind; I did not care if there had been fifteen times fifteen thousand, I should have gone just as soon as if there had been but fifteen hundred. I never spent a thought about numbers; the Americans were invincible in my opinion. If anything affected me, it was a stronger desire to see them....

I, one evening, went off with a full determination to enlist at all hazards. When I arrived at the place of rendezvous I found a number of young men of my acquaintance there. The old bantering began—come, if you will enlist I will, says one; you have long been talking about it, says another—come, now is the time. "Thinks I to myself" I will not be laughed into it or out of it, at any rate. I will act my own pleasure after all. But what did I come here for tonight? Why to enlist. Then enlist I will. So seating myself at the table, enlisting orders were immediately presented to me; I took up the pen, loaded it with the fatal charge, made several mimic imitations of writing my name, but took special care not to touch the paper with the pen until an unlucky wight who was leaning over my shoulder gave my hand a stroke, which caused the pen to make a woeful scratch on the paper. "O, he has enlisted," said he. "He has made his mark; he is fast enough now."

Well, thought I, I may as well go through with the business now as not. So I wrote my name fairly upon the indentures. [July 6, 1776, in Samuel Peck's Third Company, William Douglas's Fifth Battalion, James Wadsworth, Jr.'s Brigade of new levies.]

And now I was a soldier, in name at least, if not in practice; but I had now to go home, after performing this, my heroic action. How shall I be received there? But the report of my adventure had reached there before I did. In the morning when I first saw my grandparents, I felt considerably of the sheepish order. The old gentleman first accosted me with, "Well, you are going a soldiering then, are you?" I had nothing to answer; I would much rather he had not asked me the question. I saw that the circumstance hurt him and the old lady, too; but it was too late now to repent. The old gentleman proceeded, "I suppose you must be fitted out for the expedition, since it is so."

Accordingly, they did "fit me out" in order with arms and accou-
terments, clothing, and cake, and cheese in plenty, not forgetting to put
my pocket Bible into my knapsack. Good old people! They wished me
well, soul and body. I sincerely thank them for their kindness and love
to me, from the first time I came to live with them to the last parting
hour. I hope, nay, I believe, that their spirits now rest in the realms of
bliss. May it be my happy lot to meet them there.

I was now what I had long wished to be, a soldier. I had obtained
my heart's desire; it was now my business to prove myself equal to my
profession. Well, to be short, I went with several others of the company
on board a sloop bound to New York; had a pleasant though protracted
passage; passed through the straight called Hell's Gate, where all who
had not before passed it had to pay a treat (I had been through it before);
arrived at New York; marched up into the city, and joined the rest of
the regiment that were already there.

And now I had left my good old grandsire's house, as a constant
resident, forever, and had to commence exercising my function. I was
called out every morning at reveille beating, which was at daybreak, to
go to our regimental parade in Broad Street [New York City occupied
only the southern tip of Manhattan Island, an area about a mile
square—northward lay farmlands, woods, and marshes] and there practice the manual exercise, which was the most that was known in our
new levies, if they knew even that. I was brought to an allowance of provisions, which, while we lay in New York, was not bad; ... I began soon
to miss grandsire's table and cellar. However, I reconciled myself to my
condition as well as I could; it was my own seeking. I had had no com-
pulsion....

I remained in New York two or three months ... when, sometime
in the latter part of August, I was ordered upon a fatigue party. We had
scarcely reached the grand parade when I saw our sergeant major direct-
ing his course up Broadway, towards us, in rather an unusual step for
him. He soon arrived and informed us and then the commanding officer
of the party to take off all belongings to our regiment and march us to
our quarters, as the regiment was ordered to Long Island, the British
having landed in force there. Although this was not unexpected to me,
yet it gave me rather a disagreeable feeling, as I was pretty well assured
I should have to snuff a little gunpowder....

However, I kept my cogitations to myself, went to my quarters, packed up my clothes, and got myself in readiness for the expedition as soon as possible. I then went to the top of the house where I had a full view of that part of the Island; I distinctly saw the smoke of the field artillery, but the distance and the unfavorableness of the wind prevented my hearing their report, at least but faintly. The horrors of battle then presented themselves to my mind in all their hideousness; I must come to it now, thought I. Well, I will endeavor to do my duty as well as I am able and leave the event with Providence. We were soon ordered to our regimental parade, from which, as soon as the regiment was formed, we were marched off for the ferry.

At the lower end of the street were placed several casks of sea-bread, made, I believe of canel and peas-meal, nearly hard enough for musket flints; the casks were unheaded and each man was allowed to take as many as he could, as he marched by. As my good luck would have it, there was a momentary halt made. I improved the opportunity thus offered me, as every good soldier should upon all important occasions, to get as many of the biscuit as I possibly could. No one said anything to me, and I filled my bosom and took as many as I could hold in my hand, a dozen or more in all, and when we arrived at the ferry-stairs, I stowed them away in my knapsack.

We quickly embarked on board the boats. As each boat started, three cheers were given by those on board, which was returned by the numerous spectators who thronged the wharves; they all wished us good luck, apparently; although it was with most of them perhaps nothing more than ceremony.

We soon landed at Brooklyn, upon the Island, marched up the ascent from the ferry to the plain. We now began to meet the wounded men, another sight I was unacquainted with, some with broken arms, some with broken legs, and some with broken heads. The sight of these a little daunted me, and made me think of home, but the sight and thought vanished together.

We marched a short distance when we halted to refresh ourselves ... the hard bread was hard enough to break the teeth of a rat. One of the soldiers complaining of thirst to his officer "Look at that man," said he pointing to me; "he is not thirsty, I will warrant it." I felt a little elevated to be styled a man....

We were soon called upon to fall in and proceed. We had not gone far, about half a mile, when I heard one in the rear ask another where his musket was. I looked round and saw one of the soldiers stemming off without his gun, having left it where we last halted; he was inspecting his side as if undetermined whether he had it or not, he then fell out of the ranks to go in search of it. One of the company, who had brought it on (wishing to see how far he would go before he missed it) gave it to him....

We overtook a small party of the artillery here, dragging a heavy twelve-pounder upon a field carriage, sinking half-way to the naves in the sandy soil. They plead hard for some of us to assist them to get on their piece; our officers, however paid no attention to their entreaties, but pressed forward towards a creek, where a large party of Americans and British were engaged. By the time we arrived, the enemy had driven our men into the creek, or rather millpond, (the tide being up), where such as could swim got across; those that could not swim, and could not procure anything to buoy them up, sunk. The British having several fieldpieces stationed by a brick house, were pouring the canister and grape upon the Americans like a shower of hail. They would doubtless have done them much more damage than they did, but for the twelve-pounder mentioned above; the men having gotten it within sufficient distance to reach them and opening a fire upon them, soon obliged them to shift their quarters.

There was in this action a regiment of Maryland troops, (volunteers) all young gentlemen. When they came out of the water and mud to us, looking like water rats, it was a truly pitiful sight. Many of them were killed in the pond, and more were drowned. Some of us went into the water after the fall of the tide, and took out a number of corpses and a great many arms that were sunk in the pond and creek.

Our regiment lay on the ground we then occupied the following night. The next day, in the afternoon, we had a considerable tight scratch with about an equal number of the British, which began rather unexpectedly, and a little whimsically.

A few of our men, (I mean of our regiment), went over the creek upon business that usually employed us, that is, in search of something to eat. There was a field of Indian corn at a short distance from the creek, with several cocks of hay about halfway from the creek to the cornfield; the men purposed to get some of the corn, or anything else that was eatable. When they got up with the hayracks, they were fired upon by about an equal number of the British, from the cornfield; our people took to the hay, and the others to the fence, where they exchanged a number of shots at each other, neither side inclining to give back. A number, say forty or fifty more of our men, went over and drove the British from the fence; they were by this time reinforced in their turn, and drove us back. The two parties kept thus alternately reinforcing until we had the most of our regiment in the action.

After the officers came to command, the English were soon routed from the place, but we dare not follow them for fear of falling into some snare, as the whole British army was in the vicinity of us; I do not recollect that we had anyone killed outright, but we had several severely wounded, and some, I believe, mortally.

Our regiment was alone, no other troops being near where we were lying. We were upon a rising ground, covered with a young growth of trees; we felled a fence of trees around us to prevent the approach of the enemies' horse. We lay there a day longer. In the latter part of the afternoon there fell a very heavy shower of rain which wet us all to the skin and much damaged our ammunition. About sunset, when the shower had passed over, we were ordered to parade and discharge our pieces.... However, we got our muskets as empty as our stomachs, and with half the trouble, nor was it half the trouble to have reloaded them, for we had wherewithal to do that, but not so with stomachs.

Just at dusk, I, with one or two others of our company, went off to a barn about a half-mile distant, with intent to get some straw to lodge upon, the ground and leaves being drenched in water, and we as wet as they.... I could not find any straw, but I found some wheat in the sheaf, standing by the side of the floor; I took a sheaf or two and returned as fast as I could to the regiment. When I arrived the men were all paraded to march off the ground; I left my wheat, seized my musket and fell into the ranks. We were strictly enjoined not to speak, or even cough, while on the march. All orders were given from officer to officer, and communicated to the men in whispers. What such secrecy could mean we could not divine.

We marched off in the same way that we had come on to the island, forming various conjectures among ourselves as to our destination....

We marched on, however, until we arrived at the ferry, where we immediately embarked on board the batteaux and were conveyed safely to New York, where we were landed about three o'clock in the morning, nothing against our inclinations.

The next day the British showed themselves to be in possession of our works upon the island by firing upon some of our boats passing to and from Governor's Island. Our regiment was employed during this day in throwing up a sort of breastwork at their alarm post upon the wharves facing the enemy, composed of spars and logs and filling the space between with the materials of which the wharves were composed—old broken junk bottles, flint stones, etc., which, had a cannon ball passed through, would have chanced to kill five men where the ball would one. But the enemy did not see fit to molest us.

We stayed several days longer in the city, when one morning we discovered that a small frigate had advanced up and was lying above Governor's Island, close under the Long Island shore. Several other ships had come up and were lying just below the town. They seemed to portend evil. In the evening, just at dark, our regiment was ordered to march to Turtle Bay, a place about four miles distant on the East River, where were a large warehouse or two, called then the King's stores, built for the storing of marine stores belonging to the government before the war. There was at this time about twenty-five hundred barrels of flour in those storehouses, and it was conjectured that the design of the aforementioned frigate, or rather the officers and crew of her was to seize on this flour.

We were, therefore, ordered to secure it before the British should have an opportunity to lay their unhallowed hands upon it. We arrived at the place about midnight, and by sunrise or a little after had secured the whole of it by rolling it up a steep bank and piling it behind a ledge of rocks....

We continued here some days to guard the flour. We were forbidden by our officers to use any of it, except our daily allowance. We used, however, to purloin some of it to eat and exchange with the inhabitants for milk, sauce, and such small matters as we could get for it of them....

One evening while lying here, we heard a heavy cannonade at the city, and before dark saw four of the enemy's ships that had passed the town and were coming up the East River. They anchored just below us.

These ships were the *Phoenix* of forty-four guns; the *Roebuck,* of forty-four; the *Rose* of thirty-two; and another, the name of which I have forgotten. Half of our regiment was sent off under the command of our major to man something that were called "lines," although they were nothing more than a ditch dug along on the bank of the river with the dirt thrown out towards the water. They stayed in these lines during the night and returned to camp in the morning unmolested.

The other half of the regiment went the next night under the command of the lieutenant colonel upon the like errand. We arrived at the lines about dark and were ordered to leave our packs in a copse wood under a guard and go into the lines without them. What was the cause of this piece of wise policy I never knew, but I knew the effects of it, which was that I never saw my knapsack from that day to this, nor did any of the rest of our party unless they came across them by accident in our retreat. We "manned the lines" and lay quite as unmolested during the whole night as Samson did the half of his in the city of Gaza and upon about as foolish a business, though there was some difference in our getting away: we did not go off in so much triumph quite as he did. We had a chain of sentinels quite up the river, for four or five miles in length. At an interval of every half hour, they passed the watchword to each other, "All is well." I heard the British on board their shipping answer, "We will alter your tune before tomorrow night." And they were as good as their word for once.

It was quite a dark night, and at daybreak [September 15] the first thing that "saluted our eyes" was all the four ships at anchor with springs upon their cables and within musket shot of us. The *Phoenix* lying a little quartering and her stern toward me, I could read her name as distinctly as though I had been directly under her stern. What is the meaning of all this, thought I, what is coming foreward now?

They appeared to be very busy on shipboard, but we lay still and showed our good breeding by not interfering with them as they were strangers, and we knew not but they were bashful withal.

As soon as it was fairly light, we saw their boats coming out of a creek or cove on the Long Island side of the water, filled with British soldiers. When they came to the edge of the tide, they formed their boats in line. They continued to augment their forces from the island until they appeared like a large clover field in full bloom. And now was coming on the famous Kip's Bay affair, which has been criticized so much by the historians of the Revolution....

It was on a Sabbath morning, the day in which the British were always employed about their deviltry if possible, because they said, they had the prayers of the church on that day. We lay very quiet in our ditch waiting their motions till the sun was an hour or two high. We heard a cannonade at the city, but our attention was drawn toward our own guests. But they being a little dilatory in their operations, I stepped into an old warehouse which stood close by me with the door open inviting me in and sat down upon a stool. The floor was strewed with papers which had in some former period been used in the concerns of the house but were then lying in "woeful confusion." I was very demurely perusing these papers when all of a sudden there came such a peal of thunder from the British shipping that I thought my head would go with the sound. I made a frog's leap for the ditch and lay as still as I possibly could and began to consider which part of my carcass was to go first. The British played their parts well; indeed they had nothing to hinder them. We kept the lines till they were almost leveled upon us, when our officers, seeing we could make no resistance and no orders coming from any superior officer and that we must soon be entirely exposed to the rake of their guns, gave the order to leave the lines.

In retreating we had to cross a level, clear spot of ground forty or fifty rods wide, exposed to the whole of the enemy's fire, and they gave it to us in prime order. The grapeshot and langrage flew merrily, which served to quicken our motions. When I had gotten a little out of the reach of their combustibles, I found myself in company with one who was a neighbor of mine when at home and one other man belonging to our regiment. Where the rest of them were I knew not.

We went into a house by the highway in which were two women and some small children, all crying most bitterly. We asked the women if they had any spirits in the house. They placed a case bottle of rum upon the table and bid us help ourselves. We each of us drank a glass and bidding them good-by betook ourselves to the highway again. We had not gone far before we saw a party of men, apparently hurrying on in the same direction with ourselves. We endeavored hard to overtake them, but on approaching them we found that they were not of our way of thinking: they were Hessians. We immediately altered our course and took the main road leading to King's Bridge [main evacuation route]. We had not been on this road before we saw another party, just ahead of us, whom we knew to be Americans. Just as we overtook these, they were fired upon by a party of British from a cornfield and all was immediately in confusion again. I believe the enemy's party was small, but our people were all militia, and the demons of fear and disorder seemed to take full possess of all and everything on that day.

When I came to the spot where the militia were fired upon, the ground was literally covered with arms, knapsacks, staves, coats, hats, and old oil flasks.... All I picked up of the plunder was a block-tin syringe, which afterwards helped to procure me a Thanksgiving dinner. Myself and the man whom I mentioned as belonging to our company were all who were in company at this time, the other man having gone on with those who were fired upon; they did not tarry to let the grass grow much under their feet.

We had to advance slowly, for my comrade having been some time unwell was now so overcome by heat, hunger, and fatigue that he became suddenly and violently sick. I took his musket and endeavored to encourage him on. He was, as I before observed a nigh neighbor of mine when at home and I was loath to leave him behind, although I was anxious to find the main part of the regiment if possible before night, for I thought that that part of it which was not in the lines was in a body somewhere. We soon came in sight of a large party of Americans ahead of us who appeared to have come into this road by some other route. We were within sight of them when they were fired upon by another party of the enemy. They returned but a very few shots and then scampered off as fast as their legs would carry them. When we came to the ground they had occupied, the same display of lumber presented itself as at their other place. We here found a wounded man and some of his comrades endeavoring to get him off. I stopped to assist them in constructing a sort of litter to lay him upon, when my sick companion growing impatient moved on, and as soon as we had placed the wounded man upon the litter I followed him.

While I was here, one or two of our regiment came up and we went on together. We had proceeded but a short distance, however, before we found our retreat cut off by a part of the enemy stretched across the island. I immediately quitted the road and went into the fields, where there happened to be a small spot of boggy land covered with low bushes and weeds. Into these I ran and squatting down concealed myself from their sight. Several of the British came so near to me that I could see the buttons on their clothes. They, however, soon withdrew and left the coast clear for me again. I then came out of my covert and went on, but what had become of my sick comrade or the rest of my companions I knew not. I still kept the sick man's musket. I was unwilling to leave it, for it was his own property and I knew he valued it highly and I had a great esteem for him. I had indeed enough to do to take care of my own concerns; it was exceeding hot weather, and I was faint, having slept but very little the preceding night, nor had I eaten a mouthful of victuals for more than twenty-four hours.

I waddled on as well and as fast as I could, and soon came up with a number of men at a small brook, where they had stopped to drink and rest themselves a few moments.... Leaving them I went on again and directly came to a foul place in the road, where the soldiers had taken down the fence to pass into the fields. I passed across the corner of one field and through a gap in a cross fence into another. Here I found a number of men resting under the trees and bushes in the fences. Almost the first I saw, after passing the gap in the fence, was my sick friend. I was exceeding glad to find him, for I had but little hope of ever seeing him again. He was sitting near the fence with his head between his knees. I tapped him upon the shoulder and asked him to get up and go on with me. "No," said he, at the same time regarding me with a most pitiful look, "I must die here." I endeavored to argue the case with him but all to no purpose; he insisted upon dying there. I told him he should not die there nor anywhere else that day if I could help it, and at length with more persuasion and some force I succeeded in getting him upon his feet again and to moving on.

There happened just at this instant a considerable shower of rain, which wet us all to the skin, being very thinly clad. We, however, continued to move forward, although but slowly. After proceeding about half a mile we came to a place where our people had begun to make a stand. A number, say two or three hundred, had collected here, having been stopped by the artillery officers; they had two or three fieldpieces fixed and fitted for action, in case the British came on, which was momentarily expected. I and my comrades (for I had found another of our company when I found my sick man) were stopped here, a sentinel being placed in the road to prevent our going any further.

I felt very much chagrined to be thus hindered from proceeding, as I felt confident that our regiment or some considerable part of it was not far ahead, unless they had been more unlucky than I had. I remonstrated with the officer who detained us. I told him that our regiment was just ahead. He asked me how I knew that. I could not tell him, but I told him I had a sick man with me who was wet and would die if exposed all night to the damp cold air, hoping by this to move his compassion, but it would not do. He was inexorable....

I saw but little chance of escaping from this very humane gentleman by fair means, so I told my two companions to stick by me and keep together and we would get from them by some means or other during the evening.

It was now almost sundown and the air quite chilly after the shower, and we were as wet as water could make us. I was really afraid my sick man would die in earnest. I had not stayed there long waiting for an opportunity to escape, before one offered.

There came to the sentinel I suppose an old acquaintance of his, with a canteen containing some sort of spirits. After drinking himself, he gave it to the sentinel who took a large pull upon it. They then fell into conversation together, but soon taking a hare from the same hound, it put them into quite a "talkative mood." I kept my eyes upon them and when I thought I saw a chance of getting from them, I gave my companions a wink and we passed by the sentinel without his noticing us at all. A walk of a very few rods concealed us from his view by a turn in the road and some bushes, and thus we escaped....

We went on a little distance, but had not gone far when we came up with the regiment, resting themselves on the "cold ground" after the fatigues of the day. Our company all appeared to rejoice to see us, thinking we were killed or prisoners. I was sincerely glad to see them, for I was once more among friends or at least acquaintance. Several of the regiment were missing, among whom was our major. He was a fine man and his loss was much regretted by the men of the regiment. We were the last who came up, all the others who were missing were either killed or taken prisoners....

We lay that night upon the ground which the regiment occupied when I came up with it. The next day, in the forenoon, the enemy, as we expected, followed us "hard up" and were advancing through a level field. Our Rangers and some few other light troops ... were in waiting for them. Seeing them advancing, the Rangers &c. concealed themselves in a deep gully overgrown with bushes. Upon the western verge of this defile was a post and rail fence and over that the afore-mentioned field. Our people let the enemy advance until they arrived at the fence, when they arose and poured in a volley upon them.... The British gave back and our people advanced into the field. The action soon became warm.

Our regiment was now ordered into the field, and we arrived on the ground just as the retreating enemy were entering a thick wood, a circumstance as disagreeable to them as it was agreeable to us at that period of the war. We soon came to action with them. The troops engaged, being reinforced by our regiment, kept them still retreating until they found shelter under the cannon of some of their shipping lying in the North River.

We remained on the battleground till nearly sunset, expecting the enemy to attack us again, but they showed no such inclination that day. The men were very much fatigued and faint, having had nothing to eat for forty-eight hours; at least the greater part were in this condition, and I among the rest....

We now returned to camp, if camp it was; our tent held the whole regiment and might have held ten millions more. When we arrived on the ground we had occupied previous to going into action, we found that our invalids, consisting of the sick, the lame, and the lazy, had obtained some fresh beef. Where the commissaries found the beef or the men found the commissaries in this time of confusion I know not, nor did I stop to ask. They were broiling the beef on small sticks in Indian style round blazing fires made of dry chestnut rails. The meat when cooked was as black as a coal on the outside and as raw on the inside as it had not been near the fire. "I asked no questions for conscience's sake," but fell to and helped myself to a feast of this raw beef, without bread or salt....

A circumstance occurred on the evening after this action which, although trifling in its nature, excited in me feelings which I shall never forget. When we came off the field we brought away a man who had been shot dead upon the spot, and after we had refreshed ourselves we proceeded to bury him. Having provided a grave, which was near a gentleman's country seat we proceeded, just in the dusk of evening, to commit the poor man, then far from friends and relatives, to the bosom of his Mother Earth. Just as we had laid him in the grave in as decent a posture as existing circumstances would admit, there came from the house towards the grave two young ladies who appeared to be sisters.

As they approached the grave, the soldiers immediately made way for them with those feelings of respect which beauty and modesty combined seldom fail to produce, more especially when as in this instance accompanied by piety. Upon arriving at the head of the grave, they stopped and with their arms around each other's neck stooped forward and looked into it, and with a sweet pensiveness of countenance might have warmed the heart of a misogynist, asked if we were going to put the earth upon his naked face. Being answered in the affirmative, one of them took a fine white gauze handkerchief from her neck and desired that it might be spread upon his face, tears at the same time flowing down their cheeks. After the grave was filled up, they retired to the house in the same manner they came. Although the dead soldier had no acquaintance present (for there were none at his burial who knew him) yet he had mourners and females too. Worthy young ladies! You and such as you are deserving the regard of the greatest of men. What sisters, what wives, what mothers and what neighbors would you make! Such a sight as those ladies afforded at that time and on that occasion was worthy and doubtless received the attention of angels....

We remained here till sometime in the month of October without anything very material transpiring, excepting starvation and that had by this time become quite a secondary matter; hard duty and nakedness were considered the prime evils, for the reader will recollect that we lost all our clothing in the Kip's Bay affair.... It now began to be cool weather, especially the nights. To have to lie as I did almost every night on the cold and often wet ground without a blanket and with nothing but this summer clothing was tedious. I have often while on guard lain on one side until the upper side smarted with cold, then turned that side down to the place warmed by my body and let the other take its turn at smarting, while the one on the ground warmed. Thus alternately turning for four or six hours till called upon to go on sentry, as the soldiers term it, and when relieved from a tour of two long hours at that business and returned to the guard again, have had to go through the operation of freezing and thawing for four or six hours more...

Sometime in October, the British landed at Frog's Neck, or Point, and by their motions seemed to threaten to cut off our retreat to York Island. We were thereupon ordered to leave the island. We crossed King's Bridge and directed our course toward the White Plains.... We arrived at the White Plains just at dawn of day, tired and faint, encamped on the plains a few days and then removed to the hills in the rear of the plains.

When we arrived at the camp the troops were all parading. Upon inquiry we found that the British were advancing upon us.... We packed up our things, which was easily done for we had but a trifle to pack, and fell into the ranks. Before we were ready to march, the battle had begun. Our regiment then marched off, crossed a considerable stream of water which crosses the plain, and formed behind a stone wall in company with several other regiments and waited the approach of the enemy.

They were not far distant, at least that part of them with which we were quickly after engaged.... Finding ourselves flanked and in danger of being surrounded, we were compelled to make a hasty retreat from the stone wall.... We did not come in contact with the enemy again that day, and just at night we fell back to our encampment. In the course of the afternoon, the British took possession of a hill on the right of our encampment, which had in the early part of the day been occupied by some of the New York troops. This hill overlooked the one upon which we were and was not more than half or three fourths of a mile distant. The enemy had several pieces of field artillery upon this hill and, as might be expected, entertained us with their music all the evening. We entrenched ourselves where we now lay, expecting another attack. But the British were very civil, and indeed they generally were after they had received a check from Brother Jonathan for any of their rude actions. They seldom repeated them, at least not till the affair that caused the reprimand had ceased in some measure to be remembered.

During the night we remained in our new-made trenches, the ground of which was in many parts springy. In that part where I happened to be stationed, the water before morning was nearly over shoes, which caused many of us to take violent colds by being exposed upon the wet ground after a profuse perspiration. I was one who felt the effects of it and was the next day sent back to the baggage to get well again, if I could, for it was left to my own exertions to do it and no other assistance was afforded me. I was not alone in misery; there were a number in the same circumstances.

When I arrived at the baggage, which was not more than a mile or two, I had the canopy of heaven for my hospital and the ground for my hammock. I found a spot where the dry leaves had collected between the knolls. I made up a bed of these and nestled in it, having no other friend present but the sun to smile upon me. I had nothing to eat or drink, not even water, and was unable to go after myself, for I was sick indeed. In the evening one of my messmates found me out and soon after brought me some boiled hog's flesh (it was not pork) and turnips, without either bread or salt. I could not eat it, but I felt obliged to him notwithstanding. He did all he could do. He gave me the best he had to give, and had to steal that, poor fellow. Necessity drove him to do it to satisfy the cravings of his own hunger as well as to assist a fellow sufferer.

The British soon after this, left the White Plains and passed the Hudson into New Jersey. We likewise fell back to New Castle and Wright's Mills. Here a number of our sick were sent to Norwalk in Connecticut to recruit. I was sent with them as a nurse.... I arrived at camp with the rest, where we remained ... undergoing hunger, cold, and fatigue until the twenty-fifth day of December, 1776, when I was discharged, at Philipse Manor in the State of New York near Hudson's River.

Here ends my first campaign. I learned something of a soldier's life, enough, I thought, to keep me at home for the future. Indeed I was then fully determined to rest easy with the knowledge I had acquired in the affairs of the army.

The spring of 1777 arrived. In the month of April, as the weather warmed, the young men began to enlist.... I put my name to enlisting indentures for the last time.... Just at this time the British landed in Connecticut, and marched twenty miles into the country, where they burnt the town of Danbury with all the public stores it contained, which were considerable, among which was all the clothing of our regiment.

The militia were generally turned out and sent to settle the account with them. The newly enlisted soldiers were with the militia.... We had some pretty severe scratches with them; killed some, wounded some, and took some prisoners. The remainder reached their shipping, embarked, and cleared out for New York.... We likewise returned home, with the loss of three men belonging to the town, one of whom was an enlisted soldier.

Soon after the above transaction, we had orders to join our regiment.... We marched to Peekskill, on the Hudson River, and encamped in the edge of the Highlands, at a place called Old Orchard. Here we were tormented by the whippoorwills. A potent enemy! Says the reader. Well, a potent enemy they were, particularly to our rest at night. They would begin their imposing music in the twilight and continue it till ten or eleven o'clock, and commence again before the dawn, when they would be in a continual roar. No man could get a wink of sleep during the serenade, which, in the short nights in the month of May, was almost the whole of the night....

I was soon after this transaction ordered off, in company with about four hundred others of the Connecticut forces to a set of old barracks, a mile or two distance in the Highlands, to be inoculated with the smallpox. We arrived at and cleaned out the barracks, and after two or three days received the infection, which was on the last day of May. We had a guard of Massachusetts troops to attend us. Our hospital stores were deposited in a farmer's barn in the vicinity of our quarters.

One day about noon, the farmer's house took fire and was totally consumed. Our officers would not let any of the inoculated men go near the fire, and the guard had enough to do to save the barn. I had the smallpox favorably as did the rest, generally.

In the latter part of the month of June, I was ordered off in a detachment of about a hundred men to join two regiments of New York troops which belonged to our brigade.... We arrived upon the lines and joined the other corps which was already there. No one who has ever been upon such duty as those advanced parties have to perform, can form any adequate idea of the trouble, fatigue and dangers which they have to encounter. Their whole time is spent in marches, especially night marches, watching, starving, and in cold weather freezing and sickness.... We remained on this hard and fatiguing duty about six weeks.... Our troops, not long after this, marched to join the main army in Pennsylvania....

When I arrived at camp it was just dark, the troops were all preparing for a march. Their provisions (what they had) were all cooked, and their arms and ammunition strictly inspected and all deficiencies supplied. Early in the evening we marched in the direction of Philadelphia. We naturally concluded there was something serious in the wind. We marched slowly all night....

About daybreak our advanced guard and the British outposts came in contact. The curs began to bark first and then the bulldogs. Our brigade moved off to the right into the fields. We saw a body of the enemy drawn up behind a rail fence on our right flank; we immediately formed in line and advanced upon them. Our orders were not to fire till we could see the buttons upon their clothes, but they were so coy that they would not give us an opportunity to be so curious, for they hid their clothes in fire and smoke before we had either time or leisure to examine their buttons. They soon fell back and we advanced, when the action became general. The enemy were driven quite through their camp. They left their kettles, in which they were cooking their breakfasts, on the fires, and some of their garments were lying on the ground, which the owners had not time to put on.

Affairs went on well for some time. The enemy were retreating before us, until the first division that was engaged had expended their ammunition. Some of the men unadvisedly calling out that their ammunition was spent, the enemy were so near that they overheard them, when they first made a stand and then returned upon our people, who for want of ammunition and reinforcements, were obliged in their turn to retreat, which ultimately resulted in the rout of the whole army [the battle of Germantown]....

I had now to travel the rest of the day, after marching all the day and night before and fighting all the morning. I had eaten nothing since the noon of the preceding day, nor did I eat a morsel till the forenoon of the next day, and I needed rest as much as victuals. I was tormented with thirst all the morning, fighting being warm work....

After the army collected again and recovered from their panic, we were kept marching and countermarching, starving, and freezing, nothing else happening, although that was enough, until we encamped at a place called the White Marsh, about twelve miles to the northward of Philadelphia.... Our two Connecticut regiments were ordered off to defend the forts on the Delaware River below the city.

It was a hard and fatiguing job, until Fort Mifflin was destroyed by British bombardment and Joseph with his unit was evacuated.

Later we arrived early in the morning at a pretty village called Milltown or Mount Holly. Here we waited for the troops to come up. I was as near starved with hunger as ever I wish to be. I strolled into a large yard where was a plenty of geese, turkeys, ducks, and barn-door fowls. I obtained a piece of an ear of Indian corn, and seating myself on a pile of boards, began throwing the corn to the fowls, which soon drew a fine battalion of them about me.... I took up one only, wrung off its head, dressed and washed it in the stream, seasoned it with some of my salt [he had taken from a barrel] and stalked into the first house that fell in my way, invited myself into the kitchen, took down the gridiron and put my fowl to cooking upon the coals. The women of the house were all the time going and coming to and from the room. They looked at me but said nothing. "They asked me no questions and I told them no lies." When my game was sufficiently broiled, I took it by the hind leg and made my exit from the house with as little ceremony as I had made my entrance. When I got into the street I devoured it after a very short grace and felt ... refreshed.

After a few days we crossed the Schuylkill in a cold and snowy night [December 12] upon a bridge of wagons set end to end and joined together by boards and planks.... We at last settled down at a place called "the Gulf." While we lay there, there was a Continental Thanksgiving ordered by Congress, and as the Army had all the cause in the world to be particularly thankful, if not for being well off, at least that it was no worse, we were ordered to participate in it. We had nothing to eat for two or three days previous except what the trees of the fields and forests afforded us. But we must now have what Congress said: a sumptuous Thanksgiving to close the year of high living we had now nearly seen brought to a close.

Well, to add something extraordinary to our present stock of provisions, our country, ever mindful of its suffering army, opened her sympathizing heart so wide on this occasion as to give us something to make the world stare.... You cannot guess, be you as much of a Yankee as you will. I will tell you: it gave each and every man Half a gill of rice and a tablespoon full of vinegar!

After we had made sure of this extraordinary superabundant donation, we were ordered out to attend a meeting and hear a sermon delivered upon the happy occasion. We accordingly went, for we could not help it. I heard a sermon, a "Thanksgiving" sermon, what sort of one I do not know now, nor did I at the time I heard it.... I remember the text, like an attentive lad at church...."And the soldiers said unto him, 'and what shall we do?' And he caid unto them, 'Do violence to no man, nor accuse anyone falsely.'" The preacher ought to have added the remainder of the sentence to have made it complete, "and be content with your wages." But that would not do; it would be too apropos. However, he heard it as soon as the service was over; it was shouted from a hundred tongues....

The army continued at and near the Gulf for some days after which we marched for Valley Forge in order to take up our winter quarters. We were now in a truly forlorn condition,—no clothing, no provisions, and as disheartened as need be. We arrived, however, at our destination a few days before Christmas.

For a short time he was assigned to a wagonmaster and supply depot and engaged in foraging. Upon returning to his regiment:

I was kept constantly, when off other duty, engaged in learning the Baron de Steuben's new Prussian exercise. It was a continual drill.

About this time I was sent off from camp in a detachment consisting of about three thousand men, with four field-pieces, under the command of the young General Lafayette. We marched to Barren Hill, about twelve miles from Philadelphia [May 18, 1778]. Washington heard that Howe was going to leave for New York. There are crossroads upon this hill, a branch of which leads to the city. We halted here, placed our guards, sent off our scouting parties, and waited for—I know not what. A company of about a hundred Indians, from some northern tribe[Oneidas], joined us here. There were three or four young Frenchmen with them. The Indians were stout-looking fellows.... There was upon the hill, and just where we were lying, an old church built of stone, entirely divested of all its entrails. The Indians were amusing themselves and the soldiers by shooting with their bows, in and about the church. I observed something in a corner of the roof which did not appear to belong to the building, and desired an Indian who was standing near me to shoot an arrow at it. He did so and it proved to be a cluster of bats; I should think there were nearly a bushel of them, all hanging upon one another. The house was immediately alive with them, and it was likewise instantly full of Indians and soldiers. The poor bats fared hard; it was sport for all hands. They killed I know not how many, but there was a great slaughter among them. I never saw so many bats before nor since in my whole life put all together.

The next day I was one of a guard to protect the horses belonging to the detachment. They were in a meadow of six or eight acres, entirely surrounded by tall trees....

Just at the dawn of day the officers' waiters came, almost breathless, after the horses. Upon inquiring for the cause of the unusual hurry, we were told that the British were advancing upon us in our rear.... We helped the waiters to catch their horses and immediately returned to the main body of the detachment.

We found the troops all under arms and in motion preparing for an onset. Those of the troops belonging to our brigade were put into the churchyard, which was enclosed by a wall of stone and lime about breast high, a good defense against musketry but poor against artillery. I began to think I should soon have some better sport than killing bats. But our commander found that the enemy was too strong to be engaged in the position we then occupied. He therefore wisely ordered a retreat from this place to the Schuylkill, where we might choose any position that we pleased, having ragged woody hills in our rear and the river in front.

It was about three miles to the river. The weather was exceedingly warm, and I was in the rear platoon of the detachment except two platoons of General Washington's Guards. The quick motion in front kept the rear on a constant trot. Two pieces of artillery were in front and two in the rear. The enemy had nearly surrounded us by the time our retreat commenced, but the road we were in was very favorable for us, it being for the most part and especially the first part of it through small woods and copses. When I was about halfway to the river I saw the right wing of the enemy through a lawn about a half mile distant, but they were too late. Besides they made a blunder here. They saw our rear guard with the two fieldpieces in its front, and thinking it the front of the detachment, they closed in to secure their prey, but when they had sprung their net they found that they had not a single bird under it.

We crossed the Schuylkill in good order ... formed and prepared for action, and waited for them to attack us; but we saw no more of them that time, for before we had reached the river the alarm guns were fired in our camp and the whole army was immediately in motion. The British, fearing that they should be outnumbered in their turn, directly set their faces for Philadelphia and set off in as much or more haste than we had left Barren Hill.

If anyone asks why we did not stay on Barren Hill till the British came up, and have taken and given a few bloody noses—all I have to say in answer is, that the General well knew what he was about; he was not deficient in either courage or conduct, and that was well known to all in the Revolutionary army.

The following summer, as the British were retreating from Philadelphia and combining their forces in New York, action was in progress as American militia and Continental detachments attacked the hundreds of wagons, carriages and carts strung out over twelve miles. An attack was planned but seemed to be going awry, as General Lee ordered a retreat. Private Joseph Martin had been in the rear of the advanced corps when the order had come to retreat. Said he:

Grating as this order was to our feelings, we were obliged to comply. We had not retreated far before we came to a defile, a muddy, sloughy brook. While the artillery were passing this place, we sat down by the roadside. In a few minutes, the Commander-in-Chief and suite crossed the road just where we were sitting. I heard him ask our officers, "by whose order the troops were retreating," and being answered "by General Lee's," he said something, but, as he was moving forward all the time this was passing, he was too far off for me to hear distinctly.

He rode on and took an observation of the advancing enemy. He remained there some time on his old English charger, while the shot from the British artillery were rending up the earth all around him.

After he had taken a view of the enemy, he returned and ordered the two Connecticut brigades to make a stand at a fence, in order to keep the enemy in check while the artillery and other troops crossed the before mentioned defile....

When we had secured our retreat, the artillery formed a line of pieces upon a long piece of elevated ground. Our detachment formed directly in front of the artillery, as a covering party, so far below the declivity of the hill that the pieces could play over our heads. And here we waited the approach of the enemy, should he see fit to attack us.

Washington stemmed the retreat. Lafayette was charmed by the way in which he rode "all along the lines amid the shouts of the soldiers, cheering them by his voice and example and restoring to our standard the fortunes of the fight." Upon the New Englanders, whom Washington had placed at the fence, fell the brunt of the British assault. Joseph Martin, who had not been under fire since Germantown, was becoming a seasoned soldier; he and his comrades now reaped the benefits of Steuben's training.

A sharp conflict ensued; these troops maintained their ground until the whole force of the enemy that could be brought to bear had charged upon them through the fence, and after being overpowered ... and the platoon officers had given the orders ... to leave the fence, they had to force them to retreat so eager were they to be revenged....

As soon as the troops had left this ground, the British planted their cannon upon this place and began a violent attack upon the artillery and our detachment, but neither could be routed. The cannonade continued for some time without intermission, when the British pieces being mostly disabled, they reluctantly crawled back from the height which they occupied and hid themselves from our sight.

Before the cannonade had commenced, a part of the right wing of the British army had advanced across a low meadow and brook and occupied an orchard on our left....

After the British artillery had fallen back ... we were immediately ordered from our old detachment and joined another, the whole composing a corps of about five hundred men. We ... marched toward the enemy's right wing, which was in the orchard, and kept concealed from them as long as possible by keeping behind the bushes. When we could no longer keep ourselves concealed, we marched into the open fields and formed our line. The British immediately formed and began to retreat to the main body of their army. Colonel Cilly, finding that we were not likely to overtake the enemy before they reached the main body of their army, on account of fences and other obstructions, ordered three or four platoons from the right of our corps to pursue and attack them and thus keep them in play till the rest of the detachment could come up.

I was in this party. We pursued without order. As I passed through the orchard I saw a number of the enemy lying under the trees killed by our fieldpiece....

We overtook the enemy just as they were entering ... the meadow which was rather bushy.... They were retreating in line, though in some disorder. I singled out a man and took my aim directly between his shoulders (they were divested of their packs); he was a good mark, being a broad-shouldered fellow, but what became of him I know not; the fire and smoke hid him from my sight. One thing I know ... I took as deliberate aim at him as ever I did at any game in my life....

By this time our whole party had arrived, and the British had obtained a position that suited them ... for they returned our fire in good earnest, and we played the second part of the same tune. They occupied a much higher piece of ground than we did and had a small piece of artillery, which the soldiers called a "grasshopper." We had no artillery with us. The first shot they gave us from this piece cut off the thigh bone of a captain, just above the knee, and the whole heel of a private in the rear of him.

We gave it to poor Sawney (for they were Scotch troops) so hot that he was forced to fall back and leave the ground they occupied. When our commander saw them retreating and nearly joined with their main body, he shouted "Come, my boys, reload your pieces and we will give them a set-off!" We did so and gave them the parting salute and the firing on both sides ceased.

We then laid ourselves under the fences and bushes to take breath; for we had need of it.... Fighting is hot work in cool weather, much more so in such weather as it was on the twenty-eighth of June, 1778....

As soon as our party had ceased firing, it began in the center and then upon our right, but as I was not in that part of the army, I had

196

no "adventure" in it, but the firing was continued in one part or the other of the field the whole afternoon. The enemy retreated about midnight, leaving behind them all the marks of disgrace and precipitancy....

One little incident happened during the heat of the cannonade, which I was eyewitness to, and which I think would be unpardonable not to mention. A woman whose husband belonged to the artillery ... attended with her husband at the piece the whole time. While in the act of reaching a cartridge and having one of her feet as far before the other as she could step, a cannon shot from the enemy passed directly between her legs, without doing any other damage than carrying away all the lower part of her petticoat. Looking at it with apparent unconcern, she observed that it was lucky it did not pass a little higher, for in that case it might have carried away something else, and continued her occupation.

The next day after the action ... we joined our regiments in line and marched for Hudson's River ... to King's Ferry, where we crossed the Hudson. Each brigade furnished its own ferrymen to carry the troops across. I was one of the men from our brigade.... Nearly the last trip the bateau that I was in made, while crossing the river empty, a large sturgeon (a fish in which this river abounds) seven or eight feet in length, in his gambolings, sprang directly into the boat without doing any other damage than breaking down one of the seats of the boat. We crossed and took in our freight and recrossed, landed the men and our prize, gave orders to our several messmates as to the disposal of it and proceeded on our business till the whole of the brigade had crossed the river, which was not long, we working with new energy in expectation of having something to eat when we had done our job. We then repaired to our messes to partake of the bounty of Providence, which we had so unexpectedly received. I found my share, which was about the seventh part of it, cooked, that is, it was boiled in salt and water and I fell to it and ate, perhaps, a pound and a half.

And now there was to be a material change in my circumstances, which, in the long run, was much in my favor. There was a small corps to be raised.... These men were called "Sappers and Miners," to be attached to the engineer's department. I was accordingly transferred to this corps and bid a farewell forever to my old comrades.... I immediately went off with this captain and the other men drafted from our

brigade, and joined the corps in an old meetinghouse at the Peekskill....
I was appointed a sergeant in this corps, which was as high an office as
I ever obtained in the army....

On the tenth of May Lafayette rode into Morristown after
more than a year's absence. He brought good news: six French
ships of the line and six thousand troops were en route to Rhode
Island with orders to cooperate in a joint operation to take New
York and its defenders.

We now fell back a few miles and encamped ... at a place called
Philipse Manor. We then went to making preparations to lay siege to
New York. We made fascines and gabions. The fascines (pronounced
fa-sheens) are bundles of brush bound snugly together, cut off straight
at each end; they are of different lengths, from five to twelve feet. We
now expected soon to lay close siege to New York. Our Sappers and Miners were constantly employed with the engineers in front of the army,
making preparations for the siege.

One day I was sent down towards the enemy with a corporal and
twelve men, upon a reconnoitering expedition, the engineers having
heard that there was a party of Refugees, or Cowboys, somewhere not
far from their premises. We set off upon our expedition early in the
afternoon and went as far as directed by our officers, but saw no enemy.
We stopped here awhile and rested ourselves. When we had refreshed
ourselves, we thought it a pity to return ... and report that we had seen
nothing. We therefore agreed unanimously to stretch our orders a trifle
and go a little further. We were in the fields; about a mile ahead were
three or four houses at which I and some others of our party had been
before. Between us and the houses there was a narrow wood, mostly of
young growth and quite thick. We concluded to go as far as the houses
and if we could not hear anything of the Cowboys there, to return contented to camp.

Agreeably to our plan we set out, and had but just entered the
wood when we found ourselves flanked by thirty or forty Cowboys, who
gave us a hearty welcome to their assumed territories and we returned
the compliment, but a kind Providence protected every man of us from
injury although we were within ten rods of the enemy. They immediately rushed from their covert, before we had time to reload our pieces;

consequently, we had no other alternative but to get off as well and as fast as we could. They did not fire upon us again, but gave us chase, for what reason I know not. I was soon in the rear of my party, which had to cross a fence composed of old posts and rails with trees plashed down upon it.

When I arrived at the fence, the foremost of the enemy was not more than six or eight rods distant, all running after us helter-skelter, without any order. My men had all crossed the fence in safety, I alone was to suffer. I endeavored to get over the fence across two or three of the trees that were plashed down. Somehow or other, I blundered and fell over, and caught my right foot in a place where a tree had split partly from the stump. Here I hung as fast as though my foot had been in the stocks, my ham lying across the butt of another tree, while my body hung down perpendicularly. I could barely reach the ground with my hands, and, of course, could make but little exertion to clear myself from the limbs.

The commander of the enemy came to the fence and the first compliment I received from him was a stroke with his hanger across my leg, just under or below the kneepan, which laid the bone bare. I could see him through the fence and knew him. He was, when we were boys, one of my most familiar playmates, was with me, a messmate, in the campaign of 1776, had enlisted during the war in 1777, but sometime before this, had deserted to the enemy, having been coaxed off by an old harridan, to whose daughter he had taken a fancy. The old hag of a mother, living in the vicinity of the British, easily inveigled him away. He was a smart active fellow and soon got command of a gang of Refugee plunderers. When he had had his hack at my shins, I began to think it was "neck or nothing," and making one desperate effort, I cleared my foot by leaving my shoe behind, before he could have the second stroke at me. He knew me as well as I did him, for as soon as he saw me clear of the fence and out of the reach of his sword, he called me by name, and told me to surrender myself and he would give me good quarters. Thought I, you will wait till I ask them of you. I sprang up and run till I came to my party, who were about a hundred rods ahead, waiting to see how I should come off.

The enemy never fired a shot at me all the time I was running from them, although nearly the whole of their party was standing on the other side of the fence when I started from it. Whether his conscience smote him and he prevented them from firing at me, or whether they were unprepared, not having had time to reload their pieces in their pursuit of us, or from what other cause, I know not....

Instead of aiming their strategy at New York, Washington and Rochambeau decided to join Admiral DeGrasse in advancing against the British in the Chesapeake. Joseph states:

We prepared to move down and pay our old acquaintance, the British at Yorktown, a visit. I doubt not but their wish was not to have so many of us come at once, as their accommodations were rather scanty. They thought, "The fewer the better the cheer." We thought, "The more, the merrier." We had come a long way to see them and were unwilling to be put off with excuses. We thought the present time quite as convenient (at least for us) as any future time could be, and we accordingly persisted, hoping, that as they pretended to be a very courtly people, they would have the politeness to come out and meet us, which would greatly shorten the time ... spent in the visit and save themselves and us much labor and trouble....

We soon arrived and encamped in their neighborhood, without let or molestation. Our Miners lay about a mile and a half of their works, in open view of them.... We now began to make preparations for laying close siege to the enemy. We had holed him and nothing remained but to dig him out. Accordingly, after taking every precaution to prevent his escape, [we] settled our guards, provided fascines and gabions, made platforms for the batteries, to be laid down when needed, brought on our battering pieces ammunition, &c....

One-third part of all the troops were put in requisition to be employed in opening the trenches. A third part of our Sappers and Miners were ordered out this night to assist the engineers in laying out the works. It was a very dark and rainy night. However, we repaired to the place and began by following the engineers and laying laths of pine wood end to end upon the line marked out by the officers for the trenches.

We had not proceeded far ... before the engineers ordered us to desist and remain where we were and be sure not to straggle a foot from the spot while they were absent from us. In a few minutes after their

200

departure, there came a man alone to us, having on a surtout, as we conjectured (it being exceedingly dark), and inquired for the engineers. We now began to be a little jealous of our safety, being alone and without arms and within forty rods of the British trenches. The stranger inquired what troops we were, talked familiarly with us a few minutes, when, being informed which way the officers had gone, he went off in the same direction, after strictly charging us, in case we should be taken prisoners, not to discover to the enemy what troops we were. We were obliged to him for his kind advice, but we considered ourselves as standing in no great need of it. For we knew as well as he did that Sappers and Miners were allowed no quarters, at least are entitled to none, by the laws of warfare and, of course, should take care if taken and the enemy did not find us out, not to betray our own secret.

In a short time, the engineers returned and the aforementioned stranger with them. They discoursed together some time, when by the officers often calling him, "Your Excellency," we discovered that it was General Washington. Had we dared, we might have cautioned him for exposing himself so carelessly to danger at such a time and doubtless he would have taken it in good part if we had....

It coming on to rain hard, we were ordered back to our tents and nothing more was done that night. The next night ... the sixth of October, the same men were ordered to the lines that had been there the night before. We ... completed laying out the works. The troops of the line were there ready with entrenching tools and began to entrench, after General Washington had struck a few blows with a pickax, a mere ceremony, that it might be said, "General Washington with his own hands first broke ground at the siege of Yorktown." The ground was sandy and soft, and the men employed that night ate no "idle bread" (and I question if they eat any other), so that by daylight they had covered themselves from danger from the enemy's shot, who, it appeared never mistrusted that we were so near them the whole night, their attention being directed to another quarter. There was upon the right of their works a marsh. Our people had sent to the western side of this marsh a detachment to make a number of fires, by which, and our men often passing before the fires, the British were led to imagine that we were about some secret mischief there, and consequently directed their whole fire to that quarter, while we were entrenching literally under their noses.

As soon as it was day, they perceived their mistake and began to fire where they ought to have done sooner. They brought out a field-piece or two without their trenches, and discharged several shots at the men who were at work erecting a bomb battery, but their shot had no effect and they soon gave it over. They had a large bulldog and every time they fired he would follow their shots across our trenches. Our officers wished to catch him and oblige him to carry a message from them to his masters, but he looked too formidable for any of us to encounter. After the trench was perfected a number of field guns were brought up and workmen began cutting and fitting wooden platforms for heavier ordnance.

I was in the trenches the day that the batteries were to be opened. All were upon the tiptoe of expectation and impatience to see the signal given to open the whole line of batteries, which was to be the hoisting of the American flag in the ten-gun battery. About noon the much-wished-for signal went up. I confess I felt a secret pride swell my heart when I saw the "star-spangled banner" waving majestically in the very faces of our implacable adversaries.... A simultaneous discharge of all the guns in the line followed, the French troops accompanying it with "Huzza for the Americans!"

The siege was carried on warmly for several days, when most of the guns in the enemy's works were silenced. We now began our second parallel, about halfway between our works and theirs.... I, with the rest of our corps that had been on duty in the trenches the night but one before, were ordered to the lines. I mistrusted something extraordinary, serious or comical, was going forward, but what I could not conjecture.

We arrived at the trenches a little before sunset. I saw several officers fixing bayonets on long staves. I then concluded we were about to make a general assault upon the enemy's works, but before dark I was informed of the whole plan, which was to storm the redoubts, the one by the Americans and the other by the French. The Sappers and Miners were furnished with axes and were to proceed in front and cut a passage for the troops through the abatis, which are composed of the tops of trees, the small branches cut off with a slanting stroke which renders them as sharp as spikes. These trees are then laid at a small distance from the trench or ditch, pointing outwards, and the butts fastened to the ground in such a manner that they cannot be removed by those on the outside of them. It is almost impossible to get through them; threw these we were to cut a passage before we or the other assailants could enter.

At dark the detachment was formed and advanced beyond the trenches and lay down on the ground to await the signal for advancing to the attack, which was to be three shells from a certain battery near where we were lying. All the batteries in our line were silent, and we lay anxiously waiting for the signal. The two brilliant planets, Jupiter and Venus, were in close contact in the western hemisphere, the same direction that the signal was to be made in. When I happened to cast my eyes to that quarter, which was often, and I caught a glance of them, I was ready to spring on my feet, thinking they were the signal for starting. Our watchword was "Rochambeau," the commander of the French forces' name, a good watchword, for being pronounced Ro-sham-bow, it sounded, when pronounced quick, like rush-on-boys.

We had not lain here long before the expected signal was given, for us and the French, who were to storm the other redoubt, by the three shells with their fiery trains mounting the air in quick succession. The word up, up, was then reiterated through the detachment. We immediately moved silently on toward the redoubt we were to attack, with unloaded muskets. Just as we arrived at the abatis, the enemy discovered us and directly opened a sharp fire upon us. We were now at a place where many of our large shells had burst in the ground, making holes sufficient to bury an ox in. The men, having their eyes fixed upon what was transacting were falling into these holes. I thought the British were killing us off at a great rate. At length, one of the holes happening to pick me up, I found out the mystery of the huge slaughter.

As soon as the firing began, our people began to cry, "The fort's our own!" and it was "Rush on boys." The Sappers and Miners soon cleared a passage for the infantry, who entered it rapidly.... I could not pass at the entrance we had made, it was so crowded. I therefore forced a passage at a place where I saw our shot had cut away some of the abatis; several others entered at the same place.

While passing, a man at my side received a ball in his head and fell under my feet, crying out bitterly.... As I mounted the breastwork, I met an old associate hitching himself down into the trench. I knew him by the light of the enemy's musketry, it was so vivid. The fort was taken and all quiet in a very short time. Immediately after the firing ceased, I went out to see what had become of my wounded friend and the other that fell in the passage. They were both dead. In the heat of the action I saw a British soldier jump over the walls of the fort next the river and go down the bank, which was almost perpendicular and twenty or thirty feet high. When he came to the beach he made off for the town, and if he did not make good use of his legs, I never saw a man that did.

All that were in the action of storming the redoubt were exempted from further duty that night. We laid down upon the ground and rested the remainder of the night as well as a constant discharge of grape and canister shot would permit us to do.... We returned to camp early in the morning, all safe and sound.... Seven or eight men belonging to the infantry were killed, and a number wounded. After we had finished our second line of trenches there was but little firing on either side.

On the morning of the 17th of October a red-coated drummer appeared on the enemy's parapet. Amid the noise of the bombardment he tapped upon his drum the special message for a parley. It signaled that Cornwallis was ready to surrender. Immediately a British officer, holding up a white handkerchief, made his appearance outside their works. The drummer accompanied him, beating. The rebels' batteries ceased. There was silence. An officer from the American lines ran and met the other. He tied the handkerchief over the British officers eyes. The drummer was sent back. The British officer was conducted to a house in the rear of the American lines. The terms of the treaty were signed. The battle was over.

The next day we were ordered to put ourselves in as good order as our circumstances would admit, to see (what was the completion of our present wishes) the British army march out and stack their arms.... After breakfast on the nineteenth, we were marched onto the ground and paraded on the right-hand side of the road, and the French forces on the left. We waited two or three hours before the British made their appearance. They were not always so dilatory, but they were compelled at last, by necessity, to appear, all armed, with bayonets fixed, drums beating, and faces lengthening. They were led by General [Charles] O'Hara, with the American General Lincoln on his right, the Americans and French beating a march as they passed out between them. It was a noble sight to us, and the more so, as it seemed to promise a speedy conclusion to the contest.... They marched to the place appointed and stacked their arms; they then returned to the town in the same manner they had marched out, except being divested of their arms. After the prisoners were marched off into the country, our army separated, the French remaining where they then were and the Americans marching for the Hudson.

Joseph boarded a small schooner that went to the Head of Elk and then marched to Philadelphia, and later northward to the Hudson, where he continued to serve while waiting for the signing of the final peace treaty. Joseph Martin expressed the feelings of many at the end of the war when he received news of the final signing of the treaty papers in Paris on June 11, 1783. He wrote the following:

I confess, after all, that my anticipation of the happiness I should experience upon such a day as this was not realized; I can assure the

Surrender of Cornwallis to Washington at Yorktown, October 19, 1781. Painting by John Trumbull shows detail of British General Charles O'Hara actually surrendering to Benjamin Lincoln, as Cornwallis was "indisposed" (National Archives).

reader that there was as much sorrow as joy transfused on the occasion. We had lived together as a family of brothers for several years, setting aside some little family squabbles, like most other families, had shared with each other the hardships, dangers, and sufferings incident to a soldier's life; had sympathized with each other in trouble and sickness; had assisted in bearing each other's burdens or strove to make them lighter by council and advice; had endeavored to conceal each other's faults or make them appear in as good a light as they would bear.

And now we were to be, the greater part of us, parted forever; as unconditionally separated as though the grave lay between us. I now bid farewell to the service. I had obtained my settlement certificates and sold some of them and purchased some decent clothing, and then set off from West Point. I went into the Highlands, where I accidentally came across an old messmate who had been at work there ever since he had left the army in June last. I stopped a few days with him and worked at the farming business. I got acquainted with the people here, who were chiefly Dutch and as winter was approaching and my friend recommended me to them, I agreed to teach a school amongst them; ... I stayed and had a school of from twenty to thirty pupils....

Through much fatigue and many dangers past,
The warworn soldier's braved his way at last.

Bibliography

Martin, Joseph Plumb. *Private Yankee Doodle, Being a Narrative of Some of the Adventures, Dangers and Sufferings of a Revolutionary Soldier.* Ed. George F. Scheer. 1830. Reprint, Boston: Little, Brown, 1962.

23

Peter Otsiquette: Liaison Between Iroquois and Americans at Treaties

In the 1783 peace treaty, England recognized the independence of the United States of America. However, the boundaries of the country on the continent of North America were not settled. The British still held territory on the northern boundary, the Spanish, on the west and the south. The greatest threat came from all the Indian tribes throughout the land. Peace was not at hand.

The question of boundaries and ownership of the land occupied by the Six Nations of the Iroquois was to be a particularly troubling one. There were less than five thousand Iroquois occupying the millions of acres of central and western New York at this time, compared with nearly 300,000 immigrants in the state and over three million in the thirteen states. Both the New York state and the United States governments were anxious to conclude a treaty of peace with the Six Nations and settle their legal status.

Peter Otsiquette was a young Oneida, a member of the Iroquois who was to play an important part in this last phase of the Revolutionary War. Because he could speak English and French in addition to the Iroquoian languages, he became a liaison between the Iroquois and the American government leaders in bringing them together for making peace by treaty. He was the son of a French soldier captured during the French and Indian War, adopted by the Oneidas and married to a member of the Oneida Nation of the Iroquois Confederacy. Born about 1766, Peter grew up amid the turmoil of a split in the tribes. The Mohawks, Onondagas, Cayugas and Senecas favored the British. The Oneidas and Tuscaroras sided with the patriots.

Peter, as part of the Oneida Nation, experienced at first hand

the Revolutionary War when the British invaded Oneida territory
in August 1777, as part of the plan to split the colonies. At the battle of Oriskany on August 6, and the defense of Fort Schuyler
(Fort Stanwix) against the British General St. Leger, sixty Oneida
warriors joined the American General Herkimer to stop the
advance of the British through central New York. Many were killed
or wounded.

The British set up a siege of the fort that lasted until August
22, when they became alarmed by the possibility that General
Benedict Arnold might be leading a force of several thousand up
the Mohawk to relieve the fort. The British retreated immediately.
St. Leger returned to Montreal, from which he proceeded to
Ticonderoga.

The Oneidas were asked by General Gates to join the Americans in combatting the remaining British army under Burgoyne as
he advanced down Lake Champlain/Lake George. At Albany one
hundred fifty Oneida warriors joined the Americans. Serving as
scouts and small war parties, they intercepted messages going to
and from Burgoyne. They took thirty prisoners the first week. The
Board of War issued a special certificate honoring their efforts after
the surrender of the British at Saratoga.

When the Oneidas and Tuscaroras continued to refuse to join
the other four Iroquois tribes, the hostile Indians finally attacked
and destroyed their villages, forcing them to flee down the Mohawk
to Schenectady. Temporary quarters were erected. Hungry and
cold, they waited for the war to end. When peace was finally at
hand, Peter's father had died. With his mother and his sister he
joined the other Oneidas in trying to restore their way of life.

In determining a policy with regard to land occupied by the
Indian tribes, George Washington outlined his opinion in a letter to
James Duane, chairman of the committee of Congress to confer
with the Commander-in-Chief:

> That as they (the Indians) ... were determined to join their arms to
> those of G Britain and to share their fortune, so consequently, with a
> less generous People than Americans they would be made to share the
> same fate; and be compell'd to retire along with them beyond the
> Lakes. But as we prefer peace to a state of Warfare, as we consider

them as a deluded People; as we persuade ourselves that they are convinced, from experience, of their error in taking up the Hatchet
against us, and that their true interest and safety must now depend
upon our friendship. As the country is large enough to contain us all
... we will draw a veil over what is past and establish a boundary line
between them and us, beyond which we will endeavor to restrain our
people from Hunting or settling, and within which they shall not come
but for the purpose of Trading, Treating or other business ... and if they
should appear dissatisfied at the line we may find it necessary to establish, compensation should be made them for their claims within it.

[Washington thus recognized the right of the Indians to the land.
However he opposed the sale of any property] to a parcel of banditti
who will bid defiance to all authority while they are skimming and dis-
posing of the Cream of the Country at the expense of many officers
and soldiers who have fought and bled to obtain it.... No purchase
under any pretense whatever should be made by any authority other
than that of the Sovereign power, or the Legislature of the state in
which such Lands may happen to be.

In September of 1784 Peter attended the first of many council
fires between the Iroquois and the Americans. Anxious to settle the
question of land ownership and development, New York Governor
George Clinton called the Six Nations to a council fire at Fort
Stanwix with the newly formed commissioners of Indian affairs
appointed by law "for the Extinguishment of Indian Titles in the
State of New York by Means of Treaties and Payment for the
Land." Peter, now eighteen, was concerned about the future of his
nation and wondered what the Americans were planning. As faithful allies, the Oneidas were expecting a proper reward. Yet, they
heard rumors that the State of New York wanted to take some of
their land. The governor sent several officials to the Oneidas to
allay their fears and assure them of the good intentions of the state.
On September 3, 1784, the Oneidas went to Fort Stanwix.

The next day all assembled for the usual welcome given by
both sides. Silence was observed during the speeches. The interpreter was the Rev. Samuel Kirkland, missionary to the Oneidas
and fluent in all the Iroquoian languages. When Governor Clinton
addressed the Oneidas, Peter was relieved to hear him say:

We have been informed that some designing Persons have endeavored
to persuade You that We mean to take away your Lands. This is not

true; You must not believe it. We have no Claim on your lands; its just extent will ever remain secured to you; it is therefore an Object of our present Meeting to have the Metes and Bounds thereof precisely ascertained in all its Parts, in order to prevent an intrusion thereupon.... No Purchases or Contract for the Sale of Lands, Made since the Year one thousand seven hundred and seventy-five, or which thereafter might be made with or of the Indians within this State should be binding on the said Indians or deemed valid, unless made under the Authority of the Legislature of this state; and in all our subsequent Transactions We have been equally attentive to the Preservation of your Property.

When the governor addressed the hostile tribes, he told them he expected a cession of some land to pay for the American war losses and debts. Joseph Brant, speaking for the hostile tribes, agreed to discuss the proposal with the tribal leaders, and they would determine what territory they would be willing to grant. He readily agreed to return captive prisoners and to give up any claim to land around the forts at Niagara and Oswego now in the control of the British; sales of any Indian land would require the consent of the government.

The council ended September 10, 1784, with the smoking of the pipes and covering the fire with ashes. The commissioners and the governor returned to Albany. Joseph Brant left for Niagara and then Quebec to confirm with Governor Haldimand the grant of land at Grand River for the Mohawks. Peter and the Oneidas returned to their villages to harvest their crops and hunt for food to store for the coming winter. The U.S. commissioners were expected to arrive soon for another council fire on concluding a treaty of peace with the enemy tribes.

On October 2, the Oneidas received a surprise visit from the Marquis de Lafayette. He had arrived in New York City on August 4, to see Washington at Mt. Vernon and to tour the Revolutionary War sites. Hearing that a peace treaty conference with the Indians was to be held at Fort Stanwix, he offered to attend in the hope his presence would be useful.

With his aide, Chevalier de Caraman, Lafayette journeyed to Albany with James Madison, the future president. There they met the French representative to the United States, François de Barbé-

Marbois. Together they traveled to the fort, arriving ahead of the U.S. commissioners. Wishing to see the Indians in their villages, the three French gentlemen rode their horses eighteen miles to Oneida Castle to dine and stay overnight in the longhouse. It was to be an important day for Peter.

As Barbé-Marbois wrote in his journal,

> After having gone through this deep forest, sometimes on foot, sometimes on horseback, and after crossing the rivers by fording them, and sometimes by swimming our horses, we arrived, very wet and very tired....
>
> A white flag raised on the principal cabin indicated to us the Council House.... We found the chiefs and warriors of the nation assembled there. They received us with the hospitality they show towards all those who are not their enemies.... After the customary compliments, they brought us a large salmon which had just been caught. We had milk, butter, fruit, and honey in abundance....
>
> We expressed a desire to see their dances, and at once one of the principal young men stepped out, and blowing on a horn, called the young men of the village and told them to dress for the dance. This cabin was composed of a single room twenty-four feet by eighteen. On each side were the beds on which we were to spend the night. In the middle was a sort of alley, which was the dance room. Towards the end of the central passage was a fire of which the smoke went out the roof.

Lafayette took a particular interest in Peter as his father had been a French soldier. Learning that Peter's father had died, the Marquis invited him to go with him to Paris. Torn between his desire to go and his duty to his tribe to help restore the village, Peter asked permission of the clan. All agreed they would help his mother and sister. He could go. Arrangements were made to meet in New York in December after Lafayette completed his tour.

However, Peter was not able to go at that time. As part of the treaty, the U.S. commissioners offered the hostile tribes peace, but one of the provisions was that until ninety prisoners were returned, six Indian leaders attending the treaty would be detained as hostages, including Aaron Hill, a prominent chief and ally of Joseph Brant. So it was that Peter began his career as intermediary between the government and the Indian tribes. He set off for Quebec to inform Joseph Brant and secure his aid in freeing the prisoners. Many of them had become part of Indian families. Some did not wish to return. Peter spent the winter locating the captives and escorting them back to Fort Stanwix. The last were not returned until the following May, when the six Indian hostages were released.

After his return to Paris, Lafayette wrote two letters regarding Peter. One was to Jeremiah Wadsworth, dated 16 April 1785:

> There is a young Indian, son to a french man by the name of Stephanus, whom I intended to take with me to France as a favorite servant. The young man has a regard for me as was spoken of to him by his deceased father. He was with Brant to Quebec in the fall. The whole family, who are Oneidas, consented to his coming. I send the inclosed to Kirkland by April and to forward the young Indians's departure by the October packet—because I will then be back from Prussia and Bohemia where I am going to visit troops.

The other was to William Constable, dated May 13, 1784:

> A propos of Indians, there is a young man of the Oneida Tribe whom I wanted to have with me, and who now is about Niagara. As he was willing to come, the only difficulty is to find him out and to send him to me. Chief Louis of the Indians who lives at Oneida Castle, knows everything about it. The only thing would be to send an express to him and diffray the expenses which will be ... and indeed some man or other ought to accompany him to the Havre, where the packets are now to arrive.

The packets were fast sailing ships for carrying mail and passengers between the United States and France. It is not evident when Peter made the journey to France, but he was there the following summer; on August 28, 1786, Madame Lafayette noted in a letter to United States Ambassador Thomas Jefferson that "Otchekeita (Peter) is gone to the abbe." Jefferson often visited Lafayette's home, where many French and Americans gathered to relive their Revolutionary War experiences. Often they talked about gaining for the French people the freedom and rights they had helped obtain for the Americans.

At that time France was ruled by King Louis XVI and Queen Marie Antoinette, who lived in a palace at Versailles, about eighteen miles outside Paris. As Lafayette was an important noble, he often went there to play cards with the king. Peter was presented to the king.

23. Peter Otsiquette

By 1788 the political situation in France was changing. A crisis was approaching in which Lafayette was to play an important part in working for a Declaration of Rights similar to the American Declaration of Independence. Peter was also caught up in the fever for improving the life of his own people. He decided to return to America on this eve of the French Revolution, saying:

> After two years more residence in France, my views were enlarged and I was distressed at the wretched situation of my Nation, that they were no higher than the shrubs, and I wished to return to endeavor to reform them, and did request the Marquis their Father, to let me come over to attend to the concerns of my Nation, as I did not mean to desert my country.

On August 2, 1788, Peter's return voyage to America was reported in the Boston newspaper Thomas' Massachusetts Spy:

> In the CATO from France came passenger Peter Otsiquette, who, we are told, is son to the King of the Six Nations, and whom the Marquis de Lafayette some time since sent to France to be educated. He speaks the French and English languages with accuracy and is acquainted with most of the branches of polite education, musick, etc. And is on his way to the Indian country.

Peter, now 22, did not mind putting away the tight-fitting fancy clothes he had worn in France. The decorative waistcoat, the ruffled shirt, the leather shoes and stockings would not be suitable for the rough trails of the forest. The Oneidas welcomed Peter with a feast, dances and singing. His mother and sister were very proud as everyone listened to his stories of life across the Great Water with their father, Kayewla. Many, who had never left the forest, did not believe him. At the end some of the chiefs told Peter of new worries about losing all their lands to more land grabbers. Governor Clinton had called another council at Fort Stanwix on August 28, 1788, for all the Six Nations.

A group of land speculators called the New York Genesee Company of Adventurers had arranged with certain chiefs to lease all the Indian lands in the state for 999 years. Governor Clinton informed the nations that only the government could purchase the lands and the term "lease" was an attempt to "deceive you." He pointed out that the tribes had no way to force the speculators to pay if they refused to do so. They would settle upon the lands and soon be so many they would be in control. "Nothing but the Interposition of our Great Council the Legislature, can defend you against such injuries."

In his opening speech, Governor Clinton also congratulated the Oneidas on the return of Peter Otsiquette, saying:

> His conduct has merited the approbation of their friend the Marquis de Lafayette; that by his absence he had acquired knowledge which it was hoped would render him useful to his Nation, and therefore recommended him to their attention.

Eager to help in the affairs of his nation, Peter was honored when the Oneidas chose him to represent them as one of their two speakers. In his first speech he pleaded as follows:

> 4 years ago at the Treaty at this place at which the Marquis de la Fayette was present, the Marquis proposed taking one of his sons of the Oneida Nation with him to France; that he with Reluctance left his Country, and his Companions of whose Amusements and Diversions he was very fond, and undertook the Voyage; that it was unjustly reported that the Chiefs had sold him. That when he crossed the Great Water, the Marquis received him with Kindness; that he was naked and the Marquis clad him; that he was restless for a Year after he arrived in France, but when Light or Knowledge flowed in on his Mind, he felt distressed at the miserable Situation of his Countrymen that from want of Opportunity of acquiring Knowledge they were so little informed of their true Interest.
>
> While I was still in France, I heard frequently of the situation of my native country, and of the conduct of many of our Chiefs and Warriors, that they began to cut their land in pieces, in one part and another, and that they were divided among themselves, and each tenacious of his own opinion, and I saw that their ruin was approaching.
>
> Brother Governor! Let not this be done. Look back to former days, when you first landed in New York. We then took you under our protection. You were then small and we were great, and we are now sunk down even to your ankles, while you are so risen that your hands extend over the whole island and reach the stars.

The Oneidas then chose five more chiefs and warriors to help Peter and Col. Louis, the other representative, in meetings with the governor and the commissioners. The governor asked the Oneidas to set a boundary on the land they wished to keep for themselves and cede all the rest to the state.

Twice the proposals of the committee of the Oneidas were rejected by the state. The commissioners and the governor attempted to convince them of the "impropriety of reserving all the lands on the north side of Wood Creek and the Oneida Lake with a very large extent of country on the south side of the lake."

After conferring with their nation, the Oneidas' committee agreed to give up lands on the north side of Oneida Lake. It did not satisfy the governor and the commissioners. When finally asked to point out what the state considered a proper reservation, the commissioners outlined the boundaries in the final treaty. Even the 1768 Line of Property as the eastern boundary, insisted on by the Oneida agents, had to be given up.

Under the terms, the Oneidas received $2,000 in cash, $2,000 in goods and clothing, $1,000 in provisions and $600 in rent annually forever. When the agents protested that the rent should be at least $1,000, the Governor agreed to pay $500 toward a grist mill and a saw mill. A copy of the treaty of September 22, 1788, shows each Oneida signed with X as his mark, except Peter, who signed in script.

In his closing speech, Governor Clinton noted:

> You have a very large tract of country for your own use and cultivation; you are to have the rents of a very large tract, and you are to be allowed by our Great Council to the amount of six hundred dollars annually forever.... You have therefore more than sufficient for the comfortable support of your selves and your posterity if you are prudent and sober.

It was a stupendous bargain for the future New Yorkers. Millions of acres of wilderness, rich and unspoiled, extending north and west from Fort Stanwix came under state control to be surveyed, laid out, and sold with clear title to the settlers who were pouring into the area.

Personal affairs concerned Peter. A visitor at the treaty conference noted that he found Peter "a polite and well-informed gentleman." Later he saw him riding away through the rain with a young Indian woman behind him on horseback. At this time Peter was married. Indian custom required the mothers of the bride and groom to make a simple verbal agreement. Peter was now twenty-two and an important warrior in the nation.

After a proper survey of their lands, two Oneidas, "who were known to be men of principle and interest in the Nation," were to be appointed to arrange for income from rentals and forbid sale of any land to anyone not a member of the tribe. These two were Peter and Col. Louis.

Peter was gratified that he was aiding his people. He had been given a place of honor at the treaty and again in deciding on matters of tribal government. They relied on his ability to speak other languages to aid them in their dealings with non-Indians. Whether his classical French education was a benefit is doubtful when he was concerned with legal and political measures regarding the land.

When the surveyors laid out the boundaries of the land reserved for the tribes, many perceived for the first time what vast areas they had signed away. Some of the distressed Oneidas sent a delegation to Governor Clinton in New York in January 1790. However, Clinton refused their appeals.

Many Cayugas and Onondagas complained that those who had signed the treaties with their nations did not have the power to do so. Clinton invited those who were empowered, but had not

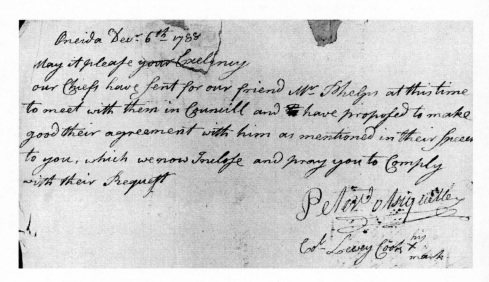

Signature of Peter Otsiquette on letter to Governor Clinton, December 6, 1778 (courtesy of the New York Historical Society).

attended the previous treaties, to meet him in June 1790 at Fort Stanwix when the annuities were to be paid.

Living with the Oneidas from about 1766 was the Presbyterian missionary Samuel Kirkland. During the war he was a chaplain at Fort Stanwix (Fort Schuyler). He was largely responsible for advising the Oneidas to help the rebels. Because he was fluent in the Iroquoian languages, he often was the interpreter in councils between the Indians and the government. Governor Clinton sent him the invitation for the tribes.

Immediately a runner was sent thirty miles into the woods to find Peter. The minister trusted him to carry the dispatches, as Peter knew the way to Buffalo Creek, he spoke the languages, and was acquainted with the chiefs.

Leaving a little after sunrise, Peter and Roger Levett set off on the Iroquois trail through the flowering woods and fields on May 12, 1790. Four days later they arrived at Buffalo Creek. In the council of the Onondagas, the Cayugas, the Senecas and the Mohawks there was disagreement. Cayuga Chief Fish Carrier objected, saying it was "not safe to go down among a people who would take every advantage of them when once in their power." Peter replied:

> I would stake my life against any ill treatment you might receive from the people of New York by attending the proposed treaty. I am fully satisfied of the peaceable disposition of the State and the Americans, and particularly the Governor of New York toward the Indians.

After several days of discussion, the Onondagas finally informed Peter they would set out for the council and appointed a young warrior to return with Peter. The council convened on June 13, 1790, at Fort Stanwix. Peter and the Oneida chiefs and warriors were summoned by the governor to witness the transactions. The Rev. Kirkland was asked to be the interpreter. After a full explanation of the treaty signed in 1788, the Onondaga Chief Clear Sky commented:

> We now see clearly that there was nothing unfriendly or wrong in any of your negotiations with us.... We have now cast away all obstructions in the path which impeded our peace with you.... We wipe away the blood which has been spilt. We have pulled up a great tree from the

roots and we have buried the voices of birds and all discords and jealousies in the hole, that they may sink down to the bottom of the Great Rivers.... We now take fast hold of the chain of peace, to be held between you and us and our Posterity forever.

At the conclusion of the council, after all had given consent to the treaty confirming the earlier 1788 agreement, Joseph Brant inserted the Indian names of those present on the parchment document. Peter was one of the witnesses who also signed.

Joseph Brant then represented the Cayugas in their meeting with the state officials. After long discussion, Chief Fish Carrier concluded:

Having determined to accede to all your proposals, and having perfectly understood them, after conversation among ourselves, we have this day determined to establish our peace and accordingly confirm the agreement between us.

Peter and three Oneida chiefs were witnesses on the treaty, as well as Joseph Brant and Samuel Kirkland. Thus peace with the Iroquois was finally settled on this day, June 22, 1790. The territory was divided, with lands reserved for the Six Nations and the remainder for settlement by others.

The following March the state awarded Peter a grant of one thousand acres adjacent to the Oneida Reservation. The governor realized the important part Peter had played in bringing the Cayugas and Onondagas from Buffalo Creek to the council fire at Fort Stanwix to finalize the peace.

Peter was to be called on once again. Threats to the independence of the new nation came from the British on the north as well as from the warring Indians in the west. The Indians scored a victory on November 4, 1791, near the present Ohio-Indiana border. One thousand warriors from the Shawnee, Miami, and other western tribes, as well as a few Cayugas, completely routed another American army led by General St. Clair. With about seventeen hundred troops he had been on his way to establish a post near the Miami villages. After this success the question was—Would the tribes now combine in a unified front with the Iroquois and the backing of the British in Canada?

In the hope of being "instrumental to the reunion of the empire," British Lt. Governor Simcoe pursued a policy of supplying the Indians with "cloathing, arms and ammunition" to make war on the frontier. Great Britain still controlled the forts on the Canadian border to the north to keep the fur trade and the good will of the Indians. Some Canadians hoped an Indian barrier state might come to separate their lands from those of the Yankees. Eventually it might join them with their own colony.

With the enormous debt of the Revolutionary War, the American government could ill afford further military action. Preventing the Six Nations from uniting with the western tribes and securing their loyalty to the Americans was vital to the future of the country.

Secretary of War Knox immediately summoned the Rev. Kirkland to Philadelphia to ask him to take charge of inviting the influential Iroquois chiefs to visit the capital as soon as convenient.

On his way back to the Oneidas, Kirkland found Peter in Albany with a delegation of Oneida Chiefs. They were meeting with General Schuyler regarding a special certificate awarded by the Board of War. To them it represented the good faith of the Americans to reward them for their aid during the war. Schuyler advised Peter to present it to Secretary of War Knox. He also urged Peter and an Oneida chief, Good Peter, to aid Kirkland in persuading the invited chiefs of the Six Nations to go to Philadelphia.

Peter and an other Oneida chief, Captain John, agreed to carry the invitation over the one-hundred-fifty-mile trail to the chiefs at Buffalo Creek. A council fire would be lighted at Geneseo to receive their answer. The Rev. Kirkland followed a week later with six other Oneida chiefs and two Tuscaroras. Along the way they invited the chiefs of the Onondagas and the Cayugas to join them at Geneseo. In his journal, Kirkland wrote Knox:

> A most fatiguing journey by reason of the extreme cold weather and great fall of snow.... I find the Indians are much alarmed with their present situation and much divided in opinion what course to take.

The question to decide was whether to support their brother tribes in further hostilities or turn toward peace and cooperation with the Americans. At Buffalo Creek Peter heard the British tell their Indian allies that it was only another Yankee trick and that Americans could not be trusted: they would cheat the Indians.

After waiting for two weeks Peter returned to Geneseo to confer with Kirkland. More chiefs from the Cayugas, the Onondagas and the Senecas were meeting daily with the missionary in his small cabin of one room and no windows. Good Peter advised sending French Peter back with another message, to convince the chiefs at Buffalo Creek of the "goodness and uprightness of the intentions of Congress toward all peaceably disposed Indians." On February 17, everyone at Geneseo was relieved when the three emissaries—Peter, Captain John, and Captain Hendrick—walked into the village with the welcome news that the old chiefs are on their return from Niagara

To provide for the large delegation of fifty, Kirkland sent Peter immediately to Canadasago to obtain sleighs and supplies for the nearly three-hundred-mile journey ahead. Going to Philadelphia by way of Tioga, they descended the Susquehanna River with "as good slaying from Tioga to Wyoming on the river as ever was known by man," according to Seth Reed, who provided the "slays."

On March 13, after two weeks of traveling from the Genesee by sleigh, on foot and in a boat, the delegation arrived in the capital. The fifty-one-year-old Kirkland was "excruciatingly worn down" and had requested in advance "a separate room for myself and French Peter."

Peter did not attend any of the ceremonies or meet any of the officials. As Col. Pickering wrote his wife, "Peter was taken with a pleurisy on his way and on Monday night 19 March 1792 he died at Oeller's Hotel." On this last mission during the last three months of his life, Peter traveled nearly five hundred miles across the snow-covered trails during extremely cold weather and storms.

To honor Peter, as well as all the Indians visiting the city, extensive arrangements were made for the funeral. Following the usual Indian ceremony of condolence, a procession accompanied the coffin from the hotel of Mr. Oeller on Chestnut Street to the Presbyterian Burying Ground on Mulberry (Arch) Street for burial with the honors of war.

23. Peter Otsiquette

The Pennsylvania Gazette dated March 28, 1792, reported:

The corpse was preceded by a detachment of the Light Infantry of the City, with arms reversed; drums muffled; music playing a solemn dirge. The Corpse was followed by six of the Chiefs as mourners, succeeded by all the warriors now in this city; the reverend clergy of all denominations; the Secretary of War, and the Gentlemen of the War Department; officers of the Federal Army, and of the militia; and a number of citizens.

Among the estimated ten thousand persons along the route was Thomas Jefferson, the future president and former ambassador to France. He wrote his daughter Martha:

I believe you knew Otchakitz, the Indian who lived with the Marquis de Lafayette. He came here lately with some deputies from his nation and died here of a pleurisy. I was at the funeral yesterday. He was buried standing up, according to their manner.

The site is now a part of Independence Mall—the last resting place for one young Indian who helped ensure that independence remained a reality.

President Washington sent the following message to the delegation:

I partake of your sorrow on account that it has pleased the Great Spirit to take from you (a member) by death since your residence in this city. I have ordered that your tears should be wiped away according to your custom and that presents be sent to the relations of the deceased. Our lives are all in the hands of our Maker, and we must part with them whenever he shall demand them; and the survivors must submit to events they cannot prevent.

Peter knew at first hand life as an Indian in the forest before, during and after the Revolution. He had visited the cities of New York, Philadelphia, and Boston, as well as Quebec. For nearly three years he had lived in a mansion in Paris learning about the politics of France at the time of King Louis XVI and Marie Antoinette before the French Revolution. Peter had taken an important role in communicating between the leaders of the war-devastated country of the Iroquois and those of the United States, as he was fluent in the languages of the Iroquois, the English and the French. He worked diligently carrying messages, interpreting them, and helping

221

to make the necessary arrangements to carry them out. He was charged especially by General Philip Schuyler to aid Rev. Kirkland in persuading the chiefs of the Six Nations to journey to Philadelphia and secure their loyalty to the United States. It cost him his life.

After a month of meetings and entertainments, the Iroquois agreed not to join the western tribes. Captain Hendrick Aupaumut, chief of the Stockbridge Indians, with several other Indian leaders, agreed to attend a great council of Indians at the Miami River near Lake Erie to convince them of the moderation, justice, and desire of the United States for peace; and that they claimed no Indian lands but those purchased by a fair treaty.

Bibliography

American State Papers, Documents, Legislative and Executive of the Congress of the United States, March 3, 1789–March 8,1813.Eds.Walter Lowrie and Matthew St. Clair Clarke. Washington: Gales and Seaton, 1832.

Chase, Eugene Parker. Our Revolutionary Forefathers: The Letters of François, Marquis de Barbé-Marbois. New York: Duffield, 1929.

Hough, Franklin B., ed. Proceedings of the Commissioners of Indian Affairs Appointed by Law for the Extinguishment of Indian Titles in the State of New York. 2 vols. Albany: Joel Munsell, 1861.

Kirkland, Samuel. Journal of Rev. Samuel Kirkland 1790–1792. Clinton, N.Y.: Hamilton College, 1980.

Lafayette, Marquis de. Lafayette in the Age of the American Revolution: Selected Letters and Papers, 1776–90. Ed. Stanley J. Idzerda. 5 vols. Ithaca, N.Y.: Cornell University Press, 1983.

Randolph, Sarah Nichols. The Domestic Life of Thomas Jefferson, Compiled from Family Letters and Reminiscences. 1871. Reprint, Charlottesville: University Press of Virginia, 1978.

A Chronology of
Events, 1763–1787

1763   British win French and Indian War

1765   British levy new taxes (Stamp Act) to pay for war with the French

1766   Colonists say "No taxation without representation." British repeal Stamp Act

1767   British enact new regulations: the Townshend Acts

1768   British send troops to Boston to enforce new laws

1770   March 5: British troops fire on Bostonians in the "Boston Massacre." Troops removed to island in harbor

1773   British repeal Townshend Act duties, except on tea
December 16: Colonials dump 342 chests of tea overboard ("Boston Tea Party")

1774   June 1: British close port of Boston until city pays for tea
September 5: First Continental Congress convenes in Philadelphia
October 25: Congress sends address to King with terms

1775   April 19: Battle of Lexington-Concord
May 10: Second Continental Congress convenes in Philadelphia
June 15: George Washington elected Commander-in-Chief of Continental army
June 17: British seize Bunker Hill and Breed's Hill
July 3: Washington takes command of the army
November 13: Montréal occupied by Montgomery

223

December 8–31: Siege of Quebec City
Dec 31: American attack on Quebec fails

1776   March 17: British leave Boston
May 6: Arrival of British reinforcements at Quebec; Americans driven away
June 8: Battle of Trois Rivières, Canada
June 12–30: American retreat from Canada
June 28: British joint expedition sails under Admiral Howe into NewYork Harbor.
July 4: Congress signs Declaration of Independence
August 27: British win Battle of Long Island and occupy New York City
September 16: Battle of Harlem Heights
October 11–12: Battle of Valcour Island, Lake Champlain
October 28: Battle of White Plains, New York
November 16: Fort Washington, Pennsylvania, captured by British
December 26: Washington's surprise victory at Trenton

1777   January 3: Americans defeat British at Battle of Princeton
April 25–27: Tryon's raid on Danbury, Connecticut
July 5: British take Fort Ticonderoga
July 7: Battle of Hubbardton, Vermont
August 6: Battle of Oriskany, New York
August 16: Germans crushed at Battle of Bennington, Vermont
August 22: St. Leger retreats from Fort Stanwix, New York
August 25: Howe's army lands at Head of Elk, Maryland
September 11: Americans defeated at Battle of Brandywine
September 19: Burgoyne checked at Freeman's farm
September 26: Howe occupies Philadelphia
October 4: Washington defeated at Battle of Germantown
October 7: Burgoyne turned back at Bemis Heights
October 17: British General Burgoyne surrenders at Saratoga
November 8: Burgoyne evacuation of Ticonderoga
November 15: Fort Mifflin captured by British
November 15: Articles of Confederation adopted by Congress
December 19 to June 19, 1778: Americans encamp at Valley Forge

1778 February 6: Franco-American alliance signed in Paris
      June 28: Battle of Monmouth ends in a draw
      July 3: Pennsylvania's Wyoming Valley massacre by Loyalists and
          Indians
      August 29: Battle of Newport, Rhode Island
      December 20: British occupy Savannah

1779 February 23–4: George Rogers Clark recaptures Vincennes
      March 3: Americans surprised at Briar Creek, Georgia
      June 21: Spain enters the war against British
      May-November: Sullivan expedition against the Iroquois in New
          York state
      July 11: Tryon's raid on Norwalk, Connecticut
      July 15: Wayne takes Stony Point
      September 14: Defeat of Americans at Penobscot Bay
      October 9: Franco-American attack on Savannah repulsed by
          British

1780 May 12: Charleston falls to British
      May 29: Massacre of the Waxhaws, Waxhaw Creek, South Car-
          olina
      June 20: Battle of Ramsour's Mills, North Carolina
      July 10: Rochambeau's 6,000 French troops arrive at Newport
      August 1: Skirmish at Rocky Mount, South Carolina
      August 6 American victory at Hanging Rock, South Carolina
      August 16: Gates defeated at Camden by Cornwallis
      September 25: Benedict Arnold turns traitor
      October 2: Execution of Major André
      October 7: British defeated at King's Mountain

1781 January 17: Morgan defeats British at Cowpens
      February 23: Battle of Haw River, North Carolina
      March 15: British win battle of Guilford Courthouse but retreat
          to Wilmington, North Carolina, for supplies
      April 12: Action at Fort Balfour, South Carolina
      April 25: Battle of Hobkick's Hill, South Carolina
      May 22 to June 19: Americans' unsuccessful siege of fort at
          Ninety-Six, South Carolina

July 29: Loyalists win at Deep River, North Carolina
August 5: Cornwallis occupies Yorktown and Gloucester Point on the York River, Virginia
September 5: French fleet drives British fleet away from Chesapeake Bay
September 6: Arnold's raid on New London, and Fort Griswold massacre
September 8: Greene drives British from Eutaw Springs
October 5–19: Siege of Yorktown
October 19: Cornwallis surrenders at Yorktown
November 18: British evacuate Wilmington, North Carolina

1782   July 11: Savannah, Georgia, evacuated by British
November 30: Preliminary peace treaty signed in Paris
December 14: British evacuate Charleston

1783   April 11: Congress proclaims cessation of hostilities
September 3: Final peace treaty signed
November 25: British and Loyalists evacuate New York City
December 23: Washington retires from command

1784   October 22: Treaty at Fort Stanwix with Iroquois

1787   September 17: Delegates from 13 states approve U.S. Constitution

A Glossary of
Sailing Ship Terms

Athwart: At right angles to. From side to side (of a ship).

Ballast: Heavy material placed in the hold of a ship to enhance stability.

Boatswain: Warrant officer in charge of everything pertaining to the working of the ship.

Bow: Forward part of the vessel.

Bowsprit: A spar extending forward from the bow of a sailing ship.

Brig: A two-masted vessel, square-rigged on both masts.

Broadside: The number of cannon mounted on a vessel's side. Also a discharge of such guns.

Caliber: The diameter of the bore of a gun or the projectile.

Cannon: Ships' guns, cast of bronze or iron. Designated by the weight of the shot they threw, i.e., 6-pounder, 32-pounder, etc.

Close-hauled: Sailing close to the wind.

Fore-and-aft sails: All staysails, gaffsails, etc., which are set parallel to the line of the keel.

Forecastle: The upper deck forward of the foremast.

Foremast: The mast nearest the bow in all vessels with two or more masts where there is a larger mast toward the stern.

Frigate: A three-masted, ship-rigged vessel, carrying its armament on the main deck, and on the quarterdeck and forecastle.

Gangway: A passageway.

Grapeshot: A cluster of iron shot, usually nine, fastened together in tiers of three by rope and/or canvas. Used against light hulls or personnel.

Hatchway: Large square opening in a deck.

Hold: The space below decks utilized for the stowing of ballast, cargo and stores.

Hulk: A vessel, often condemned as unseaworthy, and stripped of masts, spars, and cannon.

Indiamen: Large, stoutly built merchantmen, usually well armed, used in the long and dangerous voyages to the Indies.

Keel: The longitudinal beam forming the backbone of the vessel from which the ribs start.

Ladder: The term used for stairs aboard ship.

Larboard: Left side of a vessel, looking forward (also called "port").

Lash: Secure with a rope.

Lee: The side opposite that from which the wind is blowing.

Leeward: The direction away from the wind; downwind.

Letter of Marque: A commission authorizing a private vessel to operate against the vessels of an enemy even though it might be carrying cargo.

Magazine: Space or compartment devoted to the stowing of ammunition.

Mainmast: In the three-masted vessel, the middle mast. The foremast in a two-masted vessel.

Mizzen: The third mast from forward of a vessel with more than two masts.

Netting: A rope network.

Port: An opening in a ship's side. Also the left side of a vessel, looking toward the bow.

Privateer: A privately owned armed vessel, sailing against the enemy under government commission (letter of marque).

Protector: Frigate with 26 guns, built by state of Massachusetts at Salisbury in 1778–9.

Prize: A captured ship.

Quarterdeck: The after part of the upper deck. Often raised above the upper decks.

Rake: To position one's vessel across another vessel's bow or stern so that its fire can sweep the enemy's decks.

Rigging: The ropes, chains, etc., that hold and move masts, sails, and spars of a ship.

Schooner: In the eighteenth century, a two-masted vessel fore-and-aft rigged, but often with the addition of a square fore-topsail.

Six-pounder: Cannon using shot that weighed six pounds.

Sloop: In the eighteenth century, a craft with a single mast, a gaff mainsail, headsails, and usually a square topsail and course.

Spars: General terms for masts, yards, gaffs, booms, etc.

Spiking a gun: Disabling a gun by driving a long spike into the vent or touchhole.

Sponge: Usually of sheepskin, fastened to a wooden staff or stiff rope. For swabbing the bore of a gun to dampen any fire or sparks before reloading.

Square sails: Sails which are set at right angles to the line of the keel.

Starboard: The right side of a vessel, looking forward.

Stern: The afterpart of the vessel.

Topmast: The mast above the lower mast.

Vermin: Various insects or animals such as rats or cockroaches.

Wake: The track of turbulence left by the ship as it moves through the water.

Yards: Spars on which square sails are set.

Yaw: Deviating from an intended course.

Index

Index